PELICAN BOOKS

THE SOCIAL PSYCHOLOGY OF WORK

Michael Argyle, D.Sc., F.B.Ps.S., is Reader in Social Psychology at the University of Oxford and a Fellow of Wolfson College. After serving in the RAF he was educated at Emmanuel College, Cambridge, and became a research student at the Cambridge Psychological Laboratory in 1950. In 1952, he was appointed University Lecturer in Social Psychology at Oxford.

He has been a Fellow of the Center for Advanced Study in the Behavioral Sciences at Stanford, and a visiting Professor at a number of universities in the U.S.A., Canada, Australia, Europe, Africa and Israel. He has carried out a variety of research and consultancy projects especially in the areas of social skills training and selection. He pioneered the use of social skills training in Britain. He has been awarded a series of research grants for work on social interaction, social skills, non-verbal communication and related topics, and has an active research group at Oxford.

He helped to found and was Social Psychology editor of the *British Journal of Social and Clinical Psychology* (1961–7), and has edited series of books on social psychology for Penguin Books and Pergamon Press. He has been acting Head of the Department of Experimental Psychology at Oxford, Chairman of the Social Psychology Section of the British Psychological Society, and was Director of a Summer School of the European Society for Experimental Social Psychology, at various times.

Michael Argyle's publications include *The Scientific Study of Social Behaviour* (1957), *Psychology and Social Problems* (1964), *The Psychology of Interpersonal Behaviour* (1967, 1972, 1978), *Social Interaction* (1969), *Bodily Communication* (1975), *The Social Psychology of Religion* (1975, with B. Beit-Hallahmi), *Gaze and Mutual Gaze* (1976, with Mark Cook), *Social Skills and Mental Health* (1978, with P. Trower and B. Bryant), *Social Situations* (1981, with A. Furnham and J. A. Graham), and many articles in British, American and European journals.

D032469G

THE SOCIAL
PSYCHOLOGY OF WORK

MICHAEL ARGYLE

PENGUIN BOOKS

Penguin Books Ltd, Harmondsworth, Middlesex, England
Penguin Books, 625 Madison Avenue, New York, New York 10022, U.S.A.
Penguin Books Australia Ltd, Ringwood, Victoria, Australia
Penguin Books Canada Ltd, 2801 John Street, Markham, Ontario, Canada L3R 1B4
Penguin Books (N.Z.) Ltd, 182–190 Wairau Road, Auckland 10, New Zealand

—

First published by Allen Lane The Penguin Press 1972
Published in Pelican Books 1974
Reprinted 1976, 1977, 1979, 1981, 1983

—

—

Made and printed in Great Britain
by Richard Clay (The Chaucer Press) Ltd,
Bungay, Suffolk
Set in Monotype Imprint

FOR MIRANDA

CONTENTS

EDITORIAL FOREWORD

In this book Michael Argyle considers almost every aspect of work. His topics include the need for status; problems arising from technological innovation; problems of the foreman; interviewing and selection; what kind of personality is best for which job; creative groups; not wanting to work; organizational psychology; and comparisons of working conditions in Israel, Yugoslavia, Japan and Britain. This is a broad canvas, and some aspects can only be sketched in, but the book is scholarly and very easy to read, so that at the end one has a broad knowledge of the subject and a desire to know more.

The author is well known for his empirical studies of the way in which people behave towards each other, especially by means of gestures, eye movements and stance. He has also been responsible for a considerable amount of research in occupational and industrial psychology, and his advice is constantly in demand, especially on social–psychological topics, here and abroad. His breadth of interest and knowledge allow him to stand back and look at these topics dispassionately. It is also typical of his approach that he prefers to take an empirical rather than a theoretical attitude – a very great advantage in a subject in which there is so much evidence to be considered in as unbiased a way as possible. This book will provide entertainment for anyone who wants to know how the other ninety-nine per cent work, but should also be taken very seriously by those concerned with conditions of work.

B. M. FOSS

PREFACE

THIS book is intended for those who work and would like to understand it better, and for those who organize work and would like to organize it better. There are a number of pressing problems of work in modern countries: widespread discontent and alienation; low motivation and lack of cooperation; conflict between management and unions, and between other groups; and difficulties about introducing new technologies, leading to a slow rate of economic growth in Britain and other countries.

These problems are becoming more acute as we move into a period of automation and post-industrial society, and are faced with the decline of the Protestant ethic. An immense amount of research has been carried out in recent years in the field of industrial psychology and sociology. The study of social behaviour at work constitutes a further dimension not covered by industrial relations, management techniques or work-study, though it has implications for all these. Most work involves cooperation in groups, leadership and organization, and a number of different kinds of social relationship. Social psychology is concerned with the social interaction and social relationships involved, and their effect on work efficiency and satisfaction.

I have had three groups of readers particularly in mind.

Managers and administrators have been bombarded, during recent years, by theories, packages and training methods from behavioural scientists and consultants. We shall try to evaluate these approaches in the light of the mounting mass of empirical evidence. We shall look at work as it is done in some other countries today, to obtain a wider perspective. There is considerable agreement over the empirical facts in this field, and they point clearly to a set of optimum conditions for work.

Young people are not all convinced of the importance of work, or that working organizations as they exist today are the best means of doing it. We shall discuss the biological basis of work, and its historical development. Problems with contemporary working organizations will be described and a number of alternative designs considered. We shall consider whether work should be allowed to disappear, whether it should be made more like leisure or leisure made more like work.

Social psychologists. Work is one of the central activities of life, and social behaviour at work is one of the most important and interesting forms of social behaviour. Research on work extends our vision of social behaviour by drawing attention to factors which are not found inside laboratories – the effects of technology and of social structures, the historical development in the culture of social relationships, the effects on behaviour of socialization for roles and of powerful motivations, the performance of professional social skills.

I have tried to produce a book that is both popular and scholarly; popular in that it is intended to be of use to a wide audience, scholarly in that all the assertions in it are based on good evidence and some of the main sources are given.

I am grateful to Lady Margaret Brown, Robert McHenry and Dr Mansur Lalljee for commenting on the manuscript, to Julia Vellacott of Penguin Books for her work on the manuscript, and to Ann McKendry and Jessica Taplin for typing it.

Michael Argyle
Department of Experimental Psychology
Oxford

CHAPTER I

THE SOCIAL PROBLEMS OF WORKING ORGANIZATIONS

WORK has to be done; sometimes it is enjoyable, sometimes it is not. It has to be done to provide food, clothes, shelter, protection from enemies without and disruptive elements within, care, protection and education of children, and all the elaborate arrangements for entertainment, travel, etc., to which we have become accustomed. Animals work too, for some of these reasons, and do so largely through instinctive patterns of behaviour, which are the product of evolutionary processes. It is not clear whether man has innate patterns of work behaviour or not; it is possible that man's capacity for learnt, persistent, goal-directed behaviour in groups is such an innate pattern; it is certainly very well suited to man's extensive material needs for clothes and shelter for example. The carrying out of these persistent patterns of behaviour (whether they are called work or leisure) gives men a sense of identity and purpose, and may be necessary for mental health. By far the greater part of our behaviour at work is the product of cultural factors; through historical processes a society develops certain attitudes to work and ways of working, and these are passed on to children in the course of education and other kinds of socialization. We shall see in later chapters that different civilizations in the past, and different nations in the contemporary world, have evolved very different attitudes to work and very different types of working organization. The Romans thought work was only fit for slaves, while feudal serfs worked because of a sworn obligation to their overlord; Yugoslav factories are owned by the state and controlled by the workers, while Japanese factories are paternalistic and authoritarian.

Working organizations as we know them now in Europe and the U.S.A. have developed since the early Industrial Revolution. Changes have been gradual and pragmatic, in response to changes in technology, increases in the scale and complexity of work, and the ideas of organization theorists. Until very recently there were no empirical studies of the efficiency of alternative kinds of organization or the satisfaction of those working in them. We have now entered a new phase in the history of work – a great deal of research is available on the conditions under which people work effectively and happily. Unfortunately nearly all this research has been done in the U.S.A., Britain and western Europe, i.e. within a particular cultural setting, with a particular set of attitudes to work. We shall try to broaden the generality of the findings by keeping an eye on other historical periods and other countries.

Social psychologists have been studying social behaviour at work since the early 1930s. They have studied such things as behaviour in working groups, the relations between managers and supervisors and those supervised, and the organizational structures associated with work. This has been one of the main spheres of research by social psychologists outside the laboratory – social behaviour at work is affected by many factors not found in the laboratory. They have sometimes been asked to find out the conditions which result in high productivity, measured for example in terms of amount of useful output per man-hour. They have also studied the conditions which result in the greatest job satisfaction. It is an important empirical question how far high output and high job satisfaction are compatible goals. The evidence on this will be discussed later. Social psychologists have also studied the conditions under which absenteeism and labour turnover are lowest; these are found to be low when job satisfaction is high, and when they are low, overall productivity is high and labour costs low.

The social psychology of work really began with the Hawthorne studies in the 1930s, which showed the importance of interaction within working groups. The Human Relations movement demonstrated in numerous studies how the style of supervision and composition of different groups affected their work performance and satisfaction. The Tavistock Institute showed the importance of linking work groups to technology in the best way. Industrial sociologists have studied the operation of different kinds of working organization, and vocational guidance and selection psychologists have shown how people of different abilities and personalities can be placed in the most suitable jobs.

The social psychological scene in this area at the present time is somewhat chaotic. A number of theories of motivation (e.g. Maslow, Herzberg) have become very popular with managers; various forms of social skill training (e.g. T-groups) are now widely used; there are demands for new forms of working organization, for example with more participation in decision-taking and more flexibility. However there is now a considerable body of research findings about the accuracy of these theories and the effectiveness of these training methods, and we shall give a critical account of these ideas and practices in the light of the research.

THE SOCIAL PROBLEMS OF WORK

There are a number of very important social problems in industry today which fall into the sphere of the social psychologist.

Alienation and low job satisfaction. In modern industry a considerable proportion of workers do not really enjoy their work. In one survey it was found that only 16 per cent of unskilled steel workers said that they would choose the same kind of work if they were beginning their career again, as compared for example with 91 per cent of mathematicians (p. 228). Many are *alienated* in the sense that they feel that they have no control over the work process, that the work is meaningless to them, that they do not belong to the work community, and that the work is not an important part of their personalities or lives (p. 225 f.). Work also affects mental and physical health; many workers suffer from high blood pressure, ulcers, heart disease, anxiety and other signs of bodily or mental stress as a result of their work (p. 245 f.).

These various aspects of unhappiness at work are most common in the lowest ranks of industry, though manual workers can enjoy their work very much if the conditions are right. Dissatisfaction is greatest in the most repetitive, machine-controlled jobs, such as assembly-line work. It also depends on the style of supervision received, the nature of the working group and the organizational structure. This is not only a matter for humanitarian concern; low satisfaction is associated with high absenteeism, high labour turnover, and a general lack of co-operation. Research in this area has shown in detail the kind of working conditions necessary for maximizing job satisfaction and minimizing absenteeism and labour turnover (p. 226 f.).

Lack of motivation. In earlier historical periods men (and women) worked because they needed clothes, food, etc. Much work today is not so directly linked to the satisfaction of material needs, and direct motivation has been replaced by economic motivation. Ingenious and sophisticated economic incentive schemes have been devised, but these are all difficult to administer, often fail to create the necessary cooperation, and often bring about a state of affairs where men are working for money and not because they feel that the work is worth doing. There are various methods of appealing to intrinsic motivation, such as creating a concern for the goals of the organization, or by giving opportunities for the exercise of skills and abilities, or challenges to achievement motivation such as setting targets. The problem of motivation has become particularly acute now that many young people feel no great economic need to work, and are not endowed with the motivation to achieve, which was partly responsible for industrial expansion in previous periods of history (p. 23 f.).

Difficulties of communication. For technological reasons working organizations have become large; through the influence of organizational theories these large organizations have also become very hierarchical, with many ranks. This kind of structure creates great difficulties of communication – for example, delays and distortions when information goes upwards, and difficulty in communicating effectively with people two or more steps lower in the hierarchy (p. 192 f.). Other difficulties of

4

communication are due to spatial separation – to people being in different groups or departments, or on different shifts. The formal channels are slow and impersonal, and it is difficult for sufficient informal lateral links to be established. The larger the organization the more acute are these difficulties. When working groups within the larger organization become internally cohesive they tend to become isolated from other groups, thus creating difficulties of cooperation (p. 121).

Conflicts between groups. The conflict between management and labour is institutionalized for Western capitalism in the form of collective bargaining. The unions want to get better pay and working conditions for their members; management may resist because this will add to the cost of the product and make it less competitive. There is also a harmony of interests – the unions do not want to drive the firm out of business, and management do not want an undue level of labour turnover, absenteeism, or other manifestations of dissatisfaction.

However, it can be argued that preserving the management–union conflict in an institutionalized form places too much emphasis on conflict, and not enough on cooperation. An alternative way of dealing with the same problems is to arrange worker participation in some kind of industrial democracy. A number of different forms have been tried out, some of which appear to have been very successful. The unions may play an active role as in the West German system, or a much diminished one as in Yugoslavia.

Problems of technological change. Ever since the days of the Luddites there has been resistance to the installation of new equipment. The prospect of technological change arouses anxieties, realistic and unrealistic, about the difficulties of life under the new system. Management has often found it impossible to install equipment needed to keep up with trade competition because of the resistance of workers, e.g. the use of containers at docks, or various forms of automation. There are successful strategies of social change, involving worker participation

5

in studying the situation and planning the arrangements, and better social skills on the part of management. However, some technological changes *do* make life less pleasant; this is not necessarily the fault of the technology, since the same equipment can be operated with quite different social systems. Other changes, like automation, inevitably have long-term consequences for the number of workers needed, or on their level of skill. It may be argued that such changes should not be considered solely in an economic context, but in terms of their total effect on life in society. It should be a common goal of management and workers' representatives to plan the next step in industrial technology, not only in the pursuit of greater profits or wages, but also to create an optimum working community (p. 44 f.).

Low rates of economic growth. A persistent problem in Britain has been a very slow rate of economic growth. Social factors – resistance to technical change, strikes and other kinds of lack of cooperation, unsuitable organizational structures, inadequate management selection and training – have probably contributed to this.

The situation has, however, changed radically in one important respect. There is now a great deal of empirical knowledge about these matters and about how to create conditions for maximum satisfaction, cooperation and effectiveness. There is still a lot of detailed research to be done, but the most important generalizations are probably now known. While some of these research findings apply only to a particular industry, country or historical period, others appear to be of much wider application. While some of this research has been done from the point of view of management and directed towards productivity, much has been more concerned with the happiness of workers. Fortunately it seems possible to aim for the two goals at the same time; we shall consider the welfare of the whole working organization, and emphasize measures which are in the interest of all. Research is neither pro-management nor pro-anyone else, but may point to designs for working organizations which are most satisfactory from various points of view.

CHAPTER 2

THE BIOLOGICAL AND HISTORICAL ORIGINS OF WORK

'Work' in animals – the evolution of man and his work – work in the most primitive societies – pre-civilized village communities – the ancient civilizations – feudalism – medieval industry – the industrial revolution – liberal capitalism (1850–1939) – recent developments in working conditions (1950–70)

'WORK' IN ANIMALS

THE concept of work is not generally used in accounts of animal behaviour. Nevertheless, the antecedents of work can be seen in all species: they have to find food by hunting or gathering ('agriculture'), build nests or other forms of shelter ('building'), look after their young ('child-rearing' and 'education'), and repel their enemies ('defence'). All these activities are necessary for the survival of particular groups, and the survival of the species. The patterns of work behaviour in a particular species are largely, and in some cases entirely, innate. In the course of evolution there is selection for survival of those members of a species who are best equipped for life in their particular environment. Evolutionary processes result in changes and development both of bodily features, such as antlers and skin colour, and also of patterns of behaviour. These include forms of 'work' behaviour such as nest-building, and forms of social behaviour such as cooperation over nest-building, organization of social groups and means of communication.

The species most famous for their work are ants, termites, bees and other kinds of insect. In an ant colony nest-building and food-gathering is performed entirely by a sub-group of sterile worker-ants; food-gathering may involve ranging round the countryside in large groups, killing other animals and

7

carrying them back to the nest. Some kinds of ant keep members of a second species as slaves to do the work. However, insects are basically different from higher animals and humans in several ways – their behaviour is highly stereotyped, and is not modified by experience; in some ways the whole colony has the properties of a super-organism, the individuals being incomplete in themselves; and communications and social interaction take a very primitive form; for example when the worker-ants meet they feel each other with their antennae, and if one has fed it regurgitates a drop of food to be eaten by the other.

Forms of work and social behaviour rather more similar to those of man are found in higher mammals and birds. Work among apes and monkeys is in fact remarkably similar to work in the most primitive human societies, suggesting that there may be innate factors in human work-patterns also. The following kinds of work are found in all species:

Food-gathering. This may occupy a large proportion of an animal's working hours, depending on how easy food is to find. They may eat grain, fruit, nuts, or other vegetables, or may hunt and kill members of other species. They may be stereotyped in their feeding habits, or may be flexible and learn to eat whatever is available, as some birds learn to peck milk bottles and feed at rubbish tips.

Providing shelter. Many animals make themselves nests, holes, or other forms of shelter, where they and their families will be protected from other animals and from the weather; this may be an individual or a group activity.

Care of infants. Infants have to be fed by their mothers and protected from other animals; in the higher species infants are less well equipped with innate patterns of behaviour, and early socialization is needed to turn them into properly functioning members of their species. Monkeys reared in isolation are unable to cooperate with others; females show no interest in their own children, males do not know how to copulate.

8

Protection of territory. Most species live in groups, each group occupying a piece of territory containing sufficient sources of food and water, and within which nests or other shelters are built. This territory is often fiercely defended by the adult males against other animals of the same or other species who are rivals for the resources of the territory or who may be predators.

The non-human primates, the monkeys and apes, are of particular interest, since they are the animals most similar to man in the evolutionary scale. Compared with lower mammals the primates have more highly developed and sensitive hands, which grasp and have a larger area of the brain associated with them; they have a weaker sense of smell but better vision, which is stereoscopic, again with a larger associated brain area; by standing upright they can see further and free their hands for manipulating objects; they can communicate by a range of noises, gestures and facial expressions, but cannot use symbols (unless taught to do so by humans); chimpanzees, gorillas and orang-utans can make some use of tools; there is a longer period of infant dependence, and males are regular members of the social group and protect the young, though they do not recognize their own children. They live in the jungle (e.g. chimpanzees) or in open grass land (e.g. baboons). In either case their main diet is vegetable – fruit, nuts, leaves or roots, which are usually in plentiful supply. They also eat insects, while baboons eat lizards, scorpions, crabs and mussels. Chimpanzees use a simple tool to eat ants, poking a stick into the ant nest until it is covered with ants and then licking them off. The collecting of food is an individual activity, but the group keeps together, the dominant males deciding where the group shall go to feed.

Most apes and monkeys construct simple nests to sleep in at night, high up in the trees away from predators. Exceptions are baboons, who live in open country and may sleep on ledges or in caves; gorillas sleep in nests or on the ground – they are not afraid of other animals. Nests are very simple, made by bending branches, and are constructed in a few minutes. Most animals sleep alone, in private nests, though infants sleep with their mothers, males may sleep together, and members of a group make their nests close together. It is thought that the animals probably learn how to make nests rather than knowing innately.

Infants are reared mainly by their mothers, though other females help, and adult males protect the infants in their group. They are born with instinctive responses to cling to their mothers with all four hands, and for some time hang on underneath, later graduating to riding on top, and then gradually become independent. Infants have an innate sucking response; they also beg for food from their mothers, but the mothers of most species do not provide food other than milk. Later the infants observe what their mothers eat and do the same themselves; there is little actual instruction. The mother also protects her infants from others, and infants cling tight to her when frightened.

Monkeys and apes live in groups, which may be as large as 750, and each group has a territory which may be as large as 15 square miles. They do not have permanent nests, but there is a core area where the nests are made which contains sources of food and water. Outside the core area they wander over a wider territory which may be shared with other groups.

Groups of primates keep together, sleeping and eating in the same place. For most species there is a stable social order based on a dominance hierarchy of adult males. Males cooperate to defend the group, females cooperate over child-rearing, and there is a lot of purely sociable behaviour consisting of play or grooming, when there is no work to be done. The formation of male groups for attack and defence is found in primates living on the ground in grassland or semi-desert country, where there is a greater need for them to defend their group (Tiger, 1969).

THE EVOLUTION OF MAN AND HIS WORK

Man descended from a branch of the primate family which is now extinct. The earliest remains of primitive ape-men date from about two million B.C. These men made tools, stood more upright than the apes, had smaller canines, but brains no larger than those of apes. During the next two million years primitive men evolved further, and succeeded in adapting genetically and culturally to a variety of climates and habitats, and to the Ice Age. Several important evolutionary developments occurred during this period affecting work and social behaviour.

Increased size of brain. The brain increased four to five times in size, and also changed in organization: the visual and hand areas increased further, as did the areas for coordinating motor responses, and the brain developed neural organization for dealing with language. This all resulted in better tools, better mastery of the environment, and a greater capacity to learn.

Speech. The tongue muscles and other parts of the mouth developed so that the repertoire of sounds was greatly increased; neural links between hearing and vision made the naming of objects possible; and basic grammar was evolved so that words could be combined in meaningful sentences. The original purpose and the biological advantage of language was presumably to enable men to communicate and cooperate over their joint tasks; however it had further consequences such as making the retention and transmission of culture much easier.

The family. Among the non-human primates there had already been an increase in the period of infantile dependence; adult males were regular members of stable groups, protected females and infants, and kept order inside the group. In all human societies there is some more or less permanent form of marriage; the male–female pair is expected to rear children, and to cooperate in the maintenance of their household. Although the family takes a variety of forms, there is always a social group of mother, father and children. This may have an innate basis, though the pattern of kinship relations varies between cultures. It is biologically advantageous for the father to be a permanent member, and this may have been helped by a change in the oestrus cycle whereby human females are sexually receptive at all times, which is not the case for any lower animals. Another universal feature of the human family is the taboo against incest, forbidding marriage to close relatives; it is not known whether this is innate or not, but it has the effect of creating bonds between families, and thus creating a larger community.

Physiological changes. Some of the developments noted for primates were continued – the decline of smell at the expense of vision, better hands, and so on. Humans also succeeded in adapting themselves – in cold climates men became short and squat, in hot climates tall and lanky. In sunny regions darker skins were favoured, since they provide protection from the sun. There were adaptations to high and low altitudes, and people were bred with resistance to the local diseases.

In more recent historical times evolution has been proceeding in a similar manner, producing better immunity to disease, and changes of physical and mental equipment that make us able to survive better in our various environments, though evolutionary developments take many generations to have effect. Darlington (1969) has argued that historical changes can be partly explained by regulations governing breeding, which may encourage or discourage genetic mixture, keep certain social groups apart, prevent part of the population from breeding, and so on. However, changes during the last 4,000 years are much more the result of cultural development – the gradual accumulation of new patterns of behaviour introduced by innovations diffused through a social group, and taught to children. Evolution proceeds by selecting those species with the greatest survival value; cultural development operates by selecting those ways of life which are found to be most satisfactory, biologically and otherwise; however, culture is passed on by learning, while evolutionary developments are passed on genetically. Learning from the culture has become important as a direct result of the evolutionary development of the larger brain, speech and the prolonged period of childhood dependence. Human beings with the same physiological equipment are capable of learning to live in a great variety of different styles. Humans live in communities, and each community has its own culture. Cultures are 'historically created designs for living, explicit and implicit, rational, irrational and non-rational, which exist at any given time as potential guides for the conduct of man' (Kluckhohn, 1954). Culture is learnt, though it may also reflect innate dispositions or abilities in the community. For our present purposes the most important aspect is the technology and material culture – tools, weapons, clothes, houses, boats, etc. Another important aspect of culture is language, the way events are categorized and symbolized. Culture also embraces forms of social organization, rules and laws, ideas and beliefs, morals and religion. Within each society certain types of personality and certain forms of motivation are encouraged and become prevalent.

Culture is developed and modified when individuals or groups of individuals suggest new ways of doing things, either through their own creativity or by borrowing from other groups. Such innovations become accepted if the innovator is in a powerful position or is very persuasive, and if the innovation constitutes a real contribution towards dealing with the environment or competitors. The most useful cultural elements are retained and others dropped. According to the culture pattern theory (e.g. Benedict, 1934) the various elements of the culture tend to form a harmonious system, in which groups of elements are mutually consistent and support each other. If this is correct it would be expected that the least consistent elements would be dropped first and it explains why there are periods of stabilization or very slow social change.

Culture is passed on and conserved in a number of ways. Children are socialized into the culture by parents and teachers. This teaches them the basic structure of the culture – its language, concepts and categories. Socialization also builds up motivational systems, such as aggressive, achievement and power drives. Part of the socialization process prepares people for work. African peasants find industrial work very difficult because they have not been accustomed to working regular hours, under supervision, by set methods. In modern societies children are first prepared for work at school (p. 62), and are later given further training when they start work: they are taught working skills and how to behave in working groups and organizations. Many aspects of the culture are embodied in rules of various sorts; some are laws (e.g. against stealing) which are backed by official punishment for deviation; others are social norms (e.g. about what clothes to wear) which are backed by social disapproval and rejection of deviates.

The growth of science and technology introduced a new feature into the cultural scene – a regular and continuous source of change in the material conditions of life. The growth of social science is beginning to introduce a further source of social change, via research into the most effective forms of social organization, and perhaps of society as a whole (Beals and Hoijer, 1965).

WORK IN THE MOST PRIMITIVE SOCIETIES

In the rest of this chapter we shall try to outline the historical development of work in human societies, from the most primitive up to the present day. One of the main factors in the social organization of work is the particular technology, so we shall begin each section by referring to relevant features of the technology of the period, for three main areas of work – agriculture, manufacturing and building. We shall then describe the main forms of incentive and motivation, and the subjective meaning of work; the nature of working groups; leadership and management; the division of labour; and relations with the wider society.

During the Stone Age, down to about 8000 B.C., there were communities of 'hunters and gatherers'. There are still some very primitive tribes in remote areas which have been little touched by civilization, that are probably very similar to Stone-Age societies – the aboriginals in Australia, pygmies and bushmen in Africa, and tribes in New Guinea. These tribes were nomadic, following herds of wild game and seasonal fruits. They did not keep domestic animals or cultivate crops, but hunted and fished, and gathered wild fruit and vegetables. Various tools were used for the production of food – axes, pestles and mortars, clubs, spears and missiles for hunting and fishing, baskets and pottery containers for holding and preparing food. Clothes were manufactured by weaving rushes and bark, and from skins. There was some manufacture of tools from wood, bone and stone. These primitive men made simple dwellings such as tents from skins, huts from branches, or lived in caves. The incentive to work was the satisfaction of the immediate biological needs of the family – for food and shelter; there was no money and no barter. Work was not thought of as a separate category of behaviour; there was no word for it. There were no special groups to do it, and it was combined with purely social activity, and with ritual. Everybody worked, including children and leaders, and they had to work nearly all the time.

The working group was for many purposes the family, which was much more permanent than for most species of apes and monkeys. Families moved about in rather fluid groups, related by kinship. There was a second form of grouping when they engaged in hunting or fishing – groups of male kinsmen. Tiger (1969) has suggested that the formation of close bonds between males has evolutionary advantages for hunting and fighting and is part of man's instinctive equipment.

Families were usually led by the father, the oldest and strongest male. There was division of labour between the sexes, women doing most of the gathering and preparing of food, while men did the hunting and building. Children were taught the patterns of work behaviour in their families. This was partly by imitation, since they could constantly see adults working; instead of playing, children were given scaled-down weapons and tools to use (Hobhouse *et al.*, 1915).

PRE-CIVILIZED VILLAGE COMMUNITIES

From about 8,000 B.C. onwards there were developments in agriculture – the cultivation of crops, such as barley and wheat, and the keeping of domestic animals, such as sheep and goats. These developments took place at different dates in different parts of the world, and occurred first in the fertile areas by rivers in the Middle East, China, India and North Africa.

These changes in food production were of crucial importance since they led to more permanent dwelling-places, and to the growth of villages of increasing size. At first these communities engaged in both pastoral and agricultural work, but later they specialized into pastoral and cultivating societies. These were the main kinds of human society until the rise of the ancient civilizations from 2,500 B.C. onwards, though these village communities survived until much later in Britain and elsewhere. This way of life can still be seen in many contemporary primitive societies. Cultivation of the soil consisted in clearing, digging, planting and reaping, mainly of cereals; this involved the use of new tools, such as metal hoes and ploughs. Animals were kept for pulling, and there were herds of cattle. The manufacture of clothes became more elaborate and included spinning and weaving. Metal objects were made from bronze and iron; pottery and wooden canoes were made; and more substantial houses were constructed from wood or stone.

The incentive to work was still the satisfaction of fairly immediate needs, but on a more long-term basis than for the hunters and gatherers. Goods were also exchanged between families or villages, on the basis of either reciprocity or barter. At a later stage primitive forms of money developed, e.g. shells, and goods were sold in the market. In some societies there was a kind of primitive communism in which all goods belonged to the community, while in others individual families owned their own houses, land and animals (Weber, 1923). Work was less closely related to immediate needs than in more primitive communities; where barter or money were involved, work was still part of a traditional way of life, but led to material prosperity for the family. Work was motivated in other ways too: it was part of a collective task, performed as a duty to others, there was pride in craftsmanship, and it was accompanied by religious ritual, music and story-telling, and the enjoyment of social relationships. Work was an integral part of life and was not distinguished from leisure (Thomas, 1964).

Work was done in groups, for example groups of kinsmen, but these were not organized specially for work. The whole village might work together at large projects such as building a house or gathering in the harvest. The leadership structure for work was the same as that for the tribe or village, with two or more levels of leadership, the leaders usually being male. When a hierarchical structure of leadership developed, subordinates were paid, work became specialized and rewards were proportional to the work done (Udy, 1959). Division of labour proceeded further in these societies; there were farmers and herdsmen, craftsmen and traders, and some who did no manual work at all – priests and magicians, and chiefs. Some forms of work conveyed higher status than others – dealing with animals was often prestigious, though owning land was important in some societies. Work created links with the wider society outside the village, through the exchange and marketing of goods, which both supplied complementary needs, and created social bonds between different communities. Men did hunting, fishing, metalwork and boat-building, while women carried water, did most of the farming, prepared food, made clothes and pottery.

THE ANCIENT CIVILIZATIONS

From about 2,500 B.C. to A.D. 500 the ancient civilizations appeared – Sumerian, Egyptian, Hellenic and others, all of them achieving great things and later collapsing. The Roman Empire is the most familiar example. These societies were different from anything before them in that (1) people lived in cities as well as villages – this was due to the increased efficiency of agriculture, making it possible for craftsmen and others to congregate in cities; (2) there was administrative control of large areas of land and large numbers of people; (3) power was maintained by the army; and (4) most manual work was performed by slaves, who were subjugated peoples or prisoners of war. We shall describe conditions in the Roman Empire.

There were various technical advances in agriculture, such as the development of new crops. The most important change, however, was that most of the work was done by slaves, often in chains, and sometimes maimed to prevent escape. There was considerable development of manufacturing

17

industries, especially of woollen clothes, pots and ironwork; there were mines, mills and shipping. Some manufacturing, for example of clothes, was done at home, by women and slaves, but most metalwork, pottery, leatherwork, glassblowing, brickmaking and textile work was done in 'ergasterions' (workshops) where up to a hundred men worked under a foreman. The workshops were owned by wealthy men, successful craftsmen, or by temples, and the goods were marketed, often abroad. Several kinds of incentives were operative. The slaves were compelled by law to work and were severely punished if they did not; in exchange they were given lifelong board and keep, but were not normally paid. In the workshops there were also freemen, who were paid for doing identical work to that of the slaves. There were prospects of promotion to the position of foreman for slaves and others who were good at their work. Independent craftsmen set up specialized workshops in the cities, where they sold their goods directly. There were also wealthy owners of farms and workshops, who delegated all management to promoted slaves and did no work themselves.

A new form of motivation appeared with, and was partly responsible for, the great ancient civilizations – the need for achievement. McClelland (1961) has found evidence that this motivation was highest during the period of greatest economic growth in Greece, between 900 and 475 B.C., and declined as trade levelled off and diminished. He measured achievement motivation by counting the number of achievement themes in samples of Greek literature from different periods; the measure of economic activity used was Heichelheim's listing of the areas in which Greek vases (for exporting olive oil and wine) were found. The degree of achievement motivation was consistent with two further measures – the proportion of passages of literature oriented towards the future, and vase designs which were similar to designs drawn by high achievers now – more diagonals and S-shapes and less unused space. The need to achieve motivated men to seek fortunes, expand empires, construct huge and often useless buildings, and drove them to be associated with great enterprises of all kinds.

Manual work, in field or workshop was no longer accompanied by the intrinsic rewards and satisfactions of an earlier age. Such work was generally regarded as servile and degrading, and was passed on to slaves. It was more noble to do nothing or to engage in intellectual or administrative work (Neff, 1968).

The working group was still small in many households and small estates, but included perhaps six slaves. There were also larger groups in workshops and large farms, with up to a hundred slaves and freedmen, under foremen.

The supervision of working groups presented no difficulties in small households and estates, where the slaves were often looked after and treated well, in a paternalistic manner. However in the large workshops and farms working groups were found very difficult to handle, both because of the unwillingness of the workers and the large numbers involved. Some of the supervisors were themselves slaves, others monks or soldiers. In any case they found it very difficult to extract efficient work from slaves, punitive discipline being the only incentive available, including lashing, chains and execution. The competition from workshops of freedmen, the shortage of prisoners of war, and the expense of upkeep eventually led to the collapse of slavery in the later Roman Empire (Weber, 1923). Division of labour developed particularly in the metal and pottery industries, otherwise there was only division by crafts. Women no longer worked in the fields, but confined themselves to household crafts. The organization of work reflected the structure of the wider society – large-scale organization by authoritarian military rule, a subservient slave class, and large export markets in the Empire (Ingram, 1926).

FEUDALISM

Slavery collapsed in the West during the later years of the Roman Empire, and was replaced by serfdom under the feudal system, which was at its height in England between A.D. 1066 and 1300. Feudalism was a system of economic and social stratification in which a knight, usually the lord of the manor, gave his serfs the right to use land and provided protection and security, in return for which they gave him some of their produce, money, a certain number of days' service per year, or some combination of these. The knight was related in a similar way to a baron or other land-holder at a higher level in the hierarchy. The inequalities were accepted – each person had his place in society.

There were no technological advances of note during this period. Farming was conducted on the three-field system; buildings were made of stone in the towns, but of wood, wattle and thatch in the country; manufacture of cloth and household goods was carried out on the estates, as well as by craftsmen in the town. Power was provided by water, wind and animals.

There were two main incentives to work – direct provision for the family, and sworn obligation. The bond of personal loyalty and dependence on the landowner was the central and essential feature of feudalism, and people would work and fight for their superiors in the system with no direct economic reward, beyond permission to farm a small area of land. Work was regarded as a moral and religious duty, and necessary for salvation; it was also enforced by law. Agricultural work and handicrafts were thought of as necessities of life, and were accompanied by many of the satisfactions of more primitive village life – it was closely linked with social life, church festivals and sport (Thomas, 1964). The upper classes, on the other hand, despised manual work, and the monks taught that intellectual and religious work was superior to manual work.

There were small working groups composed of individual families, and larger groups based on the manor-house, including those serfs who were temporarily or permanently engaged in agricultural and craft work around the manorial estate. This was a close-knit social network in which everyone had his place, and was looked after by the others.

The style of leadership was personal and paternalistic, and based on a high degree of acceptance of authority, and the dependence of subordinates on landowners. There was little hostility between landowners and peasants; their positions were fixed but complementary, and each side recognized its social responsibilities towards the other. There was little division of labour on farms, but there was specialization in different crafts within the manorial system. The manorial village was the basic social and economic unit; it provided cohesive protection against the wider society outside, and created a system of political and military organization. The produce of the manor was sold to people in other villages and in the towns, different manors specializing in different kinds of manufacture. The feudal system collapsed after the Black Death, when labour became very scarce, and as a result of the expansion of town and industry, and the possibility of working for payment (Prawer and Eisenstadt, 1968).

MEDIEVAL INDUSTRY

During and after the feudal period craftsmen with small workshops in the towns operated on a very different basis. There were no technological advances of note until the fifteenth century, when new ways of making woollen cloth were devised.

The main incentive was now payment, either by the day as in the building industry, or by results as in the wool trade. Rates of pay and other conditions of service were regulated by the craft guilds. Work was regarded not only as natural and necessary, but as serving God and society; men should work hard but not seek to enjoy the profits made. The working group was small, consisting of the master craftsman, journeymen and apprentices, usually working in the master-craftsman's house; often the master had only one or two assistants. Leadership fell to the more experienced master craftsman, who also owned the premises and tools, but he worked alongside his assistants. There was no division of labour within workshops, only between them.

A second stage in industrial growth was the 'domestic system' of 'merchant capitalism', from about 1600 in England. Some master craftsmen became prosperous, ceased to do the manual work themselves, and became employers. They put out work to individual families in town and country on a piecework basis, providing the materials and sometimes the tools, and selling the produce. Some employees sub-contracted the work to others. Under the domestic system the family was the main form of working group, working in the home. Incentives were now entirely financial in contrast with feudalism, workers being paid by piecework when the work was completed, or sometimes when it was sold. Payment was irregular, and workers were often in debt to their employers. Some were retained on a permanent basis, which usually meant that they were legally tied to their employer and unable to move to another. There was virtually no supervision of workers – they often embezzled the materials supplied, there was no check on the quality of work, and the rate at which they worked was irregular. The domestic system made considerable specialization possible, in that different family groups developed particular skills. This system survived until the technological advances of the Industrial Revolution made it necessary to bring larger numbers of workers to one place (Pollard, 1965).

The craft guilds were social and professional societies containing all the members of a craft in a town. They maintained standards, looked after the economic interests of their members, and cared for those in need, as well as arranging social and religious functions. There was a series of grades of craftsmen – apprentices, journeymen and master craftsmen – and men could work their way up. There was far more social mobility than under the feudal social structure of the countryside.

It is generally believed by historians that the ideas of the Protestant reformers, Calvin, Luther and Zwingli, influenced the development of capitalism. Max Weber (1904) observed that the rise of Protestantism and the rise of capitalism coincided in England and in several European countries; he thought that Protestant working girls worked harder and saved their money, and that Protestant entrepreneurs did better than Catholic ones. Weber's explanation was that certain Protestant ideas encouraged capitalistic activities. The reformers taught that men would be individually judged, and would be judged on the basis of their whole life's work, of which their 'calling' was the most important part; on the other hand money should not be spent on oneself. This led to a life of hard work, self-discipline, asceticism and concern with achievement; it also led to the accumulation of money which could not be spent on luxury, but which could be put into one's own business. Calvin taught predestination, and here the link with capitalism is more obscure: it was thought that the elect could be recognized by certain outward signs, which included self-denial and devotion to duty, and it was also believed that God caused the elect to prosper (Brown, 1965). A rather different interpretation was given to these events by Tawney (1926) who maintained that the spirit of individualism, rather than any specific Protestant doctrines was the cause of capitalism. If Catholic and Protestant countries are compared today, there is no doubt that the Protestant countries are more prosperous. McClelland (1961) reports the *per capita* electricity consumption in 1950 for 25 countries: for the Protestant countries the average is 1,893, for the Catholic countries, 474. There are some exceptions however – Belgium, Austria and France are higher than Denmark and Holland.

McClelland offered a social psychological explanation for the link between Protestantism and capitalism. This is shown below.

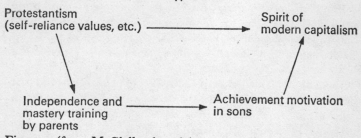

Weber's hypothesis

Protestantism (self-reliance values, etc.) ⟶ Spirit of modern capitalism

Independence and mastery training by parents ⟶ Achievement motivation in sons

Figure 1 (from McClelland, 1961).
Copyright © 1961 by Litton Educational Publishing, Inc.
Reprinted by permission of Van Nostrand Reinhold Company

The theory is that Protestant ideas and values produce (1) a certain way of bringing up children, which (2) leads to the children acquiring strong achievement motivation, and (3) high achievers become entrepreneurs and create an expansion of business. McClelland found that in England during the period 1500–1800 achievement motivation as measured from the content analysis of samples of literature rose and fell with the level of coal imports, except that the achievement changes were about fifty years ahead of the coal import changes. There was a similar relation between achievement imagery in children's reading books and the number of patents issued in the U.S.A. between 1800 and 1950, as is shown in Figure 2.

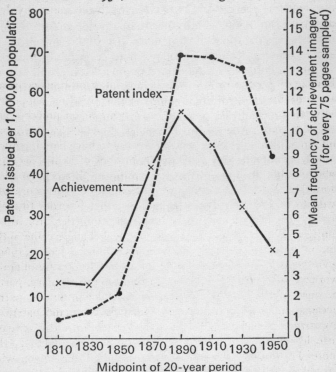

Figure 2. Mean frequency of achievement imagery in children's readers and the patent index in the United States, 1800–1950 (from McClelland, 1961).

In a study of 40 nations, there was found to be a correlation of 0·53 between motivation in 1925 (assessed by content analysis of children's reading books) and growth in the electricity supply between 1925 and 1950. One way in which McClelland has modified Weber's hypothesis is in suggesting that capitalist activity is not produced simply by affiliation with a Protestant church but by a feeling that the individual is in touch with God, without need of priest or ritual, and a belief that salvation depends on his life's work. Meanwhile McClelland's ideas have stimulated a great deal of research though the issues involved are by no means settled (Brown, 1965).

THE INDUSTRIAL REVOLUTION

The conditions under which an industrial revolution occurs are not fully understood. In England, where this first happened, between 1769 and 1850, the discovery of steam-power – and various inventions in the textile industry – were clearly important. In addition, it is probably necessary to have banking and a supply of capital, and a sufficient number of skilled workers who are able to adjust to the new conditions of work. In addition, there must be a number of innovators, entrepreneurs who want to build up industrial concerns, either in order to make money themselves or, in communist countries, for other motives. The first important technological changes came in the cotton industry, such as Arkwright's spinning jenny (1769), giving cotton the lead over wool for a time. Larger numbers of workers were brought together in the same work place, partly because of the need for expensive capital equipment, partly because small-scale production was not economic, partly to improve supervision. There was also a revolution in agriculture, less dramatic than that in industry, but essential to it – the increased productivity of farming supplied the towns with capital as well as food. In 1688 76 per cent of the population of England worked on the land; in 1800 35 per cent; now it is only 4 per cent (partly since some of our food is imported) (Edholm, 1967). The main changes were improved machinery, such as ploughs and threshing machines, new crops and breeds, better drainage, fertilizers, specialization in different areas, and larger estates. During the Industrial Revolution the results of scientific and technological research were for the first time applied systematically to improve the techniques of production.

The entrepreneurs played a very important role in the Industrial Revolution. The early entrepreneurs in England were mostly middle-class merchants with some capital; a minority were ex-craftsmen, self-made men; in the coal and steel industry in particular, capital was essential. They were not well educated, but they knew their own trade. They were non-conformists. They shared a faith in progress and an enthusiasm for technical inventions. They were a rising prosperous class, despised by the landed aristocracy; many lived austerely, reinvesting rather than spending their profits, and few sought to infiltrate the aristocracy (Bendix, 1956). They fit perfectly the description of the high need achiever given above (p. 23). In addition they must have had unusual originality, to have had the vision of building up a totally new kind of working organization. While some were unscrupulous and many were authoritarian, others like Robert Owen had a utopian vision of the ideal working community, in which there was cooperation, a happy and healthy environment and character training. The factories were administered by the owners, assisted by a new class of managers, products of the leading schools, who worked hard and often ended up as partners. They were not professional managers so much as experts in their particular industry.

There was little positive desire to go to work in the new factories; small craftsmen were driven out of business and many peasants driven off the land by enclosure; both were offered better wages, though worse conditions, in the factories. Many preferred poverty at home to being uprooted to work in factories.

'Factory discipline must have seemed as irrational, as irrelevant to one's interests, as unfree, as army discipline today. Self-respecting men would not send their children into factories which looked like workhouses. Women and pauper children filled the factories, plus Welsh and Irish immigrants who lacked the English tradition of freedom' (C. Hill, in Thomas, 1964).

In their efforts to control workers and make them work, employers used fines for lateness and absenteeism, low wages (so that hunger would keep them at work), long hours (to keep them out of the public houses), corporal punishment (especially for children), dismissal – and resultant starvation and prison. A few firms used wage incentives. Employers had considerable powers over employees, since joint action by employees was forbidden, travel to other places dangerous, and many workers were legally tied to their employers. With fluctuating unemployment there was extreme insecurity for workers.

In the new factories much larger groups of workers were gathered together than before, many of them women and children, under the direction of foremen. The process of converting craftsmen and peasants into industrial workers was a difficult one. They had previously worked at home and were not accustomed to the conditions of industrial work. In addition they were no doubt deeply disturbed by the conditions of work and the kind of supervision experienced. The relation between managers or supervisors, and workers was a curious one. On the one hand it was a personal relationship in which managers knew their men personally, and exercised some degree of paternalistic benevolence; on the other hand workers were clearly treated very badly, and sacked at once if inefficient. The traditional feudal relationship was used as a means of controlling workers by eliciting obedience and deference – but without the duties of the master being taken very seriously (cf. Bendix, 1956).

Workers were frequently absent, late, idle or drunk, fought each other, produced poor quality work, and had no ambition to become prosperous or respectable. The discipline enforced was tyrannical and brutal, and many children died in mines and factories. This was a very unhappy period for workers: instead of working at home, where work was a meaningful part of life, they worked only for money, at meaningless tasks from which they were totally alienated. The organizations which the employers built up were military hierarchical structures, with maximum division of labour, where workers were controlled by rewards and punishments. Very little concern was paid to the welfare of the workers, who were regarded as part of the factory equipment. This set of practices was later embodied in the 'classical organization theory' of Fayol and others (p. 185).

The Industrial Revolution transformed society, creating large towns, and an urbanized working class who had no power and were alienated and discontented with their work. It also increased the prosperity of both employers and workers and led to the growth of trade unions and the Marxist ideology. Workers were treated better in small village factories where there was a more personal relationship with the owners. Conditions improved partly as a result of humanitarian influences, partly because it was realized that workers would do better work if looked after better.

England was the first country to have an industrial revolution. Other European countries followed a similar pattern of development later. In the U.S.A. the process was somewhat different because of a shortage of labour and the availability of free land, resulting in an emphasis on mechanized methods of production. Countries whose technological take-off came later still were able to profit from the painful experience of the first countries to undergo the process, and could make use of the latest technological and administrative methods.

LIBERAL CAPITALISM
(1850–1939)

During this period, in the West, the conditions of work changed in a number of ways. There was continuous technological innovation, resulting in larger and more efficient factories of all kinds. Iron was succeeded by steel, steam by electricity, and new industries – such as cars and aircraft – appeared.

Attitudes to work in other countries developed rather differently. In the U.S.A. wages were high and people worked in order to sustain a high level of consumption; in the U.S.S.R. work was performed as part of a national effort in the face of a continual state of emergency (Fox, 1971); in Japan workers were looked after for life in paternalistic and feudal working organizations.

Many firms introduced systems of incentive payment. Due to new government regulations and the increasing power of trade unions, management was not able to use negative sanctions as much as before: there was still the fear of dismissal, but it was easier to move to other jobs.

Working groups took various forms, including a new pattern characteristic of the period – assembly-line production groups. The style of supervision was usually authoritarian; workers were assumed to be inherently lazy and incapable of self-discipline, and to be motivated solely by economic needs. Relationships were impersonal and rules were devised to define the rights and duties of employees.

It was believed that there should be the greatest possible division of labour, so that each worker carried out a very simple task at which he could become expert. The invention of time and method study at the turn of the century made it possible to standardize every job in order that the simplest set of movements could be used and appropriate piecework rates established. The conditions of work and the treatment of workers were greatly improved as a result of government regulations, e.g. against child labour, and the activities of the trade unions. Nevertheless many workers were extremely alienated and discontented with their work.

RECENT DEVELOPMENTS IN WORKING CONDITIONS (1950–70)

There have been a number of developments during this period, which will be discussed in greater detail later. The main technological change has been automation, which is still proceeding rapidly in advanced countries. This reduces costs, through needing fewer workers, and has widespread effects on the condition of work and the relations between workers (p. 49 f.).

Some firms have introduced wage incentives during this period, others have removed them – because machine-pacing has made them unnecessary. There has been a search for non-economic, 'intrinsic' forms of motivation (p. 91 f.).

While automation has often led to the breaking up of working groups there has also been a greater awareness of the importance of groups. Some organizations have constructed 'functional groups' to make the best use of group processes (p. 44 f.).

Styles of supervision have been much affected by the Human Relations movement (p. 186 f.), via training courses and management consultants. There has also been something of a reaction against this movement, and a realization that concern for people and concern for productivity need to be combined in supervisory skills (p. 144 f.).

The hierarchical structures of classical organization theory have been much criticized and there have been experiments with other kinds of organizational structure – decentralization, industrial democracy, and structures based on systems analysis (p. 198f).

Continued technological progress has various pros and cons. On the positive side there are the economic advantages of reduced labour costs, a lot of very boring jobs are abolished, and a large proportion of highly skilled technologists employed. On the negative side workers are continually laid off, and become unemployed, some of the new jobs are fairly monotonous, promotion prospects are reduced, and the forms of social grouping may be unsatisfying – though this can be avoided by skilful reorganization.

CHAPTER 3

THE EFFECTS OF TECHNOLOGY

Man-machine systems – socio-technical systems – technology and working groups – technology and social organization – automation.

MANUAL work involves the use of tools or other equipment to manipulate material objects; clerical work uses office equipment to deal with words and numbers; supervision and management consists of organizing men and machines to get the work done. The nature of work is greatly affected by the technology, from Stone-Age axes to automated motor-car factories, from counting on fingers to using computers. The technology affects job satisfaction, relations between workers, relations with supervisors and managers and the kind of organization needed.

The growth of civilization has been accompanied and partly caused by the development of more sophisticated technology. One aspect of this has been a growth in the use of steam and other power: between 1850 and 1950 the percentage of industrial power derived from machines rather than from men or animals in the U.S.A. rose from 14 per cent to 80 per cent; the power controlled by each man was about 50 times that in countries like Turkey and Albania (Dubin, 1958). Other technological developments have taken over the functions of individual craftsmen, as in automatic machine tools, textile machinery, and so on. Inventions such as television, aircraft and space travel create whole new industries for the manufacture and operation of the new equipment. Part of the drive towards more elaborate technology is economic – to make the same goods more cheaply, usually with fewer workers. The increase in industrial output in Japan of 217 per cent between 1953 and 1961 was not achieved by Japanese workers rushing

31

round 3·17 times as fast: it was achieved by the installation of a massive amount of new equipment, so that there was an enormous increase of productivity per man. The greater productivity of American compared with British firms is largely, perhaps wholly, due to the greater amount of capital equipment per worker in the U.S.A. Another goal is the development of new products or services, or the solution of military, medical or social problems. Carrying passengers from London to New York in seven hours was not achieved by getting aircrews to work harder, or by training them better: it was accomplished by jet aircraft.

When any new piece of equipment is designed, some attention is paid to the men who will operate it; the machine is designed to suit the man. However, as we shall see, machine designers take account only of certain basic physiological aspects of the man.

MAN-MACHINE SYSTEMS

New equipment is introduced because it helps workers to do a job better, or faster, or to do some new job. The first approach to the interaction between man and machine was method study; this consists of finding the most efficient method of working, training men to use it, and selecting those most suited to the job. A later development was ergonomics; this is concerned with the optimum design of equipment. The present approach is to design 'man-machine systems' in which the best combination of men and machines is designed, where both men and machines do what they can do best. A man riding a motorcycle, a secretary typing, or a man operating twenty-two automatic looms, are examples. In each case the machine is introduced so that the operator can do something better or more cheaply than he could without it. In each case the man is there because the machine cannot do it all by itself. At any stage of the available technology there are some things the man can do better, some things the machine can do better. A motorcycle can go faster and further than a bicycle, by using machine power, but it still needs a man to steer it. The technology is not yet available to steer the motorcycle.

Equipment has to be designed with some regard for those who will operate it. Equipment design has paid attention primarily to the physiological properties of man such as what he is able to see, hear or reach, but without much regard to what he will find interesting or satisfying, or to the social relationships created by technology. The human operator has three main functions to perform, and in each of these the machinery can be adapted to his physiological capacities.

(1) *Receiving information*, from visual displays, the environment or other people. A lot of research has been done into the kinds of dials which can be read most easily, and the conditions under which information should be visual or auditory.

(2) *Processing information in decision-taking*. A worker often has to take account of several kinds of information, and then make decisions on the basis of his knowledge and skills, e.g. the pilot of an aircraft. One of man's most useful abilities is that of taking complex decisions in new and varied circumstances.

(3) *Motor responses* – made by manipulating objects or controls in some way. Much research has been done into the design of these controls for maximum ease of use. (Chapanis, 1965). However, the situation is continually changing as 'machines' become increasingly sophisticated. Machines can not only think now, they can read, talk, play games, plan ahead, control other machines, and be given 'personalities' (Minsky *et al.*, '1968). Not only are machines taking over more and more of our work, but our relationship to them is changing.

The systematic study of methods of working was begun by Gilbreth (1909). In one of his early studies he found that bricklaying could be reduced from eighteen movements to five, with the result that men could lay 350 bricks in an hour instead of 120. Even today it is sometimes possible to increase productivity by up to 200 per cent by these methods – using both hands, cutting out unnecessary movements, etc. However everyone has to do the job in exactly the same way, whether he likes it or not. Furthermore method study has been combined with a move towards greater division of tasks – the idea being that each worker should be an expert at carrying out a few simplified and standardized movements, and should be able to do them very well and quickly. It has been realized for some time that this development has gone too far, producing great discontent and boredom, and loss of motivation. Friedmann (1961) reported a slaughterhouse where one man did nothing but remove pigs' testicles, while another linked a sausage every three seconds.

Workers do not respond like passive machines to the working conditions imposed upon them; they react constructively and creatively to satisfy any of their needs which are not being met. Assembly-line workers create interest and variety in their work by playing practical jokes, such as fixing cars so that stepping on the accelerator blows the horn and starts the wipers, or may engage in various kinds of horseplay such as glueing each other's toolboxes to the floor. Together with horseplay and other games workers attempt to gain control of their rate of work by saving it up, and not handing in completed work during a busy period, so that they can take it easy later. They may modify parts of the job, change round with other workers, make a game out of the job, set goals for themselves, let the machinery break down or deliberately sabotage it (Sayles and Strauss, 1966).

It is possible to change the working arrangements, without changing the technology, to make it more satisfying and motivating. This can be done by job enlargement – each worker carries out a wider variety of operations, when for example assembly tasks are allocated to a smaller number of people. Job rotation – workers learn to perform a number of different skills and change round periodically; this is very useful in work-teams. Job enrichment ('vertical job enlargement') – elements of supervision are included in the job; the worker may be partly responsible for planning, supplies, repair and maintenance and becomes something of an independent craftsman. The pace can be varied by the introduction of rest periods. Sub-goals, and a sense of progress and the completion of meaningful task units can be created by setting targets (p. 95 f.). The individual can become a member of a social group, where the members cooperate over a task and provide social satisfactions for each other.

Technology has created quite different types of work at different stages of its development. *Craft work* and *one-off production* was typical of an earlier era but is still found in many skilled jobs, e.g. those of printers, electricians, toolmakers and others. A craftsman has complete control over the speed and method of working, there is a very varied product, he is highly skilled and responsible for doing the job. Blauner (1964) concludes as follows from his study of printers: 'When work provides opportunities for control, meaning and self-expression, it becomes an end in itself, rather than simply a means to live' (p. 53).

Machine-tending and assembly-line work. The typical technology of the period 1850–1950 consisted of machine-minding, as in textiles, and assembly-line work, as in the car industry. The jobs created were described above in connection with method study: they are typically machine-paced, with a short cycle of movements, and no control over pace or method of working.

More advanced technology, as found in the chemical industry, electric power stations and automated factories, has brought a return to more favourable working conditions, similar to those of craft workers (p. 49 f.).

SOCIO-TECHNICAL SYSTEMS

Most technological systems need more than one person to operate them. A bicycle can be ridden by one person, but a space-craft requires a large number of personnel who do different jobs and are closely coordinated with one another. Some technical systems impose certain social arrangements; others can be operated by alternative social arrangements which are each compatible with the technology. The combination of technology and social arrangements is called the socio-technical system (Rice, 1958). Until recently almost no attention was paid to the effects of technology on the social relations between workers. The main relationship envisaged was between a fore-man and the individuals he supervised. In fact the matter is far more complex than that.

When a worker has to deal with his job, and with other workers, he is carrying out a combination of a technical skill and a social skill. Although socio-technical systems have been studied as a whole as sociological units, little research has yet been done on the performance of the socio-technical skills involved. Three main kinds may be distinguished, with subdivisions.

Cooperation over a task.

(1) Parallel performance of similar tasks, e.g. independent assembly work, typing, research.
(2) Cooperative performance of similar tasks, e.g. two-handed sawing, 2–3 men handling sheet steel in a press-shop.
(3) Cooperative and simultaneous performance of different but complementary tasks, e.g. pilot and navigator of a plane.

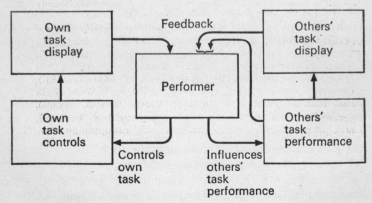

Figure 3. Performance of a socio-technical skill.

(4) Sequential performance of different but complementary tasks, e.g. assembly-line work, the different jobs in coal-mining.

In all of these cases the worker receives input information *both* from the work of other persons *and* from his own task displays such as dials; he can control events either by influencing the other or by manipulating the controls of his own task. The general model may be shown as above (Fig. 3).

The different feedbacks have to be considered together – for example it may be necessary for different jobs to be synchronized in time.

Supervisory relationships.

(5) Supervision, e.g. by foreman.
(6) Inspection.
(7) One person is an assistant to others, e.g. doctor–nurse, research worker–technician.

In these cases one person does not do the work himself but has to make sure that someone else does it properly.

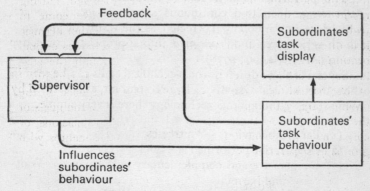

Figure 4. Supervisory skill.

The supervisor receives feedback both from the task display *and* from studying his subordinates' behaviour.

Other social relationships. Other kinds of social skill are commonly found in socio-technical systems:

(8) Conveying objects or information.
(9) Discussion, by members of a cooperative problem-solving group.
(10) Negotiation, where there is some conflict of interest.
(11) Providing expert advice, without authority.

These situations are all examples of social skills, for which the model is:

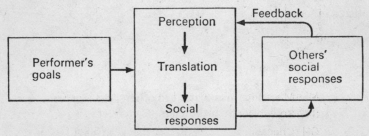

Figure 5. Performance of a social skill.

The performer is *motivated* to influence the *others' social responses* and emits a continuous stream of *social responses* which are continuously corrected as the result of *feedback*, which is *perceived* and *translated* into appropriate corrective action (Argyle, 1969; 1978).

Several of these different socio-technical skills can be seen in the socio-technical system of a large restaurant, as described by Whyte (1948), though the 'technology' here is very simple.

(1) Parallel behaviour – Waitresses
(2) Cooperative performance – Cooks
(3) Cooperative and complementary performance – Waitresses and Barmen
(4) Sequential performances – Cooks and Dishwashers
(5) Supervision – at several points
(6) Inspection – e.g. Checkers and Waitresses
(7) Assistance – probably in kitchen, but not shown

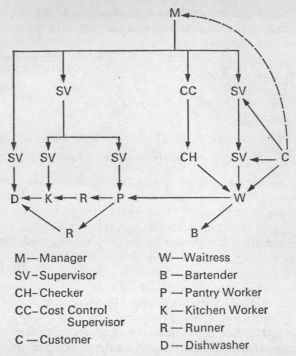

M—Manager
SV—Supervisor
CH—Checker
CC—Cost Control
       Supervisor
C—Customer

W—Waitress
B—Bartender
P—Pantry Worker
K—Kitchen Worker
R—Runner
D—Dishwasher

Figure 6. The social system of a restaurant (from Whyte, 1948). Used with permission of McGraw-Hill Book Company

(8) Conveying objects and information – e.g. Runners take food from kitchen to pantry, and orders from pantry to kitchen
(9) Discussion – between Supervisors
(10) Negotiation – between Waitress and Customer
(11) Providing expert advice – no example here

There may be difficulties in any of these relationships which may result in the system not working well. Some of these difficulties can be solved by better social skills on the part of performers, others by organizational changes, others may require changes in the technology such as new equipment or means of communication. Here is an example of the use of better social skills. Whyte discovered that some waitresses found their jobs full of stress and strain, and cried a great deal. One reason for this was that they were under constant pressure from customers, who wanted food that the cooks were not able to produce rapidly, this being worse at busy periods. Some waitresses, however, managed to deal with the situation by influencing the customers – they persuaded them to have the food that was readily available.

TECHNOLOGY AND WORKING GROUPS

The technology affects the size and internal structure of working groups. For example an assembly-line may be designed to be operated by a group of 75 men who pass the work on to one another, and each of whom can only interact with the person before and after him. Other kinds of working group, corresponding to the different socio-technical skills listed on p. 36 f., are discussed further in Chapter 6. It is necessary for efficiency and satisfaction that the members of a group should cooperate smoothly and get on well together. The technical system will affect relationships in the group and may create conflict and tension rather than cooperation. Here are some ways in which the technical arrangements can affect the working of groups in an unfavourable way.

Oversized working groups. The technology often dictates the size of the working group, in assembly lines for example. In a large group differences in informal status between different men become more marked, the group breaks up into sub-groups, and cohesiveness is less. In a number of comparisons of different sized work groups it has been found that the smaller ones, five to ten in size, do better at a variety of tasks. Larger groups may be more effective if the task is very complex and benefits from division of labour. Group size has a great effect on satisfaction and associated variables: people prefer smaller groups of five to six – the rates of absenteeism and labour turnover have been found to be three to four times as great in larger groups. The reason for this is probably that small working groups are able to work out a satisfactory social system, where each person has some influence over what happens; when the inter-personal problems have been solved group members can devote their full energies to the task.

Lack of cooperation between sub-groups. In a number of field studies it has been found that difficulties of communication and lack of opportunity for interaction result in failure of co-operation. An interesting example is the Longwall system of mechanical coal-mining, where three different shifts carried out the separate tasks of cutting, filling and stonework, but never met, so it was impossible for cohesiveness and cooperation to develop (see p. 44 f.).

Conflict and lack of cooperation between sub-groups are particularly likely to arise if there are differences of power or status between the sub-groups. Differences of power are created if one man has to direct, inspect or supervise another; there are differences of status, if one man's job is more highly paid, or more interesting, important, glamorous, etc., than another's. Such differences result in loss of cohesiveness, and lead to inefficiency and dissatisfaction in the group. The trouble gets worse if there is incongruence, i.e. if a person has high power or status in one respect, but low in another – for example in the restaurant, where waitresses or runners have to give orders to cooks who are of higher skill and status, and do not like being given such orders. The usual managerial solution to this problem is for orders to be written down and left for the cooks to deal with when they have time.

Indirect access to information. A group member may be dependent on information which must be obtained from others, sometimes via a chain of others. An example of this is the cooks receiving orders from customers via three intermediaries (the runner, the pantry worker and the waitress). This produces delays, distortions of the message and makes feedback impossible, so that there can be no discussion of points which are not clear, or two-way negotiation. Lanzetta and Roby (1956) carried out some laboratory experiments designed to replicate the organization of aircrews. They found that in three-man groups, accuracy of performance is reduced if things are arranged so that one man is dependent on others for information rather than being able to obtain it directly himself, and if information is dispersed so that more than one source has to be used. A number of experimenters compared the performance of laboratory groups when an individual received feedback on accuracy or errors (*a*) about his own performance, (*b*) about the average performance of the group, or (*c*) about errors made by others. The results vary according to the tasks used, but it is usually found that there is better team performance under (*a*) than (*b*), and under (*b*) than (*c*) (e.g. Rosenberg and Hall, 1958).

Inappropriate communication structures. Many laboratory studies have been carried out comparing the effects of different communication structures in small groups. When very simple problems are used, such as finding which one of five symbols the group members have all been given, it is found that highly centralized structures like the 'wheel' do better than 'circle' or 'all-channel' structures.

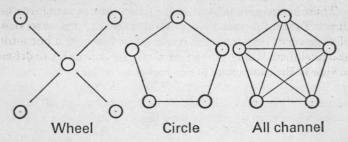

Wheel   Circle   All channel

However, if more complex problems like solving arithmetic problems are used, the other two designs do better than the wheel. A number of experiments have shown that centralized structures are better for solving simple or deductive tasks, decentralized structures for tasks requiring creativity or more difficult problem-solving (Glanzer and Glaser, 1961). One result which is probably of fairly wide application is that in a highly centralized structure the central member becomes the leader and enjoys himself more than the peripheral members do.

Conflicts in three-person structures. Many conflicts can arise in three-person structures. One appeared in Whyte's restaurant research: the waitresses were under the control of both customers and cooks, who were liable to exert contradictory pressures.

Another kind of three-person conflict occurs when there is a conflict of roles: P_1 is linked with two other persons (or classes of persons) P_2 and P_3 who have different ideas about how P_1 ought to behave, or how they would like him to behave (p. 189f.). A foreman, for example, is under conflicting pressures from his superiors and subordinates.

$$P_2 \rightarrow P_1 \leftarrow P_3$$

There is also a three-person problem where P_1 supervises or directs P_2 and P_3, since he has to treat them differently in view of differences between their work, personality, etc., but must also treat them 'fairly', though this may be impossible to define in view of the complexity of the situation.

The position is further complicated by differences of skill or seniority between P_2 and P_3, or by differences in their position in the group's informal hierarchy. It is not at all clear how far these differences should affect P_1's behaviour.

However, groups, like individuals, do not react passively to the conditions of work imposed by the technology. The group may create its own ways of coping with the task situation. In laboratory studies of the effects of communication structures it has been found that the group is often able to set up its own communication structure within the limits set by the structure of the task. Experiments in Holland showed that the groups which arrived at a centralized communication structure did better at simple tasks, and this happened more often when such a structure was imposed on the group (Mulder, 1960). Experiments in France found that groups of four tended to develop a centralized structure for deductive problems and a decentralized structure for inferential ones (Faucheux and Moscovici, 1960). However, the achievement of a new working structure takes time, needing either a long series of trials or time out for discussion. Groups also develop elaborate informal friendship structures, which satisfy various social needs.

However, groups may not always succeed in working out the best structure for their task, and may operate unhappily and ineffectively. It may then be possible to suggest an alternative social system. The Tavistock Institute of Human Relations have provided several very interesting demonstrations showing that the same technology can sometimes be operated under a quite different set of social arrangements which may be much more satisfactory. One of their most important studies was on the Longwall system of mechanical coalmining. In this system, groups of 41 men under a single supervisor were divided into three shifts, each doing a different job – cutting, filling and stonework, though each shift was highly dependent on the others. Since the teams never met, it was impossible for cohesiveness and cooperation to develop, especially as different prestige was attached to the different jobs. One shift would not clear up properly, or fail to leave the roof safe for the next shift. It was extremely difficult to supervise shifts working at different times; in addition these working groups were larger than those in earlier arrangements, and were more spread out spatially in the dark, so that the old cohesiveness, which served to reduce the anxieties of mining, was lost. There was a high level of absenteeism and discontent. This arrangement was compared with a modified version, in which the men were regrouped into composite groups, so that all three tasks were carried out on each shift. The result was an output of 5·3 tons per man-shift compared with 3·5 in the conventional Longwall design; absenteeism was 40 per cent lower than in the other groups. The reasons are probably that (1) better relations were established between those doing the three different jobs, and tensions between shifts were removed, (2) there was less division of labour and more variety of work, and (3) status differences between those in different shifts and using different skills were abolished (Trist *et al.*, 1963). This study shows that the same technology can be combined with quite different kinds of social organization. This is not always the case – it would be difficult to operate an assembly line very differently for example (Brown, 1967).

In another Tavistock study, Rice (1958) designed a new system of working groups in the Ahmedabad textile mills in India. Automatic looms had been introduced but production had not increased. Two hundred and twenty-four looms were looked after by 29 men, divided into 12 different jobs, and with a very confused pattern of relations between them. Rice's solution was to create four groups of seven, three on weaving and one on maintenance, the groups being formed by mutual choice. Each group was collectively responsible for 64 looms, each performing its own ancillary services. The result was an increase of 21 per cent in productivity and a drop of 59 per cent in damaged cloth; the new organization was rapidly applied to other weaving sheds. The reasons for the success of this arrangement were probably that (1) workers belonged to small cohesive groups working on a cooperative task, and (2) the task was more varied and added up to a meaningful total performance. This change in structure is shown in Figures 7 and 8.

In this section we have considered how socio-technical problems can be solved by reorganizing jobs and relationships in working groups. In the previous section we gave an example of the use of better *social skills* to solve a socio-technical problem. In other cases there may be no solution with the existing technology: for example, very long assembly lines or automated plants which make social contacts very difficult. It is extremely important that designers of equipment should take advice on the social relationships that their equipment will create, and

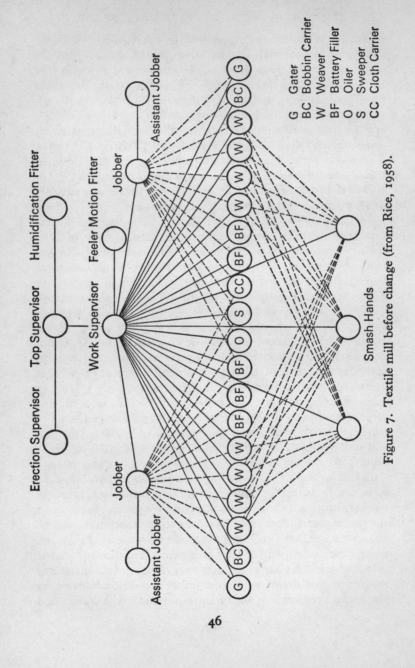

Figure 7. Textile mill before change (from Rice, 1958).

G   Gater
BC   Bobbin Carrier
W   Weaver
BF   Battery Filler
O   Oiler
S   Sweeper
CC   Cloth Carrier

46

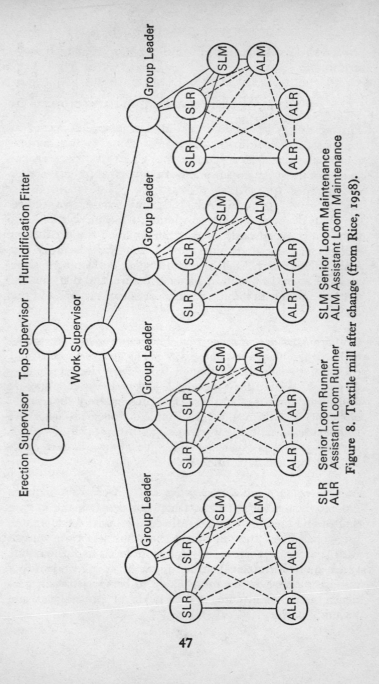

Erection Supervisor   Top Supervisor   Humidification Fitter

Work Supervisor

Group Leader

SLR   Senior Loom Runner   SLM   Senior Loom Maintenance
ALR   Assistant Loom Runner   ALM   Assistant Loom Maintenance

Figure 8. Textile mill after change (from Rice, 1958).

47

how far these will produce effective cooperation and job satisfaction.

TECHNOLOGY AND SOCIAL ORGANIZATION

The technology influences the kind of organization needed to supervise and coordinate different working groups, and to control and direct all aspects of the work. We have seen examples of the social organization of restaurants (p. 39), and of weaving sheds (p. 45 f.).

Woodward (1965), Blauner (1964) and others have studied the kinds of social organization found with different kinds of technology. Woodward, for example, studied the production systems and social organization of 100 English firms and found that at each level of technological development there was a characteristic kind of social structure, and that this did not vary much with the size of organization or the kind of work done.

Craft work and one-off production. The craft worker either works by himself, or with a few helpers; working groups are small and cohesive, though the craftsmen work fairly independently; there is little need for supervision and craft workers may be difficult to supervise, but there is no pressure from supervisors or conflict with them; there is a simple management hierarchy, with no specialization between managers; it is a 'flat' hierarchy, with 25–30 men per manager; any specialists work in research and development departments.

Machine-tending and assembly-line work. Men work in large groups, though social contacts between them on the job are limited and there may be no real social groups; there is more use of incentives and machine-pacing, and less close contact with supervisors; there are typically four levels in the hierarchy and a more hierarchical structure, with 14–18 workers per manager; managers are more likely to be specialists in particular areas, and more use is made of professional and technical people.

More automated technology. In oil refineries and similar plants there is a return to smaller working groups, less close supervision, and better relations in the hierarchy, with 8 workers per manager.

Organizations, like individuals and groups, adjust to different technological systems. In a later chapter we shall describe the various kinds of 'informal organization', such as new communication channels, that may develop in this way (p. 192f.). It is also possible to re-design whole organizations to provide more effective structures, just as groups can be reorganized. Chapple and Sayles (1961) describe the reorganizing of the sales department of a company, where there had been a lot of conflict between the credit manager and the sales manager. What happened was that orders were handled first by the sales department, and later by the credit department which sometimes had to cancel orders at a late stage in the proceedings.

The solution was (1) to reverse the order in which orders went to the sales and credit departments, (2) to put all the work connected with a single order under one supervisor, who saw that everything was done on one day, and (3) sales *and* credit representatives took a hand in writing letters to customers when higher-level attention was needed.

At one time working organizations were designed like quasi-military hierarchies, in which all the people doing similar work were placed together under a supervisor. More recent thinking about organization favours designing them for the particular technology and work to be done, with appropriate structures for control and decision-taking further up.

AUTOMATION

Since about 1950 the group of technical innovations known as automation have been making great changes to the industrial scene in advanced countries. The effects have been so great that this has been called a 'second industrial revolution'. The distinctive elements of these technical innovations have been the use of automatic machines responsive to feedback, and electronic computers. There are three main kinds of application. 'Detroit' automation consists of automatic machine-tools which are linked by transfer machines coordinating one process with the next. One such system consists of five linked machines making engine blocks, and the machines carry out together 495 pieces of machining and 106 inspections, working on 100 blocks at a time (Dubin, 1958). Another aspect of automation is where continuous control is kept on production processes by means of a computer. This is most often found in the chemical industry. When this is combined with 'Detroit' automation there can be a 'closed-loop' system in which the entire production process is automatic and needs no human operators at all, except for maintenance. Oil refineries and electric power stations come closest to this. Automation is also used in offices for working out wages, keeping records of supplies, or collecting data of other kinds. This is usually done by card-sorting equipment, under computer control.

Like other technological innovations automation can only be introduced when the conditions are right – when the relevant equipment has been invented, when there is enough capital to pay for it, when it will save money to use it, when there is a sufficiently standard product, and when skilled men are available to install and operate it. None of these conditions apply in India or Africa for example, where labour is so cheap that there would be no economic gain from automation. It is in the U.S.A., where labour is very expensive (and difficult to deal with), that automation has gone furthest, though Japan, Germany and Britain are not far behind. The industries in which it has been most extensively applied are chemicals, car and other manufacturing industries, electric power and mining. It has not been applied in service industries – such as shops, hotels and restaurants.

Automation of different kinds and degrees of sophistication is now very common in advanced countries. In 1964 about two thirds of American firms with over a hundred employees had some automation (Froomkin, 1968). The rate of change is rapid: in 1960 there were 35 process-control computers at work in the U.S.A.; in 1966 there were 600. On the other hand it has been estimated that only 8 per cent of all jobs are in any sense ripe for automation (Friedmann, 1961).

The main advantage of automation is that fewer workers are needed, so labour costs are reduced and the firm is placed at a competitive advantage – so that the other firms have to automate too. There has been much debate over the effects of automation on unemployment. There is little doubt that fewer workers are needed in a particular firm as the result of automation – it would not be profitable to have automation otherwise, in view of the immense capital costs involved. In the decade ending in 1954 a million fewer workers were employed in manufacturing and mining in the U.S.A., with no drop in productivity. Those employed in oil refining fell from 147,000 to 137,000 with an increase in output of 22 per cent (Jacobsen and Roucek, 1959). There will be some increase in employment in firms manufacturing computers, etc., but there is no doubt that the long-term effects of automation are a continuous increase in unemployment, unless this can be taken up by increases of employment in other sectors of the economy, such as service industries, the forces, teaching and research or new industries. Another way of looking at it is to predict that there will be more leisure, rather than more unemployment, or that people will start work later in life and retire earlier. One of the social costs of automation is damage to the self-respect of those replaced by machines.

We will now consider the impact of automation on the people who are at work.

The labour force. It has long been believed that automation displaces large numbers of semi-skilled workers and creates jobs for a smaller number of more highly skilled people who install, maintain and control the new equipment, like computer programmers, etc. Before and after studies show that there are fewer workers after automation has been introduced, but that there is no overall upgrading of the level of skill (e.g. Bright, 1958). This is partly because some jobs are greatly simplified under automation – merely a matter of pressing buttons and watching dials – though these jobs can be very responsible – and new semi-skilled jobs are created, such as card-punching in the office. However, the long-term outlook may well be rather different since these simple jobs are likely to be automated in due course. Wiener (1961) foresees the time when 'the average human being of mediocre attainments or less has nothing to sell that is worth anyone's money to buy' (p. 28). At this stage there will be very little need for people at work.

There is an immediate need for a number of new kinds of specialist – to install and maintain the automatic equipment and computer systems. Dubin (1958) argues that the educational curriculum should be modified to provide more workers with the necessary skills for automated work. Some of the men displaced by automation can be retrained to do the new jobs which are created, but this is not possible for the less able and the older workers.

Supervisors and managers need to be more technically skilled than before. Promotion prospects in one way are improved since there is a higher proportion of senior jobs; on the other hand, all senior staff need technical qualifications. Women may be displaced from their office jobs, as specialists move in to deal with the automated office equipment – though there are still jobs for card-punchers.

Working groups. Earlier commentators gloomily predicted that the jolly working groups of traditional factories would be replaced by lonely operators tied to isolated control points. Operations men, and those controlling 'Detroit' automation, can certainly be isolated in this way, though they may have leisure in which to walk about. Maintenance men on the other hand work in small, autonomous teams. Card-punchers work in rather traditional types of working group. Relations in groups are often reported to be improved as a result of the removal of pay differentials and tensions over piecework jobs, and the feeling of taking part in a cooperative enterprise.

Supervision. The relationship between supervisors and working groups has been found to be affected in quite different ways in different automated systems. In a power station workers were more autonomous (Mann and Hoffman, 1960); in a car factory there were more supervisors, closer supervision, and more tension between workers and supervisors (Faunce, 1958). Technologists become more important in the managerial hierarchy.

The nature of work. Many routine, repetitive, dirty and heavy jobs are eliminated. The trend towards dividing up jobs into ever smaller and more meaningless units is reversed: most automated jobs are concerned with larger aspects of production. Instead there are jobs for operations men who watch dials; their work is very responsible, though physically easy and leisurely. There are also specialized and highly skilled maintenance men who look after automatic equipment and electronic circuits. The only routine jobs are those connected with electronic data processing – punched-card operators. There are more supervisory and higher technical jobs than before, and all supervisory and managerial grades deal with work of more technical complexity. Except for punched-card work, most jobs under automation are more interesting and responsible, usually require more skill and training, allow greater freedom and are physically easier than before. For most workers job satisfaction is greater.

CHAPTER 4

PERSONALITY AND WORK

*Dimensions of personality – learning how to work:
occupational choice – personnel selection.*

DIMENSIONS OF PERSONALITY

THERE are great individual differences between people at
work: in how well they can do different jobs, how hard they
work, and how much they enjoy different kinds of work. They
differ in *abilities* – which determine how well they will be able
to do a particular job, and which job each person is best suited
for. They differ in *interests* and *motivation*, which determine
what kinds of work each person most wants to do, and how
hard he will work at it. They differ in patterns of *social
performance*; this is partly a matter of temperament – differences of mood, energy, reactions to stress – but is also a
question of styles of social performance in different social
situations. From the point of view of personnel selection these
aspects of personality are important, since they enable predictions to be made of which people will be most *effective* at
a particular job. From the point of view of vocational guidance
these factors are important since they enable predictions to be
made of which job will give a particular person the greatest
job satisfaction. From the point of view of social psychology
these factors are interesting since they help us to understand
why people behave differently at work.

Not all aspects of personality are relevant to behaviour at
work, and we have picked out those areas of personality which
have been found to be most relevant, for purposes of selection
or guidance. The traditional approach to this problem has been
to look for correlations between personality traits and measures
of work performance. Recent research has shown that the
relation between personality and work behaviour is more com-

plicated than this. In the first place, behaviour may depend in a complex way on a number of traits in combination. Secondly, the model of general traits which has worked so well in the field of abilities does not work so well in the fields of motivation or social behaviour, where the same person may behave quite differently in different situations.

Intelligence and other abilities. Jobs vary in the intellectual and other abilities they require. To select the best person for a job it is obviously important to choose someone who has the necessary abilities; it may also be necessary to exclude those whose abilities are too great, since they will be discontented. For the most effective use of the personnel available, the most talented of those available should be given the most difficult jobs; where different jobs call for different abilities the problem is more complicated (p. 73). From the point of view of the individual, he should do the work which makes the best use of his abilities. In fact people are found to choose the jobs which require the abilities which they have (p. 70), and in vocational guidance this is one of the main considerations.

Intelligence is the capacity to solve problems, apply principles, make inferences and perceive relationships. General intelligence consists of a number of abilities which enable a person to succeed at a wide variety of intellectual tasks; it can be measured by intelligence tests with abstract, verbal, mathematical and problem-solving items. There are other more specific mental abilities, which are correlated with general intelligence, but which are also partly independent of it – verbal fluency, numerical ability, spatial ability and mechanical aptitudes. Intelligence can be measured by intelligence tests, but a fairly accurate assessment can often be made from a person's academic record, where this is consistent. Details are needed of the precise results of examinations and the ages at which they were taken. By studying the results in different subjects some assessment can also be made of different aspects of intelligence.

There are two other dimensions of mental ability which are widely held to be important for predicting occupational success but for which satisfactory tests have not yet been developed.

Judgement is the capacity to make realistic assessments of practical situations, and produce workable solutions to particular problems where it is more a matter of weighing different factors and guessing probabilities than of applying logical principles. Judgement can be assessed by interviews, by asking candidates their views about a number of complex practical situations with which they are familiar. *Creativity* is the ability to see situations from a new point of view and to propose original solutions. It can be assessed by tests such as the 'uses of objects' test – in which candidates are asked to write down all the unusual uses they can think of for a brick, a piece of string, etc. It is not yet known whether such tests correlate with inventiveness on the job; an alternative measure is an interview which focuses on past occasions where a candidate could have displayed originality. *Motor skills* form a further, and largely independent set of abilities; there is no single dimension here – there appear to be eleven separate dimensions (Fleishman, 1965).

Motivation and interests. It is not enough for a person to have the necessary abilities for a job, he must also be sufficiently interested and motivated to want to do it, or he will not work very effectively and will not find it satisfying. Effective performance is a joint product of abilities and motivation. French (1958) found that the ability to solve problems was a function of *both* intelligence and achievement, the effect of intelligence being greater for more highly motivated subjects, which shows that the relationship is multiplicative, i.e. Performance = (ability × motivation). The strength of motivation in turn depends both on an individual's enduring drive strength and on the incentive conditions. Both the choice of occupation and the choice to work hard are products of incentives and drive strength. The amount of satisfaction is a product of the motivation and rewards obtained.

These are the main drives which affect performance at work:

(1) *Biological needs – hunger and thirst.* These motivate work directly for primitive men, and less directly via money for less

primitive men. Money appears to be partly a route to such goals, partly an independent acquired drive – which is satisfied by just having it rather than spending it. Under civilized conditions, in which people are rarely hungry or thirsty, it is hard to see that these drives will have much direct effect on work performance.

(2) *Social motivation – affiliation, dependency and dominance* are among the factors that cause people to work, and under certain conditions affect their productivity (p. 101f.). The main effect, however, is on the pattern of social relationships that people seek with each other at work (p. 127 f.).

(3) *Achievement motivation* is one of the main drives affecting how hard a person works, in situations where it is possible to achieve success of some kind. This is discussed below (p. 93 f.).

(4) *Self-esteem, 'ego-needs'.* There appears to be a need for self-esteem and for approval from other people. This can be linked to achievement motivation, when certain targets are set; here work motivation has become part of identity.

Individuals vary in the strength of these drives, and one can see how different kinds of work satisfy such needs. Work with other people, such as personnel and sales work, probably satisfies affiliative needs, while work that gives the opportunity for the accomplishment of great tasks satisfies achievement motivation.

Occupational choice and job satisfaction are also greatly affected by individual interests – for example, in literary, scientific, mechanical or outdoor things. There are two tests for these personal interests, the Kuder Preference Record and the Strong Vocational Interest Blank. These have been widely used in the U.S.A. for vocational guidance, and both give very good predictions of the jobs that people in fact choose (p. 69). They do not, however, measure the *strength* of motivation to work, though people are usually more intrinsically motivated to work at jobs in which they are able to follow their own interests.

Personality traits. The traits most relevant to work are those governing social behaviour. At one time it was believed that traits such as 'dominance' functioned like 'intelligence' in that each person would display the trait consistently in different situations. However, the situation has been changed by the realization that this is not the case and that individuals behave very differently in different situations. The same person may behave quite differently when at home or at work, with superiors or subordinates, with males or females, and so on. The traditional approach, in terms of universal personality traits, does not do justice to these variations. It has been realized for some time that 'leadership' is not a personality trait: whether or not a person will be leader in a particular group and in a particular situation depends primarily on whether he has more of the abilities needed to deal with that situation than the others present. The following kinds of social behaviour in which individual differences appear *cannot* be accounted for primarily in terms of personality traits: dominance, dependence, leadership, conformity, persuasibility, honesty, likeability (Mischel, 1969; Argyle, 1969).

A person's social behaviour depends on his enduring features, but also on the personalities of others present, and on the nature of the situation. A person's behaviour can be predicted to some extent from variables like age, sex, job and social class, since there are regular and specified relations between people occupying different positions in the social structure. For example, whether A will dominate B depends mainly on whether A is older, male rather than female, more senior, or of higher social class than B – without introducing a trait of 'dominance'.

(1) *Temperament.* There is more consistency between different situations for features of temperament such as level of energy, mood and reactions to stress. Two dimensions which have repeatedly emerged from psychological research are intro-

version–extroversion and neuroticism. These dimensions are somewhat similar to intelligence in that they are general factors of personality, a source of consistent behaviour, and tests can be given for them (Eysenck and Eysenck, 1969). However, there is an important difference from intelligence – although these dimensions do predict behaviour in a wide range of situations, the predictions are very weak, usually corresponding to correlations of 0·2–0·3, accounting for 4–9 per cent of the variance, whereas intelligence tests are much more strongly predictive. We refer later to a study showing that managers are somewhat more extroverted and less neurotic than other people (p. 68), but the differences found are too small to base a selection procedure on these two variables. They can be regarded perhaps as a 'biological core' of the personality, associated with physique and other physiological measures.

Extroversion contains two components which are correlated but partly independent. These are behavioural extroversion, which consists of impulsiveness and a preference for action as opposed to thinking about action, and social extroversion, which consists of a liking for social situations, especially large and noisy ones.

By neuroticism we mean an inability to tolerate stress, a tendency to be anxious, to work ineffectively, to suffer from minor ailments such as headaches, sleeplessness and pains, and to find people difficult to deal with. Neuroticism is a matter of degree; about 5–10 per cent of the population would be classified as neurotic by psychiatrists, and could benefit from treatment. Neuroticism can be measured by questionnaire (e.g. the Eysenck Personality Inventory), interview, or from performance at laboratory tasks. Although neuroticism has often been regarded as a consistent feature of personality, it is much less so than intelligence and a person is often neurotic only in some areas of his behaviour. For example he may have a quite isolated phobia for heights, animals or travel.

Social anxiety is a partly independent aspect of neurosis: some people are anxious in social situations, are shy and self-conscious, tense, embarrassed and generally unable to cope. The socially poised person, on the other hand, is thoroughly at home and enjoys himself in social situations, is confident and relaxed, and able to control situations smoothly.

(2) *Social performance.* Our research has shown that individuals vary greatly in their entire style of social performance from one situation to another (Argyle and Little, 1972). There appears to be very little consistency so that personality cannot be described in terms of general traits like 'warmth', 'dominance', etc. Individuals *are* however consistent in groups or similar situations, and it is possible to describe their behaviour at work, in committees, as chairman, etc. A person may be more or less socially skilled over a given range of social situations. *Rewardingness* may be an important part of this general ability – rewarding people are both more popular and influential. In addition there are a number of more specific social skills, such as dealing with subordinates ('leadership skills'), taking the chair at committee meetings, interviewing, giving lectures, etc. We shall consider later these different social skills, and the ways in which they can be acquired (Chapter 7).

(3) *The self-image.* This is not a 'dimension' of personality but a cognitive structure consisting of the ideas a person has about himself. It exercises a controlling effect on his behaviour, by restraining behaviour which is inconsistent with it, and seeking to elicit appropriate reactions from others. For each class of social situations a different part of the self-image is emphasized (e.g., father, research worker), corresponding to the social performance in those situations. One way of describing an individual's social behaviour is to list the main roles he plays in the groups to which he belongs; each role is linked to part of his self-image. The self-image also includes self-perceptions such as being 'intelligent' or 'lively', which may extend across all these roles, and lead to their being played in a characteristic way. The occupational role, and the way it is played, is a core feature of identity; the crystallization of identity and choice of an occupation proceed side by side during late adolescence. Individuals differ, not only in the contents of their identities, and their degree of self-esteem, but also in how secure and well-

integrated their identity is, and how realistic. There are questionnaire measures for various aspects of identity, and these can also be discovered by interview.

(4) *Attitudes to authority*. People probably have consistent attitudes to authority in their work situation, though they may have different attitudes to other kinds of authority. Most work takes place in organizations with a hierarchical structure. Some people have great respect for tradition, are subservient and deferential to those in authority and bully their juniors; they have conservative attitudes, are conformist in appearance and other behaviour, are opposed to change, and have been found to be hostile to racial and other minority groups. At the other extreme are rebellious people who reject tradition and authority; in between are different degrees of acceptance and rejection of authority. It is probably necessary for members of working organizations to have some balance between the two – enough acceptance of authority to carry out orders, enough rebelliousness to appreciate that what the boss says is not always right, and that what was done last year may be out of date. Authoritarianism can be measured by questionnaire, or by interview, asking about relationships with superiors and subordinates, and attitudes towards respectable and less respectable social groups or institutions.

LEARNING HOW TO WORK: OCCUPATIONAL CHOICE

Stages of development. In primitive societies children learn how to work at an early age. The work their parents do is simple and clearly visible, children are provided with scaled-down implements, are taught the basic work skills and help their parents. In more advanced societies there is much more division of labour, children do not see their parents at work, often have no clear idea of what their work consists of, and are allowed to spend a lot of their time at 'play'. The work they are expected to do is school work. Children may play at being the teacher, doctor, vicar, or other work roles which are visible to them. Many children later go into occupations similar to those of their fathers; it is interesting that doctors' children very often become doctors – surgeries are often at home and the work can be clearly seen by the children. Childhood experiences affect later occupational choice and work behaviour in a number of ways. It has been found that those who become social scientists or social workers had more strained relations with their parents than engineers, physical scientists or biologists (Roe, 1964).

There are a number of difficulties in socialization for work in modern societies which are absent in more primitive societies – the need to choose between about twenty thousand different occupations, the difficulty of knowing what these jobs are like, the difficulty of seeing how these jobs contribute to society, and the lack of continuity between school work and later work.

In modern societies, children from six to twelve years of age have no serious ideas about choosing a job, but they are expected to carry out school work. As McClelland and his colleagues (1953) have shown, the need for achievement is established during this period. As a result of exhortations from parents and teachers, imitation of successful models, and rewards for successful achievement the child acquires a drive to carry out school tasks with persistence, and to do well at them. Neff (1968) maintains that it is at school that the child learns the difference between work and play, and acquires a 'work personality'.

Certain basic components of the work personality appear to be laid down in the early school years – the ability to concentrate on a task for extended periods of time, the development of emotional response-patterns to supervisory authority, the limits of co-operation and competition with peers, the meanings and values associated with work, the rewards and sanctions for achievement and non-achievement, the affects (both positive and negative) which become associated with being productive (p. 161).

This preparation for work plays a more important part in modern society than is often realized. The Industrial Revolution was traumatic for many workers and produced a great deal of conflict between workers and employers because people were quite unused to the conditions of industrial work (p. 26 f.). Industrialization in Africa has proceeded slowly because Africans are not accustomed to working at regular hours, under supervision, at a regular speed with standard methods. West Indians and Pakistanis in Britain are reported to have a rapid turnover from their first employers, but to do better with their second employers; unlike Africans, however, they are entering a situation in which there is a tradition of work already established, and they have a powerful economic incentive to accept it.

During adolescence, from 12–13 to 17–19, children get nearer to doing real work. As Erikson (1956) has shown, many adolescents go through an 'identity crisis' in which they have to make some important decisions about their direction in life. During this period adolescents try out various kinds of work, first at home, then at school, in part-time jobs, and sometimes by a period of floundering in the labour market with a succession of jobs. During this period they become aware of their own capacities and what they are best suited for, and of the possibilities available (Ginsberg et al., 1951; Super, 1957). A number of studies have shown that adolescents are attracted to occupations which they see as similar to their self-image, or as requiring skills which they believe they possess. Their degree of realism here can be checked by measuring the actual properties of jobs and of the qualities needed to perform them. It has been found that as adolescents grow older they develop greater understanding of different jobs and their own abilities. They are helped in choosing an occupation by parents, teachers and other adults, and the process is accelerated by offers of jobs and the need to fill in application forms for courses. Ginsberg (1951) maintained that the choices made at any stage are irreversible, in that early decisions make some later choices impossible. However, it has been found that only 17 per cent of 15-year-old boys and 26 per cent of girls had the same occupational plans a year after leaving school (Super and Overstreet, 1960). Final choices were more predictable from aptitude tests than from vocational plans in adolescence.

There are several ways in which adolescents may fail to learn how to work or choose a suitable job (Erikson, op. cit.; Elder, 1968). Some decide too early on a career, before they have fully explored the possibilities, and before they have achieved an independent identity. They may decide to work in father's firm, in which they would still be in a dependent relation to adults, and for which they may not have the right interests or aptitudes. They may fail to develop an integrated identity, fail to make any occupational choice, and be unable to work. This happens with many hippies and drop-outs, who seek an alternative kind of identity in the 'anti-culture'. They may decide to delay the decision about what to do. University life and graduate work may provide such a period of 'moratorium', and this may be followed by one or more years spent in remote countries overseas, wandering about looking for an identity.

Neff (1968) describes various kinds of people who are unable to adjust to work. Some lacked work motivation and regarded work as something unpleasant; others were anxious in response to the demand to be productive; some were aggressive; others dependent; others still were socially naïve, unfamiliar with work and work standards. These groups of people would not usually be found at work, but in treatment centres which are trying to adjust them to work.

Among those who leave school at 15–16, some go straight into jobs, others to further training or education. Veness (1962) surveyed 1,300 British school leavers and classified their reasons for choosing jobs into the three categories established by Riesman. About 11 per cent made 'traditional' choices, following family and local patterns; about 53 per cent were 'inner-directed' and tried to suit their own abilities and interests; about 36 per cent were 'other-directed' and were responding to recent social influences.

For those who go to college the beginning of work proper is postponed, though they do realize that work is likely to start at the end of college and that they will have to have reached a decision about what to do by then. Some do vocational courses, but others do courses which are not very relevant to any job apart from teaching the same subjects to others. In a study of 500 student mental patients at Oxford it was found that the breakdown rate was lowest in the more vocational courses like Law and Natural Science, and the highest in the least vocational courses like English and Greats (Davidson and Hutt, 1964). A lot of students change their ideas about their career while at college. In an American survey it was found that the students most likely to change were those whose values (i.e. self-expression, interest in people, money and status) were in conflict with the values of their initial occupational choice, and that they shifted to an occupation with more similar values. However, those who had started specialized training were less likely to change (Rosenberg, 1957).

Once a person has started a job he is usually exposed to further socialization. He may undergo an initial period which has some of the characteristics of an initiation: trainees may be isolated, exposed to stressful experiences, issued with a uniform, and helped through these experiences by senior members of the organization. This happens in the military, the medical profession, the clergy and some other professions; it has the effect of enhancing the feeling of belonging to a special élite group, and of inculcating a powerful attachment to the organization. In a study of medical students it was found that 31 per cent thought of themselves as doctors at the end of their first year, 83 per cent at the end of the fourth year. However, even in the first year 75 per cent thought of themselves as doctors in relation to patients if they were given some patients to look after (Merton *et al.*, 1957). After the trainee period, when the person starts doing the job, further kinds of socialization take place. The new member of an organization is likely to imitate the behaviour of prominent existing members. He is expected to conform to a particular role, and the complementary behaviour of performers of interlocking roles will elicit standard role behaviour from him (p. 190). The effects of training on the job, and other forms of training, are discussed in Chapter 7.

Working in an organization over a period of time leads to a person assimilating a whole work culture and outlook; this will be quite different for clergymen, miners, soldiers and farmers for example. In addition, working in a particular job leads to a style of behaviour and set of attitudes which are associated with that job; these will be different for managers, foremen and shop stewards, for example.

Many people who enter jobs are also entering *careers*, that is they see the job as a step in an ordered series of jobs lasting over the working life. Miller and Form (1962) distinguish (i) the initial work period – part-time or vacation jobs during the period of education; (ii) the trial work period – in which jobs are tried out for longer or shorter periods, after full-time education is completed; and (iii) the stable work period. They found that the trial work period lasts from four to six years for different occupational groups. It is only in the stable work period that commitment to a career develops. The extent to which a job is seen as part of a career varies between occupations. There are class differences here; middle-class adolescents think in terms of careers, working-class adolescents are more likely to think of jobs – perhaps offering good pay and job satisfaction, but not promotion.

Management. In industrial firms, the Civil Service and other large bureaucratic organizations there is a recognized series of steps, for example moving into administration in the early forties, and the hope of promotion is one of the main incentives. In a study of the middle managers in a British oil company and an American car manufacturing firm it was found that these men were preoccupied with their prospects of promotion; they were all striving to get on to the next step of the ladder (Sofer, 1970).

Entrepreneurs. Some people want to run their own businesses, and are prepared to risk their own capital, plough the profits back into the business, and become responsible for employing others. They may run small shops, garages or cafés, or establish large manufacturing concerns. Many men employed on assembly jobs with little hope of promotion, consider starting their own businesses as the next step.

Professionals. Scientists, accountants, lawyers, doctors and others undergo a long period of professional training and are highly committed to their skills, standards and professional group rather than to the organization that employs them.

Professionals have careers, but may be self-employed, or move between different organizations.

Skilled craftsmen do not normally have careers in the usual sense, though they are highly committed to their skills and may achieve standards of excellence with them. They may play an active part in their working community and in union activities (Blauner, 1964).

Unskilled manual work. Here there is usually very little prospect of promotion, except for energetic people who acquire further qualifications in their spare time. Since the work is often very uninteresting many unskilled workers come to adopt an 'instrumental' attitude to their work and do it simply for the pay.

How far people want to go, and how far they do go, depends mainly on their level of aspiration and the strength of their achievement motivation and their abilities. When a person is promoted to a new rank, he experiences a change of identity – he has a new status, a new way of life, and knows new people. He sees himself, his past and his anticipated future differently. The transition to a new job involves some degree of re-socialization, and the shift is sometimes assisted by a public ceremony, such as a celebration party, known to sociologists as a *rite de passage*.

The influence of personality on occupational choice. Psychologists have tended to emphasize the importance of personality variables in determining occupational choice, while sociologists have emphasized environmental factors, such as the jobs available. In reality, both factors are important, but their relative weights are different for different sections of the population. For working-class people there is a rather narrow choice of occupations, so that personality factors are relatively unimportant, while in the middle class there is a wider range of possibilities so that people are more able to choose what best suits their personality (Elder, 1968).

Intelligence and other abilities are the most important personality factors. Young people express preferences for jobs which roughly correspond to their level of ability (Vroom, 1964). There is an approximate correspondence between the distribution of intelligence in people doing different jobs, and the intelligence needed to do them. Himmelweit and Whitfield (1944) analysed the intelligence test scores of 5,000 British army recruits; the average scores for different occupations varied from 40·7 for school master to 12·0 for carter, but there were wide variations within each occupational group. There is also a characteristic profile of more specific abilities for different jobs. Thorndike and Hagen (1959) studied the abilities of over 10,000 American air force recruits, and found that different occupations varied in general intelligence, but also in mechanical ability, numerical fluency, visual perception and psychomotor ability. Manual workers tended to score low in general intelligence but high in mechanical tests.

Individual differences in other aspects of personality are less closely related to occupational choice – there is a very wide range of personalities in most occupations. For those people who fall in the middle range of the population on personality traits occupational choice is not much affected by personality. For many jobs there are no special personality requirements, and this may be particularly true of strongly sex-typed jobs like secretary and salesgirl (Roe, 1964); other jobs may attract a certain type of personality – lighthouse keepers, psychoanalysts, boxers and monks, for example. There is only a small association between occupation and traits like extroversion and neuroticism. In a survey of 1,500 managers it was found that they were somewhat more extroverted and less neurotic than the population norms; those in sales and personnel were the most extroverted, research and development men and consultants the least (Eysenck, 1967a). American studies have found that successful managers are intelligent, well adjusted and strongly motivated. They are also reported to be friendly, dominant and socially skilled, but it is not clear how far these should be regarded as traits or as part of the role.

Differences in motivation also affect occupational choice. Those high in achievement motivation choose high-status and risky occupations; in the U.S.A., at least, they choose finance

68

and business in preference to other professions. They want to take risks in the hope of making a lot of money; they want to build up large enterprises and make their mark in the world (Atkinson *et al.*, 1958). There is also evidence that they play a crucial role in initiating economic growth (p. 23 f.). A different pattern of motivation is found among successful physical scientists, who in addition to working extremely hard are often male, from Protestant backgrounds, avoid interpersonal aggression and complex human emotions, and are intensely masculine (McClelland, 1962). The effect of other kinds of motivation is shown by questionnaire studies of values. For example Rosenberg (1957) found that students high in his people-oriented scale chose social work, medicine, teaching and social science; students scoring high on his self-expression scale chose architecture, journalism and art; students scoring high on extrinsic-reward orientation chose sales, hotel management, estate agency and finance. Finer discrimination can be made from the Strong Vocational Interest Blank or from the ten dimensions of the Kuder Preference Record, which measure preference for outdoor, mechanical, computational, scientific, persuasive, artistic, literary, musical, social service and clerical work. This scale is widely used in the U.S.A. for vocational guidance for school leavers. The Strong Vocational Interest Blank is better for university students since its scales relate to more specific occupations.

A person's self-image affects his choice of occupation, though as described above the two develop side by side. If he chooses his occupation fairly late, e.g. at the end of college, he will already have a fairly well developed self-image by this time; the choice of job is a further crystallization of his self-image. While the self-image partly reflects abilities or other objective properties of the person, these may be perceived inaccurately; in addition the self-image is a somewhat complex product of past experience, and is not always very closely related to objective qualities of personality – as for example in people who feel 'inferior'. A study was carried out in which students scored themselves for fifteen attributes such as creativity, leadership and intelligence and the extent to which various occupations required them. There was an average correlation of 0·54 between the two sortings for the occupation that they had chosen themselves, and lower correlations for other occupations (Vroom, 1964). This shows that people choose occupations which they think require the qualities which they think they possess. The self-image may also include elements of the job chosen. A student may come to see himself as an embryo-scientist as the result of playing the role of scientist and close association with and admiration of scientists. Similarly he·may come to see himself as a future businessman, journalist, clergyman, etc. as a result of vacation jobs or university club activities. A central feature of the self-image is the set of values or higher goals that has been chosen, and these also affect choice of occupation. The Vernon–Allport values questionnaire measures economic, theoretical, aesthetic, political, social and religious values, and shows that the pattern of values is quite different for people in different occupations.

People's understanding of different jobs includes a good deal of mythology. Hudson (1968) found that British schoolboys thought that the typical arts graduate would probably wear fashionable clothes, flirt with his secretary, like expensive restaurants, and get into debt; the novelist was seen as 'imaginative, warm, exciting and smooth', the psychologist as similar to the novelist, but intelligent and lazy. Physicists were seen as dependable, hard-working, manly and valuable; engineers as similar to physicists but less intelligent, colder and duller. In Britain the ablest schoolboys tend to choose pure science rather than engineering and technology, more than in the U.S.A. and Europe (Hutchins, 1963). This is probably due to the stereotypes of engineers and technologists, which have been given some support by the low status of technology in universities. Of course stereotypes may be partly correct – though there is a far wider range of personalities in an occupation than the stereotype suggests. Engineers (supposedly dependable, dull, etc.) are actually found to be interested in things rather than people or ideas, to be stable, orderly and tough-minded, and like working out of doors and with their hands (Morrison and McIntyre, 1971).

Men and women tend to seek different things in their work. Men want to have a job that is well paid, secure, and gives prestige; they are quite happy working with things rather than people, and do not mind risk. Women are more concerned with self-expression and creativity, want to work with people rather than things, and to be helpful to others (e.g. Goldsen *et al.*, 1960). As a result men and women tend to choose different occupations. Women often become nurses, teachers, social workers, secretaries, shop assistants and hairdressers; men become engineers, managers, builders, farmers, scientists and lawyers. It has been found that taking both sex *and* patterns of interest into account enabled a good prediction of occupational choice: 70 per cent of women with 'service' interests chose teaching, compared with 5 per cent of men who were oriented towards money (Davis, 1963). For most women work is a short-term affair before getting married, perhaps to be resumed later. American studies of career-oriented girls show that they are high in educational ambitions, and concern with self-expression, but somewhat lower on interest in people. These sex differences can partly be accounted for by the different roles played by mothers and fathers in families: the mother has a nurturant, socio-emotional, people-oriented role, while the father is more concerned with the economic support of the family, and looking after physical aspects of the home – a thing-oriented role. Sex differences in occupations are partly due to cultural factors – women in Russia, India and Israel do heavy manual work and may occupy senior management positions.

Environmental factors in occupational choice. The social class of a child's family may affect his aspirations and final occupational choice in a number of ways. Working-class adolescents are much affected by local employment opportunities, while those from middle-class homes become aware of a wider range of possibilities. They are also likely to get a better education, may be able to go into father's business or be helped by family contacts or capital. In an American survey it was found that 71 per cent of students whose fathers earned over $30,000 planned to enter law, medicine or business, compared with 38 per cent of those whose fathers earned less than $7,500 (Rosenberg, 1957). In another survey it was found that while this was true of people living in large towns in the U.S.A., in the country and in small towns intelligence was a better predicter of occupational goals, perhaps because intelligence is needed to see beyond immediate employment prospects in the country (Sewell and Orenstein, 1965).

Children have been found to choose the same occupations as their fathers more than would be expected by chance. This is well known in the case of doctors' children; in an American study Werts (1968) found that 35 per cent of the sons of physical scientists chose scientific careers; the opposite prob-do not want their children to enter this occupation. If they do not enter the same occupation children are likely to enter one with similar values or patterns of activity, e.g. being concerned with people rather than things. There is some evidence that boys who identify strongly with their fathers choose the same occupation, though this may not be true of their final choice. Those with high achievement motivation aim higher than their fathers if the latter are in low status jobs, and are less likely to move downwards if their fathers are in high status jobs (Vroom, 1964). Schools influence occupational choice in a number of ways – preferences for school subjects are extrapolated to occupations, courses taken may limit later choices, information about one's abilities is received from teachers, and about occupations from careers masters. In any school there are about three or four jobs or further courses of training which are common, though many of the children have almost no idea what the jobs entail, apart from their names, e.g. 'scientist', or 'manager' (Morrison and McIntyre, 1971).

PERSONNEL SELECTION

In all working groups it is periodically necessary to select new members and to promote existing ones. In the past this has usually been done by rather informal methods, which are now known to be extremely inaccurate. New methods of assessment and new statistical procedures for combining the data are now available, though they are not yet very widely used.

Where there are a number of candidates (Cs) for one job, the procedure is to select the C with the combination of qualities making him most likely to do it well. However, if there are a number of rather different jobs to be filled, and there are a number of Cs with various combinations of attributes, selection is more complex. What is now needed is *differential* selection, i.e. finding the best way of allocating available Cs to the vacant jobs, so that the most important jobs get the Cs best suited to them. Selecting for a number of jobs at once has several advantages – it enables Cs to be placed more accurately, to the advantage both of the organization and themselves, and it is more economical. From the C's point of view the problem is choosing the most suitable job for him; this must be taken into account by the selectors, otherwise the C may become discontented, or leave. A psychologist giving vocational guidance would of course consider the problem solely from this point of view. The overall policy of selection therefore should be one of differential selection, in which due account is taken of the preferences of the Cs (cf. Dunnette, 1966).

The accuracy or efficiency of a selection procedure can be measured in various ways. One is to calculate the correlation between the final score given by the selectors, and an index of subsequent effectiveness on the job. Figure 9 shows diagrams corresponding to correlations of 0·25 and 0·75. Individual scores on the test are measured on the y-axis, scores of later success on the x-axis. The distribution of scores is plotted, and the envelopes containing most of the sample are shown here. If the correlation was perfect (r = 1·00) the distribution would take the form of a straight line at 45 degrees; if there was no correlation (r = 0) there would be a completely random scatter of points. The envelopes corresponding to correlations of 0·25 and 0·75 are shown together with the percentages of individuals falling above and below the average on each axis. The correlation between a selection test (or combinations of tests) and a measure of job success is known as the *validity* of the test.

Let us suppose that the top half of the Cs on the test (the

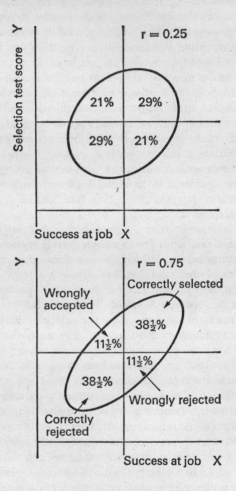

Figure 9. The validity of selection (from Vernon, 1964).

y-axis) were selected; we can see the proportions that fall in the top half in terms of effectiveness on the job (x-axis). With the correlations shown, the proportions correctly accepted and rejected are as shown. There are two rather different kinds of error: those wrongly accepted might be disastrous in positions of seniority, while it is socially undesirable for people to be wrongly rejected for educational purposes.

It would be possible to improve the accuracy of selection almost indefinitely by adding more and more tests, and devising ever more sophisticated statistical procedures. However the point comes where this is not justified in terms of *utility*, i.e. it takes more time, money and effort to do the selection than is gained by doing this selection.

There are two main issues to discuss: which tests or measures to use, and how to combine the data in the most effective way. The first stage, however, is to find out the qualities which are required in a job.

Job specification. In order to fill a job it is necessary to know what qualities are needed for success at the job. There are four main ways of discovering these. First, a job analysis can be carried out, by observation or interview, of the detailed activities of which the job consists. This may lead, via statistical analysis, to establishing the dimensions along which jobs differ. A study was carried out of the jobs of 93 managers, and 575 job elements were found, such as 'adjust customers' complaints'; statistical analysis showed that these consisted of ten dimensions, such as 'technical aspects of products and markets' (Hemphill, 1960). Judgements can then be made of the personal qualities required to carry out the main components of the job. Second, 'critical incidents' can be recorded by supervisors or others who are familiar with the job. These are occasions when the employee's performance led to clear success or failure. Kirchner and Dunnette (1957) asked a large number of sales managers to describe critical incidents in selling, and grouped the incidents into thirteen categories of behaviour which made a difference between successful and unsuccessful selling. Third, groups of successful and unsuccessful performers in a job can

75

be compared, in terms of observed behaviour, education, age or other demographic data, or in terms of test scores. Examples of this approach are given later in connection with the study of supervisory skills (p. 144 f.). Finally, follow-up studies can be carried out, in which a number of possible selection measures are validated in terms of their power in predicting success on the job.

Selection tests and other measures. We have to assess in some way the main abilities and traits thought to be needed for a job. These may include intelligence; other cognitive abilities – creativity and judgement; other aptitudes, e.g. mechanical abilities; achievement motivation, or other motivations; social skills; adjustment; and attitudes to authority.

There are different methods of assessing these, each of which has its special advantages and disadvantages.

Interview. An interview is nearly always used in selection, despite scepticism about it on the part of some psychologists. It is generally used as a means of improving on other sources of data; the interviewer has the candidate's dossier in front of him, explores points which are not clear, and bases his questions on the candidate's record. Used in this way, the interview has been found to raise validity typically from about 0·3–0·4, using the dossier alone, to 0·5–0·6 when the interview is added (Ulrich and Trumbo, 1965). The validity of the interview varies greatly according to the interviewer and is greater when the interviewer is of a similar age and comes from a similar background to the subject, and has been trained in interviewing. There is some unreliability, in that different interviewers often disagree about a C; accuracy can be increased if there are two or three separate interviews, after which the interviewers discuss their judgements and try to arrive at an agreed set of ratings. The social skills needed in the selection interview are described later (p. 158 f.).

Apart from its validity, the interview is useful from the C's point of view for deciding about the job, for interesting Cs in the job, and in some cases for judging their compatibility with immediate superiors or co-workers.

Biographical information. Information about C's past performance can be obtained from his application form, or from a longer questionnaire covering a number of items of his personal history. In one follow-up study 484 items were used which were then found to fall into five statistical factors; comparison with the criterion of number of patents submitted by 418 research scientists showed that two of the factors predicted best to success in this job: these were 'inquisitive, professional orientation', and 'tolerance for ambiguity' (Morrison *et al.*, 1962). This kind of procedure can be a substitute for an interview; it is more objective and covers more ground, but it is less flexible and does not allow for the possibility of studying problems unique to individual Cs.

Testimonials are another source of biographical information. Referees should have known about C's recent performance at work. The main difficulty is that each C is reported on by different referees with somewhat different standards, styles of reporting, etc. Testimonials can be more helpful if a questionnaire is devised, and standard rating scales provided. In one investigation supervisors and other co-workers were interviewed about C's past performance, and validities were obtained between 0·33 and 0·79 for predicting success at different jobs (Mosel and Cozan, 1952).

Biographical information can be used in two ways. Firstly, it can be used to predict that Cs will behave in the future much the same as in the past. Secondly, it can be used as a prediction on the basis of statistical regularities. The prediction tables used for releasing prisoners on parole include both methods: prisoners are less likely to commit a further offence if (1) they have committed fewer offences in the past, and (2) they have had regular employment in the past, have been free of drugs and drink, and did not live in an industrial area (Mannheim and Wilkins, 1955).

Tests. Intelligence tests are often used with success for personnel selection; the validity correlations are frequently as high or higher than for any other measure. However, they may be unnecessary, since sufficient evidence about the intelligence of Cs may be available from their educational record; and anxious Cs do badly on mental tests, unless tested individually. Tests may, however, be needed for specific kinds of mental ability, such as verbal, mathematical and spatial. Tests for mechanical aptitude, the different psychomotor abilities, vision, and particular skills like reading and typing, are also widely used for the selection of different kinds of worker (Tiffin and McCormick, 1966).

Interest inventories such as the Strong and Kuder are widely used in the U.S.A. for vocational guidance, but are less suitable for selection purposes since they can be easily faked, once Cs discover what the most acceptable answers are. Personality questionnaires are open to the same objection. As Whyte (1957) advised, it is best to give answers which show that:

I loved my father and my mother, but my father a little bit more.

I like things pretty much the way they are.

I never worry much about anything.

I don't care for books or music much.

I love my wife and children.

I don't let them get in the way of company work.

Personality tests are now open to the additional objection that the traits which they are supposed to measure may not exist as consistent features of personality, e.g. 'dominance' (p. 58); the validity of such tests for selection purposes is, not surprisingly, minimal. Another type of test is the mock-up situation, such as the pilot's cockpit used for pilot selection. Social skills are sometimes assessed from performance in group situations, as used for officer selection and the Civil Service selection boards. C's performance is assessed in a leaderless group, as an appointed leader, and as member of a group with an appointed leader. The assessments made probably include more than social skills, e.g. intelligence comes into the quality of verbal utterances (perhaps this *is* part of social skill).

Methods of combining the data. When all the information, from biography, interviews and tests, has been assembled, how can it be combined to select the best Cs? In the 'clinical' method the selectors study the data, usually after their final interviews, and make judgements in the light of their past experience, taking account of all the available information, and making use of implicit or explicit psychological theories of which traits go together or how personality works. Comparisons of clinical prediction and statistical procedures (to be described below) usually show that statistical procedures give greater validity (Meehl, 1954). Nevertheless, clinical methods are most often used in practice, because statistical procedures mean carrying out elaborate follow-up studies on large numbers of candidates. Clinical methods can also be very successful. In one study clinical judgements based on a personal history form, a long interview, and brief intelligence tests for 31 marketing managers had a predictive validity of 0·43 to 0·58 for different criteria of effectiveness one year later (Albrecht *et al.*, 1964). There is probably a place for clinical methods in any selection procedure in that for many Cs there are certain special features or complications that would not be covered by the statistical procedures.

Statistical methods of combination of selection data can be set up after a large-scale follow-up study has been completed. The classical approach is by multiple correlation: suppose two tests have been used, T_1 and T_2, and are found to correlate with success on the job 0·25 and 0·50, then a better prediction can be achieved by combining the two tests in an equation which gives T_2 more weight than T_1. This equation will also depend on the correlation between T_1 and T_2; under some conditions a test with a small positive validity comes out in the final equation with a negative sign; it is functioning as a 'suppressor' variable. This happens when the second test has little validity itself, but has a high correlation with invalid components of another test; the second test can best be used to improve the predictions of the first test.

Recent developments in selection statistics have produced other procedures which can produce higher validity from the same data than can multiple correlation. In sequential selection procedures, scores are obtained on *moderator* variables, which have no predictive power themselves, but can be used to allocate Cs to different test procedures. It has been found that some tests give good predictions for some Cs but not for others. In attempting to predict success among engineering students ability tests were found to be quite successful for stable extroverts but not at all for neurotic introverts (Furneaux, 1962). Thus extroversion and stability can be used as 'moderator variables', to decide whether or not to use other tests. Using moderator variables, two- or three-stage schemes of this kind can lead to higher validity than equations combining different test scores for all Cs where the same test data is used. A validity of 0·66 was obtained with a regression equation and 0·73 with moderator variables when identifying successful managers among 443 oil company managers (Hobert, 1965). Further developments of this kind are described by Dunnette (1966).

Statistical procedures are clearly very useful, but they cannot be used in small organizations, and they cannot be used until a large-scale follow-up study has been completed. Sidney and Argyle (1969) recommend that informal weights are given to each dimension for each job to be filled. It would probably be agreed that, for example, a research worker needs to be intelligent and creative, while a line manager needs to have judgement and stability, and to be socially skilled. Estimates of intelligence would come from the academic record, and from intelligence tests if given. Estimates of creativity would come mainly from the interview, unless tests for creativity are used too. The 'multiple-hurdle' principle may also be applied, in that a number of minimum requirements for each job may be agreed upon. It may be helpful to plot a profile for each C across the various abilities needed for the job, as in Figure 10.

Here candidate A would be the most suitable for a research job, while B would be more suitable for line management.

The validity of selection measures. The validity of a selection test is usually regarded as the accuracy with which it can predict subsequent success at the job. As we have seen, the best predictions can be made by the use of moderator variables, so that different combinations of measures are used for different groups of candidates. Validities can be worked out separately

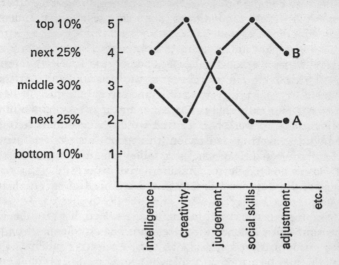

Figure 10. Profiles of ability.

for each sub-group. Predictions may be made to a number of separate indices of success at the job, or to success at a number of different jobs.

One problem about measuring validity is the difficulty of assessing success at the job. Sometimes overall ratings or rankings of effectiveness by superiors and colleagues are used, but the agreement between different raters is usually rather low. In addition, those now in the organization will tend to think well of people like themselves, whereas under changing conditions the organization may need a rather different kind of person. A better method is to decide on the main areas of performance on the job, as described above (p. 75 f.), and to ask judges to make separate ratings on each of them. Thus in the study by Albrecht (1964) district marketing managers were ranked separately on forecasting, sales, interpersonal, and overall effectiveness. Another way of measuring success at the job is by objective indices of effectiveness – sales, output, number of publications, etc. The main difficulty here is that it is often difficult to compare the effectiveness of people working under somewhat different conditions, such as salesmen working in quite different areas.

Establishing validity against such criteria can be done in several ways. The ideal way would be to give the selection tests to a fairly large group of applicants, perhaps 200, and allow all of them to enter the organization, and have their effectiveness assessed. Normally this is not done, and it is not known how well those who were not selected would have done; there is sometimes a strong suspicion that good people are being wrongly rejected. Nevertheless a follow-up study can be made of those who are selected. An alternative procedure is to study some of those who are already in the organization, to see if the tests proposed correlate with present effectiveness. However, those studied would not be taking the selection procedure in the same spirit as when the selection is known to depend on it. For unsophisticated and old-fashioned selective methods the validity may be 0·10–0·20, while with better measures combined in the optimal way it may be as high as 0·70. The interpretation of these figures however depends on certain other features of the selection situation:

(1) *The selection ratio*, i.e. the proportion of Cs who are accepted. Selection is easier with a high selection ratio. To get the best intake it is best to have a high selection ratio, e.g. 1 in 10, *and* a high test validity, e.g. 0·75. The percentages who will be successful at the job are as shown below.

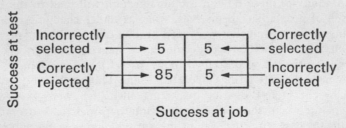

In fact the lower the selection ratio the more difficult selection is. On the other hand, from the point of view of the candidate a high selection ratio is a disadvantage since the chances that a good man will be selected are reduced.

(2) *Cut-off point.* The selection ratio can be altered by accepting a greater or smaller proportion of the Cs. It depends on whether it is more important to avoid wrong selections or wrong rejections; wrong selections can be reduced by using a higher cut-off point, but this will be at the cost of more wrong rejections.

(3) *Variability of Cs.* If all the Cs were identical selection would be impossible; if they were all very different selection would be fairly easy. This is reflected in the size of the correlations that are obtained: with small variations among the Cs, any correlation is reduced in size. Thus selection from highly selected or otherwise homogeneous populations, e.g. graduates with first-class degrees, is difficult and high validities should not be expected. However there is no difficulty in selecting good Cs in this case.

A great deal of selection is going on all the time. Most of it is conducted by old-fashioned methods of very low validity. It is possible to improve on these by means of the methods described above. In addition to selecting people who are best able to do the job, it is very desirable to select people with the right interests and temperament for the job, since they will be happier and stay longer.

CHAPTER 5

THE MOTIVATION TO WORK

Economic motivation – intrinsic motivation –
social motivation.

AMONG animals and very primitive men work is motivated
directly by the need for food, shelter and defence, and by
supporting social needs – since work is carried out in a group
setting in the interests of the group. In Chapter 2 we saw how
in pre-industrial society work was motivated by a variety of
needs, provided a variety of satisfactions, and was closely
linked with other social activities. In modern society it has
become divorced from other spheres of life – most people do
not consume the fruits of their labour, but are paid for it.
Various kinds of incentive schemes have been devised to make
people work hard, but they do not seem to be very satisfactory
unless other forms of motivation are aroused as well. During
recent years managers and social scientists have come to
realize that work can be intrinsically motivating, either because
it is directly enjoyable in itself or because it provides opportunities for achievement and recognition, through the sus-
taining of a self-image, or because it is felt to be 'worthwhile',
or because people become committed to the goals of the
organization. Workers may become committed to the goals of
the organization as the result of participation in decisions, or
co-partnership schemes, and through their relationships with
groups or supervisors.

ECONOMIC MOTIVATION

Classical organization theorists assumed that workers had to be
driven to work by the carrot and the stick – which may often
have been true during the Industrial Revolution. A similar

view is still taken by economists with their concept of 'economic man'. Human Relations writers have taken the opposite line and argued that money is *not* an important incentive or source of satisfaction (e.g. Brown, 1954). This second point of view appeared to receive some support from surveys in which workers were asked which factors were most important in making a job good or bad – 'pay' commonly came sixth or seventh after 'security', 'co-workers', 'interesting work', 'welfare arrangements', etc. (Viteles, 1954). These results may, however, be misleading since people do not have accurate insight into their motivations, and in addition may want to give socially desirable answers. The same may be true of a survey in which 60 per cent said that they would continue to work after receiving a large inheritance (Morse and Weiss, 1955), though there are certainly cases on record where this has happened.

Other evidence shows that money can act as an incentive for people to stay with their organization and work hard while they are there. It was found that labour turnover at one factory fell from 370 per cent to 16 per cent after an increase in wages (Scott *et al.*, 1941). This does not mean that people will do anything for money, and many people choose a lower paid job rather than a higher paid one because the lower paid job is more interesting, is thought to be more worthwhile, carries higher status, is in a nicer place, or because their friends work there. Promotion is quite often not accepted because it would mean separation from friends.

Incentive schemes. There is little doubt that people work harder when paid by results than when paid by the time they put in. There have been numerous studies of the effects of wage incentives. An American survey of the introduction of 514 incentive schemes found an average increase in output of 39 per cent, a decrease in labour costs of 11·6 per cent, and a wage increase of 17·6 per cent (*Modern Industry*, 1946). A careful British study of six factories where no other changes had been introduced found an increase in output of 60 per cent, and an increase in earnings of 20 per cent (Davison, 1958). However, all these figures are probably exaggerations since whenever an incentive scheme is put in other improvements are made as well, for example improvements in methods of working, or delivery of supplies. There are distinct limitations on the effect of incentives on rate of manual work – for example because of group norms about how much work it is proper to do. There are very few people with economic needs strong enough to overcome group pressures against rate-busters; the amount of money people want to earn depends on how much their friends and neighbours have, how large their family is, whether they are trying to buy a house or car, the availability of hire purchase, etc. Managers too are affected by economic incentives (Porter and Lawler, 1968)

Incentives can also be offered for the discovery of better methods of working. Workers can be given some training in method study, and emphasis placed on the continuous improvement of working methods. This approach reduces resistance to change and also produces new ideas about working methods. However, it is only really appropriate under certain conditions – where the work is technically fairly simple, and where there are frequent changes in it.

All the same, it seems fairly clear that within certain limitations payment by results, in one form or another, leads to a higher rate of work and lower labour costs. In England 84 per cent of firms make some use of incentive schemes, and one third of all workers are on some kind of incentive scheme, though this figure includes annual profit-sharing schemes (Shimmin, 1968) as described on page 100. During the last few years a number of large firms have abandoned wage-incentives in favour of some kind of regular weekly or monthly payment for an agreed rate of work (p. 88).

There are a number of difficulties about payment by results. First, it creates bad relations between workers and management. The timing of jobs cannot be done objectively, workers develop grievances over the more tightly timed jobs, improvements in methods are concealed from management, quality deteriorates, and elaborate schemes of self-protection and concealment are devised. Workers often restrict output to what they feel is a reasonable rate of work, because they fear rate-cutting and running out of work, and wish to maintain a stable level of earnings. Roy (1955) took a job as an operator and found that workers in a machine shop restricted their rate of output, but also engaged in secret competitive races with each other. When jobs were being timed they would run cutting tools at a slower speed, but when the rate had been fixed they speeded up the tools and 'streamlined' the jobs in order to earn maximum piecework rates. They enjoyed competing and proving their skills, but only if this did not endanger their earning power or jobs. In another field study it was found that members of a sales group worked out a quota system so that each member earned the same amount, thus defeating the management's incentive scheme (Babchuk and Goode, 1951). Second, workers tend to resist changes in working arrangements; they do their jobs faster, so that they are making good money, in addition to devising the informal arrangements referred to above. This makes it difficult for management to introduce changes. Third, payment by results also creates bad relations between workers. There is constant friction with management over the timing of jobs, and there is friction between workers and competition to get 'loose' jobs and avoid the 'tight' jobs. Fourth, the clerical and accounting costs are considerably increased.

Lupton (1968) concludes that payment by results is suitable under certain conditions only – with repetitive work, slow changes, a good time-study department, good industrial relations, and a tradition of incentive payment, as exists in the West Midlands.

One alternative is group piecework, which avoids friction inside groups and encourages cooperation and help. As an incentive, however, it is usually less effective than individual payment by results, and it has been found that the larger the group the weaker the effect (Marriott, 1968). However, there are situations in which group piecework produces better results than individual piecework. Individual incentives in department stores, for example, lead to salesmen grabbing the best customers, hiding the goods, and neglecting stock and display work. Group piecework is most appropriate with small, cohesive work groups, where workers are closely interdependent such as the coal-mining and textile groups described on page 44 f. In large groups of independent workers it simply acts as a weak incentive and results in hostility towards slower workers.

There are several schemes in which workers are given a bonus on the basis of the overall production or sales of the company or part of it. These will be discussed later (p. 99 f.).

Measured day work. The main alternative to wage incentives is a regular weekly or monthly wage in return for an agreed rate of work. Jobs are graded in terms of the skill, training and effort required, and pay differentials are established. Once the rate for the grade has been agreed, management pays a regular weekly wage on condition that certain standards are met by the worker. If he falls short of the agreed rate of work, management first investigates to see if this is due to failure of supplies or services; if it is due to the worker himself the sanction is transfer to a lower grade or dismissal. The whole scheme depends on a bargain over what is felt to be a fair relationship between reward and effort. This method is often used when mechanization is introduced and payment by results is no longer possible. While there are no systematic studies of its effectiveness, it is said to result in better relations between management and workers, to increase workers' feeling of responsibility, making them feel more like members of the staff, to provide more security and a stable wage, and to reduce administrative costs (Marriott, 1968; Lupton, 1968). On the other hand, there has been bitter resistance to measured day work in some British factories, where it has been felt that the rates of work required were too high, and that arrangements about shut-outs, etc. were unsatisfactory to workers. It may be suggested that for measured day work to be introduced successfully there needs to be a high degree of cooperation, trust and consultation.

Adams: equity between inputs and outputs. All the methods of payment described above depend on an agreement or bargain being reached on what rewards should be given for the exercise of a certain amount of effort and skill. Adams (1965) conceptualized this in terms of exchange theory: workers will try to achieve *equity* between their 'inputs' (training, ability, effort, age, etc.) and their 'rewards' (pay, fringe benefits, status, etc.). The ratio of inputs to rewards for different workers in an organization should be the same, or there will be disequity – older or more skilled workers should be paid more by a suitable amount, for example. Views about how much weight should be given to a particular input, e.g. sex or skill, vary between different sub-cultures, and employers and employees may not agree, e.g. about equal pay for women. This theory has been tested in a number of laboratory experiments, mostly over short periods and without industrial subjects. Different predictions are made by equity theory about the effects of over- and under-payment, under hourly pay and piecework, on the quantity and quality of work.

If workers on hourly rates are overpaid they should work harder, and the reverse if they are underpaid. An experiment was carried out in which students were hired as interviewers, some of whom were told that $3·50 per hour was above the proper rates; these subjects carried out 40 interviews in $2\frac{1}{2}$ hours, compared with 28 by those who were told that $3·50 was the right rate (Adams and Rosenbaum, 1962). However, later experiments showed that the overpayment effect did not appear unless subjects were led to feel personally inadequate – and to work hard to show they were up to the job. If workers are overpaid under piecework the theory predicts that the rate of work will go down and quality will improve (and the reverse for underpayment). These predictions have been confirmed in a number of experiments, but the effects appear to be only temporary. Adams (1965) cites a non-experimental field study of a supermarket where there was inequity through wrappers being older or more educated than cashiers: this resulted in less effective work – the labour costs were 27 per cent more than in similar shops.

Jaques: wage differentials and time-span. Jaques (1961) also argues that people seek a state of balance between inputs and reward. He maintains that there are wage norms for jobs, and that these are a function of a single input – the 'time-span of responsibility', i.e. the period of time which may elapse before the supervisor can know whether his subordinate is working efficiently. In practice this is the length of the longest jobs he does. The theory also predicts that the time-span of a job will correlate with level in the organization, the time-span which an individual prefers, and the person's level of abstraction, i.e. remoteness from manual work. These predictions were tested on 141 managers in an American firm, using tests for the last. It was found that the correlations were positive but were extremely small, in the range 0·10–0·20, thus providing very weak support for the theory as stated (Goodman, 1967). If there is a connection between time-span and actual or expected pay, it does not follow that the first is the cause of the second, via the assumption that wages should be paid in this way. Greater expertise, for example, could lead to both more pay and a longer time-span. More important, this theory does not do justice to the other inputs listed by Adams (e.g. sex, ethnic background), or the other rewards (e.g. working conditions, fringe benefits).

Equal pay. It is interesting that in almost all cultures it is accepted as just that some people should be paid more than others. The only exception to this, as far as I know, is in the Israel kibbutzim (p. 211), though the differentials in Japanese factories are also extremely small; in communist countries there are quite large wage differentials (p. 215 f.). Although there are variations between cultures in the jobs which are paid most, it does seem to be generally assumed that the more skilled and those in higher levels in the supervisory hierarchy should be paid more. Total egalitarianism would work only if people were carefully socialized and indoctrinated to believe in it – as in the kibbutzim. A more acceptable kind of reform might be to find out whether rather smaller differentials than are now common could be established.

The need for money. Little is known about the psychological basis of the need for money. It can be argued that there is no such need, and that people only want money to buy food, clothes and other things. On the other hand, there is evidence that there is an autonomous need for money, for some people at least: as well as mythical misers who enjoy counting their gold there are many who acquire considerable fortunes and do not spend them, and there are those who say they are out to make money. There is also the common subjective experience of not taking foreign currency as seriously as one's own, probably because experiences in childhood with spending money were with a particular currency, which thus becomes rewarding for itself. However, for most people in the world it is the instrumental value of money that is most important. For the more prosperous people in the more prosperous countries the situation is interesting: they may change their level of aspirations and want more or bigger houses and cars, and this will depend on their social reference group. Or they may want money as an index of success. Or they may find new ways of spending money. In a very interesting social survey in the U.S.A. it was found that the most poorly paid workers said they would be satisfied with an increase in income of 162 per cent, those in the middle ranges wanted about 60 per cent, and the most highly paid 100 per cent more, the overall average being 86 per cent (Centers and Cantril, 1946). There is evidently no point at which people do not want more money.

INTRINSIC MOTIVATION

Early managers and management theorists thought that workers disliked work and worked only because they were paid to do it; these managers and writers did not apply the theory to themselves. Early experimental psychologists assumed that activity was motivated by 'tension-reduction', and that rest was the ultimate goal of activity; they worked very hard themselves doing experiments to prove it. These ideas have had to be considerably revised. Management theorists now realize that workers as well as managers work partly because of the intrinsic satisfaction derived from working: they have also come to feel that there is something unsatisfactory about workers being motivated only by economic rewards – this does not always create a surplus of willing cooperation, and the work is done in a spirit of coercion rather than real interest or concern. Herzberg, McClelland and Maslow have drawn attention to other needs, such as the desire for achievement and recognition, and the need to carry out interesting work.

Needs for activity, stimulation, exploration, etc. Experiments with rats have shown that they spontaneously engage in behaviour like running in activity wheels, for no reward other than enjoying the actual activity. Other experiments show that rats like to explore interesting mazes, while monkeys like to solve puzzles and manipulate equipment. Experiments with humans in conditions of sensory deprivation show that the absence of stimulation and activity is very disturbing. It seems that exploration, manipulation and the receiving of novel and interesting stimuli is rewarding, and possibly that sheer activity is rewarding. Psychologists are not agreed as to what the motivational basis of this behaviour is: Berlyne (1960) maintained that animals and men seek an optimal level of stimulation. While too much activity produces fatigue and stress, too little results in boredom. Where this level lies varies between individuals: Eysenck (1967b) has produced extensive evidence to show that extroverts are more easily bored or satiated, and require a higher level of external stimulation; he maintains that extroverts are normally at a lower level of cortical arousal.

These principles affect work as well as maze-running. Everyone knows that the unemployed become depressed and bored, and try to find things to do (e.g. Bakke, 1940); in their spare time people often do gardening, decorating, hobbies or other manual work, or take part in vigorous physical sports which are evidently enjoyed and produce a feeling of well-being. While interesting work provides its own reward, those engaged in boring work do their best to make it more interesting: we described above (p. 34) the games and practical jokes often engaged in by manual workers. There are individual differences in tolerance for boring work; intelligent people are most discontented with it (Vroom, 1964); if the above theories are correct introverts should be able to tolerate it more than extroverts.

There are cross-cultural differences in the need for stimulation or activity: the hustle and pep of the Western world is less in evidence in South America and West Africa. This may be partly due to climate but is probably more a result of general cultural attitudes passed on to children by parents and teachers. We showed in Chapter 2 how Roman and medieval attitudes of aversion to work were replaced by the Protestant ethic, which in turn may now be giving way to a concern with leisure and consumption rather than work. Lynn (1971) has produced cross-cultural evidence to show that industrial growth is correlated with measures of arousal – such as number of car accidents, and questionnaire measures of anxiety.

It follows from all this that people should want to do interesting work to satisfy their needs for exploration, stimulation and manipulation. Herzberg (1959) found that when people are asked to report times when they were particularly satisfied with their jobs they often speak of occasions on which the work itself was very interesting or went well. Some of this satisfaction derives from a sense of completing an important or difficult task, and it sometimes includes elements of achievement motivation. Programmes of job enlargement, job rotation and job enrichment (p. 34) have shown that they frequently lead to an increase in the rate of work, an improvement in the quality of the work through the worker taking more responsibility for it, and increased job satisfaction (e.g. Friedmann, 1961). However, not all workers prefer to have interesting jobs (see p. 230); it has been argued that job enlargement is only successful (in the U.S.A.) with 'white collar, supervisory and non-alienated blue-collar workers' (Hulin and Blood, 1968). The reason is probably that some workers expect to be paid for working but not to enjoy it; they prefer jobs which demand the least effort, mental or physical, and which do not interfere with conversation or day-dreaming.

Achievement motivation. It would probably be agreed that some people are more ambitious and hard-working than others.

McClelland (1953) postulated that strength of the need to achieve is a basic dimension of personality. The measure used was the number of achievement themes produced in projection test stories. These stories are more achievement-oriented following experience of success or failure, or ego-involving instructions. On the other hand, this measure does not correlate well with other possible measures, and there may be two different aspects of achievement motivation, measurable by projection test and questionnaire respectively. At the moment it is not feasible to use these tests for personnel selection. High achievers (on the projection measure) tend to have the following characteristics – they do their best to obtain monetary or other rewards in laboratory games and tasks, they set themselves high but realistic targets, and are optimistic about the outcome. While they work harder at laboratory tasks, and do somewhat better at academic work, not much is known about their performance in other work situations, though there is some evidence that successful managers are high achievers (Birney, 1968). We discussed earlier the evidence that achievement motivation leads to industrial growth, via the activities of entrepreneurs (p. 23 f.).

These results encouraged McClelland and Winter (1969) to carry out experiments on stimulating achievement motivation in underdeveloped countries. They report the results of a short course for managers and businessmen in India, in which trainees played management games and were taught the behaviour of high achievers. A before-and-after comparison showed that the course members made considerable efforts to increase the productivity of their industrial concerns, compared with a control group who did not go on the course. An interesting feature of this study is that 'achievement motivation' is not mentioned as such. The results could however be due to the learning of new management techniques rather than to any increase in motivational state.

The research on achievement motivation has been mainly corcerned with individual differences; however this form of motivation can be aroused by providing challenges and targets. This was shown in experiments in which such arousal conditions were found to affect the projective measure of achievement motivation. Work situations do not always provide opportunities for achievement, and any strivings of this kind may be diverted to leisure pursuits. We shall now discuss conditions under which achievement motivation can be aroused at work.

It is achievement motivation which is largely responsible for the effects of knowledge of results (i.e. information about level of performance), and of success and failure, in work performance. Knowledge of results can improve performance in three ways. If this information is given before the action is completed it enables the performer to correct his performance to make it more accurate. If the performer is not highly skilled at the task and if knowledge of results is given after each performance, it helps him learn to perform better. A number of laboratory studies have shown that when the first two processes are eliminated knowledge of results increases work motivation. A field experiment was carried out in an electric power station: instruments were installed which showed each man how efficiently his boiler was working, and daily and weekly records were announced; the result was a saving of $330,000 per year in coal consumption, as well as a drop in labour turnover. However, this was partly due to rivalry between men and between shifts, and the men being given a new title of 'stoker operator' which increased their status (Bingham, 1932). Knowledge of results of *group* performance has been found to improve the performance of groups working in laboratory tasks. In a laboratory experiment it was found that feedback about task performance had most effect when group members were high in achievement motivation; when they were low in achievement motivation, feedback on the social interaction had more effect (French, 1958).

There is some evidence that the setting of targets for production has a motivating effect. In laboratory experiments it was found that this setting of a definite objective had more effect than telling subjects to do their best or to improve on their past score (Mace, 1935). In real-life situations success would probably depend on how far the targets were accepted. It is part of the Scanlon plan to set agreed targets (p. 207 f.). The use of group decisions by leaders (p. 149f.) and 'management by objectives' (p. 156f.) also involve the setting of targets. Where an incentive is based on competing with other people enormous motivation may be aroused, as can be seen from competitive sport. In laboratory experiments where individual competition has been aroused very high rates of performance have been produced, though the quality of work was inferior and in some cases disrupted by the unduly high motivation, since emotional arousal leads to erratic motor responses (e.g. Whittemore, 1924–5).

Standard of work is also affected by success or failure. The most common result is that success leads to greater efforts, failure to less. However among those who fail (or are told they have failed) the greatest effort is made by those closest to the target (Diggory, 1966). The effects of success and failure also vary according to personality: success can lead to taking things easy, and failure to increased efforts. Those high in achievement motivation appear to be stimulated to greater efforts by both success and failure (McClelland *et al.*, 1953).

Maslow: hierarchy of needs and self-fulfilment.

Self-fulfilment, or self-actualization
Self-esteem
Social needs (acceptance)
Safety needs
Physiological needs (hunger and thirst)

Maslow maintains that when a lower need is satisfied, the next need in his hierarchy is aroused. The main supporting evidence for this theory comes from the lowest needs in the hierarchy – when people are very hungry, thirsty, cold, or afraid they are not much concerned about higher needs, as a number of studies have shown (Cofer and Appley, 1964). There is not such clear evidence about the upper part of the hierarchy. However, studies of the motivational concerns of workers at different levels of seniority are certainly consistent with Maslow's hypothesis. At lower levels people are most concerned about pay and security; at higher levels (where they are paid more) they are more concerned about achievement and success. (Pay is not included in the Maslow scheme since it is thought to be related to a number of needs.) It has also been found that higher-level managers attach more importance to autonomy and self-actualization (Vroom, 1964; Cummings and El Salmi, 1968). However, these results could be due to more ambitious men rising higher in the hierarchy. So these studies do not test the central Maslow hypothesis that the satisfaction of a lower need results in greater concern with a higher one. This hypothesis was tested in a study of 49 young managers over an interval of five years. Only very weak connections were found between greater lower-need satisfaction and increases in higher-need strength; much the same was found for correlations at one point of time between lower satisfaction and higher needs (Hall and Nougaim, 1968). The authors propose instead a sequence of different concerns at different stages of the career, in which concern for security and acceptance is followed by promotion and achievement, perhaps followed by some concern for higher causes.

Another feature of Maslow's theory is his emphasis on the highest need in the hierarchy – 'self-actualization'. This is a postulated need for growth, continual self-development and realizing of potentialities; it is said to include the capacity to love and be loved, creativity, and to lead to mystical 'peak' experiences. As Cofer and Appley (1964) comment, these ideas 'comprise almost a programme of what life should be' (p. 691). This concept of self-actualization is popular with existential psychologists, but is regarded as mysterious and unmeasurable by their more scientific colleagues.

An alternative formulation (Vroom, 1964) is that people are motivated to make use of their abilities. Several experiments show that if subjects are led to believe that a task requires abilities which they think they possess they will work harder at it. This goes beyond experiments which show that people work harder when they feel that their performance will show their standing on intelligence or leadership.

In modern society the work a person does is a major component of his identity. In the Twenty Statements Test subjects are asked to give twenty answers to the question 'Who am I?'. Occupation is one of the most frequent kinds of answer, and it usually appears early in the list (Mulford and Salisbury, 1964). Self-esteem is greatly dependent on success at work, as shown by money earned, promotion, status symbols, or other kinds of recognition of success. In this way several kinds of motivation for work become incorporated into an autonomous drive for success at work which can become a central feature of the personality (Neff, 1968). This does not happen to every-one: those employed in low-status jobs are often not deeply committed to their work, and do it mainly for the pay and the social contacts.

The perceived value of the product. In modern society work as such is valued, and the idle are despised as parasites. In every society some jobs are valued more than others – those who do them are paid more and granted higher social status. There are intercultural differences in the work that is most valued: in communist countries manual work is esteemed more than in the West, and in primitive societies hunters or herdsmen may be most revered.

In very primitive societies men and women work to provide food, shelter, clothes and household goods for themselves and their families. In more advanced societies work is more specialized and the products of work are bartered or sold (p. 16f.). Under modern conditions most people are paid for their work, but they are still interested in the social value of their goods or services, and will work harder if they think that the work they are doing is useful. For example, it was found that an experimental incentive scheme had no effect on girls engaged in a clearly useless task (unwrapping chocolates), but when they were given the task of wrapping they worked at three times the speed after the incentive was introduced (Wyatt, 1934). Job satisfaction is related to a belief that the work done is important or useful; workers will often provide moral justifi-cation for their work. During the Second World War workers in British and American armaments factories were shown the aircraft or tanks they were making or were visited by air-crews, and this dramatization of the importance of the product probably affected their motivation.

Some working organizations are more obviously concerned with socially desirable purposes than others – hospitals, churches, voluntary organizations, and universities for example. Etzioni (1961) called these 'moral' organizations, and suggested that they are different from others in that members can be motivated by appealing to their commitment to the goals of the organization (p. 183). However, in each of the organizations mentioned there are clearly other kinds of motivation as well, such as economic rewards and the prospects of promotion.

SOCIAL MOTIVATION

We shall consider under this heading the conditions under which workers become committed to the goals of their organization, and the effect of social motives and relationships on their output.

Work is usually done in groups and organizations in which members have to cooperate. It would clearly be desirable for them to be motivated by some kind of commitment to the goals of the organization, and not solely by private needs which are liable to produce both conflict with management and competition with other workers. There are several ways in which this commitment can be created.

Monthly productivity bonus. In addition to a guaranteed weekly wage, a monthly bonus is paid, based on the output or sales of the whole firm or individual department. This bonus may be arrived at by comparison with a target figure. From studies of the incentive effects of group piecework one would think that the whole firm would constitute far too large a group for there to be any effect on productivity. The Scanlon plan (p. 207 f.) and Yugoslav industry (p. 214 f.) suggest that nevertheless there can be some incentive effect. In both these cases, however, there is also a lot of worker participation in management, and the department rather than the firm is the unit for incentive purposes. It has also been found that labour turnover is reduced, and cooperation increased where there is a productivity bonus (Marriott, 1968). There can, on the other hand, be some resentment towards slackers on the part of more effective workers, though this may take the form of constructive social pressures.

Profit-sharing and co-partnership. Here there is a guaranteed weekly wage, and an annual (or twice-yearly) bonus based on the firm's *profits*. This is very widely used in British and American industry, though the actual amount distributed may be small, and many firms have abandoned it. No very precise data is available but it is generally agreed that there is no effect on productivity – the group is too large, and the time-lag too great. Firms have often introduced profit-sharing more in the hope of creating a sense of belonging, and promoting industrial peace and team-work, but there is no evidence that industrial relations have improved. The advantages may lie in reduced labour turnover and increased job satisfaction, but this too remains to be demonstrated. Part of the trouble is that profits are partly outside workers' control, and depend on other factors besides production, such as the economic position of the firm; the profits are small during times of economic depression and workers become dissatisfied with the scheme.

There are certain conditions that must be fulfilled if schemes based on collective output or profits are to be effective: the group on which the incentive is based must not be too large; the time unit on which the bonus is based must not be too long; and there should be full worker participation in management.

Collective ownership scarcely exists in the West, apart from small family businesses. However there are rural cooperatives all over Africa, and the kibbutz scheme has been operating in Israel for over half a century. We shall describe later how kibbutz members work at boring jobs because they feel that they are contributing to the collective welfare, and because their work has a new significance for them (p. 211 f.). On the other hand, many cooperative ventures have failed, and there may have to be 'commitment mechanisms' whereby the members acquire a special attachment to the community.

Participation in decisions. Schemes for the formal participation of workers in decisions have been introduced in a number of countries, and appear to create increased identification with the organization and its goals, and to lead to increased productivity (p. 203 f.). This is also found when different styles of supervision are compared: output is higher when subordinates are consulted more (p. 148 f.).

*

We now turn to the operation of social motivations at work. They act as incentives both for people to go to work in the first place and for them to work hard when they get there. We shall consider three different social motives – affiliative, status and dependence.

People high in *affiliative motivation* spend a lot of time with others, tend to be warm and affectionate, try to establish intimate relationships, prefer to be popular rather than a leader, and are more concerned with social interaction in a group than with the work in hand (Argyle, 1969). While there are individual differences in the strength of this drive, nearly everyone has it to some extent. There is evidence that affiliative motivation is an incentive to go to work. An American survey found that 31 per cent of people who said they would still work if it was not financially necessary said that this was because of their relationships with people at work (Morse and Weiss, 1955). A number of studies have found that labour turnover is lower in cohesive groups and among popular individuals. Relationships with workmates are one of the most important causes of job satisfaction (p. 233 f.). Does affiliative motivation affect productivity however? Studies of rate-busters and restriction of output find that affiliative needs can *reduce* output (Dalton, 1948), which shows that for most manual workers the need to be accepted by the group is stronger than the need to earn more money. On the other hand, in a cohesive group one would expect there to be a social incentive for working, at least at cooperative tasks, since work involves social interaction; there is some evidence that cohesive groups on average work harder (p. 120f.).

The *need for status* is a second social need, though not a great deal is known about it. Work can give status, or respect from others, both inside and outside the working organization, though a man's internal position is sometimes rather obscure to outsiders, and has to be inferred from his income or style of life. It has been found that when people are unemployed they feel a great loss of status, and think that they are no longer respected (Bakke, 1940); this was found during the 1930s, and different results might be obtained today, both because of welfare state provisions and because of the decline in the Protestant ethic. Status is correlated with job satisfaction (p. 231f.), from which it follows that there must be a need here which can be satisfied at work. Herzberg (1959) found that recognition was often mentioned as the reason for occasions of high job satisfaction. Among salesmen competition based on number of sales has always been the custom. Among manual workers, on the other hand, there has long been a tradition in Britain of group solidarity: individuals do not want to be promoted over and separated from their workmates – they would prefer the whole group to be upgraded or better paid. In an American study, on the other hand, Georgopoulos (1957) found more productive workers among those who thought that high productivity would lead to promotion. Managers have been found to be preoccupied with their prospects of promotion (p. 66). In addition to these sub-cultural variations in the effects of status needs, there are also individual differences. The need for status may be linked to the need for achievement, though the latter was originally conceptualized as a concern for internalized standards of excellence, rather than for respect by others.

A third social need is *dependency*: this is the need for care and protection by more powerful people. Dependency is the first social need to appear in young children; although dependency is discouraged later, especially in boys, many adults have a definite need for dependence. There is extensive evidence that job satisfaction is greater under supervisors who are high in 'consideration', i.e. look after the welfare of their subordinates (p. 147 f.).

*

While it is clearly a mistake to suppose that men work only for money, financial incentives are nevertheless important in industry, though their effects are variable and complex. Intrinsic motivations such as the needs for achievement and self-fulfilment are important for many people, and much more use could be made of these needs as incentives. People become committed to the goals of an organization under certain conditions, such as participation in decision-making. Social motives are important in bringing people to work, and have an important effect on their behaviour in groups.

CHAPTER 6

WORKING IN GROUPS

*The importance of working groups – why do people work
in groups? – different kinds of work group – the elements
of social interaction in working groups – the development
of cohesiveness in work groups – group norms – informal
hierarchy and role differentiation – the optimum design
for working groups – decision-taking, problem-solving
and creative groups.*

THE IMPORTANCE OF WORKING GROUPS

ONE of the central features of work is that it is usually done in
groups, groups of individuals cooperating under the direction
of a leader or leaders. This crucial point was overlooked by
classical organization theory, and by traditional industrial
psychology; it is still being overlooked in many current ways
of looking at working organizations, for example in terms of
'man-machine systems'. Work is done in groups among animals, and among primitive men as we have seen, and has continued to be done in groups in highly automated plants, though
sometimes working groups have been disrupted through a
failure to realize their importance – for getting the work done
more effectively, as well as making it more enjoyable.

The working group is one of the main types of social group,
and social interaction at work is one of the main forms of social
interaction. Working groups differ from other groups – friends,
families, etc. – in that they are brought together in order to
collaborate over work, and the pattern of relationships in the
group is primarily determined by the task to be done. The
interaction which takes place in a working group can be
divided into work proper and sociable. Each category can be
further subdivided into various kinds of verbal and non-verbal
acts, such as helping, giving advice, joking, gossiping, etc.

(p. 112f.). By these various kinds of social interaction the group members cooperate over the group task, and sustain a pattern of relationships between them. Social behaviour in the group can also be analysed in terms of the social system – its friendship structure, informal hierarchy, different roles, and norms. One of the most important aspects of the social system is the *cohesiveness* of the group, i.e. the extent to which group members are attracted towards the group and prepared to cooperate with one another. Cohesiveness results in cooperation to attain the group goals, which may not be the same as the goals of the organization of which the group is a part; a cohesive group can be effective in opposing other groups and the wider organization.

The life of working groups is greatly affected by the job they are doing and the arrangements for work laid down by management or others. Similarly the effect of technology and working arrangements on output depends on how it affects the group system; the arrangements may generate conflict, for example, when one man has two superiors, which disrupts the group and reduces cooperation. We shall use the following model:

TASK
AND   +
TECHNOLOGY

OFFICIAL
WORKING   +
ARRANGEMENTS
↓

PERSONALITIES
OF
MEMBERS

SOCIAL SYSTEM OF GROUP
(including actual working arrangements)
↓

EFFECTIVENESS AND SATISFACTION

The TASK is the actual work to be done. The WORKING ARRANGEMENTS are the ways of performing the task as imposed by management. The group reacts to this by creating its own ways of coping with the task or using the working arrangements. This may include appointing its own informal leader, using certain communication channels but not others, establishing certain rules of working, and so on. When engineers and technologists design the task, and managers design the working arrangements, they do not yet know how the working group will react, what sort of social system will be created; consequently they do not know whether productivity or satisfaction will be high or low.

The importance of the internal dynamics of working groups for productivity was first suggested by the famous Hawthorne experiment (Roethlisberger and Dickson, 1939). Five girls were moved into a test room and subjected to various changes in rest periods and refreshments; it was found that output increased about 30 per cent, this being unrelated to any particular experimental conditions. It was generally concluded that the increase was due to social factors within the group. However, the increase could be accounted for by the change in group piecework which was shared among a group of five instead of a larger group, the smaller variety of work done, the replacement of two of the girls by faster ones, the enthusiasm of the penurious operative number two, and the general expectation throughout the works that the experiment would be a 'success' (Argyle, 1953).

Classical management theory did not mention working groups, but research has shown that the composition and inner dynamics of groups can have a marked effect on productivity and satisfaction. *Productivity:* we described earlier some of the work of the Tavistock Institute in which working groups were reorganized (p. 44f.). In the modified Longwall mining groups output per man-shift rose by 50 per cent; in the modified Indian textile groups output rose by 21 per cent, and damaged cloth fell by 59 per cent. Other studies in which size or cohesiveness alone have been varied, showed more modest increases of 10–15 per cent. *Absenteeism and labour turnover:* it is often found that the rate of voluntary absenteeism and labour turnover is three or four times as great in groups which are largest, least cohesive, or least well organized (p. 119f.). *Job satisfaction* is greatly affected by the nature of the group, particularly when the work is done in teams – as in fishing, mining, etc.

Group behaviour in animals is presumably the result of natural selection, since working in groups has obvious biological advantages. Among primitive men the whole situation is totally different because they can communicate by means of language, their work is more complex, and methods of working are continually elaborated during the history of the culture. Nevertheless they still work in groups and similar factors to those operating among animals still apply. Work groups in industrial society face more complex tasks, and their group structure is partly determined by technology and management; however, unofficial groupings appear where the formal structure has failed to arrange for people to belong to small working groups.

There are a number of advantages of working in groups. These advantages, via both evolutionary and social processes, have resulted in a number of social needs, so that belonging to groups is a source of satisfaction. Groups can cooperate over large tasks, such as nest-building in animals, or mud-hut building among primitive men. Some tasks simply require the combined efforts of a number of individuals; among somewhat less primitive men division of labour allows individuals to develop specialized skills which can then be combined to good effect. Animals cling together when danger threatens, and humans seek the company of the group, for example soldiers bunch up under fire. We shall see later that job satisfaction is higher, and tension and absenteeism lower in certain kinds of working group. Group members may also collaborate to protect their interests against action by management, the public, or other groups. The increased complexity of life in industrial society means that there are many more problems to be solved from day to day. The solutions to common problems become embodied in the culture and in the norms of groups, and are enforced as the approved way of doing things, such as how to make canoes or aircraft. There is a kind of social evolution whereby the best solutions survive. For other problems people often seek help from the group, where a variety of expertise may be found. Under the often stressful, competitive or otherwise demanding conditions of modern work there are many ways in which individuals can help one another. Such help may be reciprocated between pairs of members, and is more common in cohesive and cooperative groups. Even when work is officially performed by a number of individuals independently, in practice there is usually a great deal of mutual help; without it life is difficult and productivity low.

In animals evolutionary processes seem to have led to the development of social needs, probably to restrain aggression within the group and encourage cooperation. In human working groups similar needs appear to operate and are expressed in gossip, jokes, games and other non-work interaction. Members may also acquire a role or status in the group which adds to their sense of identity. When animals are together they work harder. Experiments on ants showed that they built nests at about three times the speed when working in groups of two or three than when alone (Chen, 1937). One interpretation of this finding is that the presence of others produces greater arousal (Zajonc, 1965). These effects are found in human groups too, and are responsible, for example, for the greater efforts people will make in problem-solving groups.

DIFFERENT KINDS OF WORK GROUP

Most people work in groups, but the grouping can take a number of forms. In addition, working groups do not always have clear-cut boundaries. We must distinguish between the groups that appear on organization charts, and the actual groupings of people who interact with one another with some frequency, like one another, or feel that they have something in common. There are people interacting who are not supposed to, and people not interacting who are supposed to.

One way of discovering the real groups is to observe the frequency and type of interaction between individuals in a place of work. In the study of the Bank Wiring Observation Room at the Hawthorne plant it was found that there were two informal groups in this sense who engaged in friendly interaction, such as helping and playing games (Roethlisberger and Dickson, 1939). Of the twelve workmen (comprising the official work group), five made up a socially superior group A, four were in group B, and three did not interact much with either.

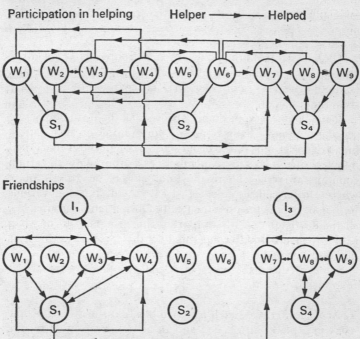

Figure 11. Bank Wiring Observation Room, Hawthorne Plant (from Roethlisberger and Dickson, 1939).

A well-known method of studying the structure of groups is *sociometry*, in which members are asked to say who they would choose or reject as companions for some common activity (Moreno, 1953). If possible these choices should be made in private, and they should actually be granted afterwards. If choices are made for different activities, it is found that different choices are made for (1) competence at work, and as co-worker, (2) like–dislike and leisure choice, (3) leadership. The choices may be plotted to form a *sociogram*, and this can show the affective structure of a group very clearly. Here is an example of a sociogram where each person was given two positive choices.

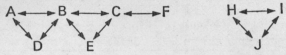

ABD, BCE, HIJ are cliques, or sub-groups. ABD and BCE are overlapping cliques, where B is the link. ABCF is a chain. B is popular; F is unpopular. HIJ is separated by a cleavage from the rest.

Social bonds at work do not always take the form of discrete social groupings. Chains of people, for example on an assembly line, are not groups in the usual sense, though those concerned may feel themselves to be members of a grouping with certain common interests. There may not always be groups quite where the organization chart shows them, but the various formal arrangements do influence the formation of groups. We shall show later that it is important for groups to form when people are supposed to cooperate over their work, but this does not always happen.

Some of the main types of social groups at work are as follows:

Technological groups, such as assembly lines, in which people work in a place, at a speed and in a way determined by the technology, but where there is little interaction between them. Under these conditions the effects of social groups are less important.

Teams are groups of people who cooperate to carry out a joint task. They may be assigned to different work roles, or be allowed to sort them out between them and change jobs when they feel like it, for example the crews of ships and aircraft, research teams, maintenance gangs and groups of miners.

Decision-taking and problem-solving groups. Managers, administrators, planners and research workers spend a lot of time in committees or working parties, where the main activity is talking, with the aim of taking decisions or solving problems. The same person may belong to a number of such groups which come to life intermittently.

Informal groups and linkages. All the groupings so far are between people brought together by the formal structure. There are also informal groups and linkages between people who find each other congenial or know each other for other reasons – neighbours, old friends, relatives, belonging to the same church or golf club, etc. These links can be very important in that they provide extra channels of communication that short-circuit the formal channels, and satisfy social needs.

The pattern of relationships in the first two kinds of group is greatly affected by the technology, as was shown on page 40 f. A number of different kinds of interaction take place in these groups (p. 38 f.).

THE ELEMENTS OF SOCIAL INTERACTION IN WORKING GROUPS

Recent research into social interaction has advanced on earlier work by looking much more closely at social interaction and analysing it in terms of its basic elements. These are verbal and non-verbal. Verbal behaviour can be categorized in a number of ways, for example whether it conveys information, asks a question or tries to influence behaviour, whether it is rewarding or punishing, and so on. The non-verbal elements are various forms of bodily proximity, orientation, posture, physical appearance, facial expression, movements of hands, head and feet, direction of gaze and eye-movements, the timing and emotional tone of speech. It is now known that non-verbal signals play three main roles in social interaction: managing the immediate social situation, e.g. by sending signals of liking or dominance; complementing speech, e.g. by gestures; and replacing verbal communication, when noise or distance makes this impossible (Argyle, 1969).

This detailed analysis has not yet been applied to behaviour in working groups, and it may be more useful to study interaction at work in terms of rather larger units of behaviour. We will distinguish between verbal and non-verbal behaviour, and between behaviour that is primarily work-orientated and behaviour that is primarily sociable. A given piece of social behaviour may fall into more than one of these categories; for example if a man passes his mate some bricks in a friendly way this is a combination of two kinds of non-verbal behaviour – work and sociable.

Verbal: work-oriented.
(1) Information, questions and discussion about the immediate task. This includes transfer of information about readings on dials, reports on progress, etc. These are the man-man links in the man-machine systems.
(2) Information, questions and discussion about how to do the work. This includes help from equals, instructions and orders from superiors, and suggestions to superiors.
(3) Information, questions and discussion about conditions of work, pay or other organizational matters.

Verbal: sociable.
(1) Sociable chat, gossip about people, and discussion of current affairs not directly related to the group situation.
(2) Jokes and games, telling of funny stories.
(3) Discussion of personal problems, sometimes in a sympathetic or therapeutic manner.

Non-verbal: work-oriented.
(1) Work activity which affects others. The sheer performance of individual work may affect others, and thus constitute a social signal. For example, a person may be seen to do twice as much work as is normal in the group, or to do it in a new way.
(2) Coordinated task activity. When two men are sawing together, lifting a load together, or in some other way coordinating their movements, each of these movements is a

social act. One of them might not pull his weight, for example, or might fail to coordinate his movements or insist on directing operations – purely through the medium of physical movements.

(3) Helping. One person may, with or without speaking, help another with his work. We shall see that helping and its reciprocation is an important aspect of the life of work groups.

(4) Guiding. Bodily contact may be used to guide another's movements when showing him a new task.

(5) Sending information. Sometimes workers are some distance apart, as in steel rolling mills; sometimes there is too much noise to speak, as in weaving sheds. Under these conditions non-verbal signals may be used instead of verbal signals to send necessary information about the task.

(6) Non-verbal comments about work. Approval and disapproval of someone's work performance is often communicated non-verbally. A rate-buster may be given a raised eyebrow, a look of disapproval, a blow on the arm, or may simply be avoided.

(7) Non-verbal accompaniments of verbal messages. The way in which an order is given for example will affect whether it is seen as 'advice' or as an 'order', and how likely it is to be carried out.

Non-verbal: sociable.

(1) Communicating interpersonal attitudes. Relations between people are established and maintained mainly by expressing attitudes non-verbally. People show others whether they like or dislike them by smiling or frowning (and other cues of bodily orientation, posture, etc.); they show whether they think they are inferior or superior, or whether they are sexually attracted, by appropriate non-verbal cues (Argyle, 1969).

(2) Communicating emotions. Similarly, people let one another know whether they are happy, sad, anxious, tired, angry, etc., by their facial expression, bodily posture and general pattern of movements. As with the communication

of interpersonal attitudes, most of this non-verbal signalling is spontaneous and uncontrolled, but it is received by others, usually with full conscious awareness.

(3) Appearance. A person's clothes, hair and other aspects of his appearance are mainly under his control and can be regarded as part of his social behaviour. In these ways a person signals his status, and various aspects of his identity – a foreman may look more like a manager or more like a worker, a scientist may look like a back-room boy or a company director.

We have carried out several small-scale surveys, with varied populations, in which respondents were asked to compare their social behaviour in various work and non-work relationships. The results so far show that behaviour at work differs from behaviour at home or with friends, in the following ways. There is more talk about the task in hand, as opposed to general chat; more concealment of personal problems, emotional states, irritation with others, financial situation and ambitions; more concern with what the others think of one, and more concern with personal appearance; a greater need for reciprocity from others before helping them a second time.

These are all most marked in relations with bosses, subordinates and less-liked fellow-workers. Behaviour with fellow-workers one likes is more similar to behaviour with friends and relations. There are also marked class differences in behaviour at work. Middle-class people are more polite at work, talk less about sex, behave in a more conventional and rule-governed way than at home or with friends. Working-class people at work, on the other hand, are less polite, swear more, and talk more about sex than at home or with friends.

THE DEVELOPMENT OF COHESIVENESS IN WORK GROUPS

Working groups, unlike groups studied in the laboratory, last a considerable period of time. During this time the social system of the group develops slowly. One of the most important aspects of this system is the *cohesiveness* of the group – the extent to which the group members are attracted towards the group. The growth of relationships inside groups has been observed to follow a regular sequence of stages; Tuckman (1965) suggests that there are usually four main stages, in groups of different kinds:

Table 1 emphasizes the fact that group members have two different problems to deal with – handling the external task with which they are confronted, and coming to terms with one another. The pattern of behaviour in the group can be seen as the group's attempt to work out solutions to both of these problems. Norms are developed, for example, about how the task is to be performed, and a pattern of interaction is developed which defines a more or less satisfactory pattern of relations between members.

In a group which is going to last for a long time the above stages may be quite slow, perhaps taking as long as a year; in more temporary groups the process may be greatly speeded up. There may be a fifth stage, when the group is about to be dissolved: there is nostalgia for the early days of the group (Mann, 1967). When a new member joins an established group, he may pass through several stages of acceptance; concern with the basic needs that bring him to the group, conformity to group norms, concern with the social interaction in the group and the group goals, taking part in the leadership of the group.

With the passage of time a group is likely to become more cohesive, though some become more cohesive than others, and the process can take place quite quickly. Cohesiveness is sometimes defined in terms of the percentage of sociometric choices to other members of the group; however, this measure does not include other sources of attraction to the job, e.g. to the task itself, or to the rewards obtained from belonging to the group. Other measures of cohesiveness sometimes used are feelings of loyalty or pride in group, the relative frequency of the words 'We' and 'I', or the amount of helping, or the effects of cohesiveness such as low labour turnover and voluntary absenteeism. Another way of looking at it is to say that people

Table 1

	Group Structure	Task Activity
(1) Forming	There is anxiety, dependence on a leader, testing to find out the nature of the situation and what behaviour is acceptable.	Members find out what the task is, what the rules are, what methods are appropriate.
(2) Storming	Conflict between sub-groups, rebellion against leader, opinions are polarized, resistance to control by group; conflicts over intimacy.	Emotional resistance to demands of task.
(3) Norming	Development of group cohesion, norms emerge, resistance overcome and conflicts patched up, mutual support and development of group feelings.	Open exchange of views and feelings; cooperation develops.
(4) Performing	Interpersonal problems are resolved, interpersonal structure is the tool of task activity, roles are flexible and functional.	Emergence of solutions to problems, constructive attempts at task completion, energy is now available for effective work; this is major work period.

belong to a work group, and may also belong to one or more informal groups. The informal groups in the Bank Wiring Observation Room of the Western Electric Company are shown in Figure 13. Similarly on an assembly line there are a series of two- and three-person groupings based on proximity. Many studies have been made of the conditions under which groups become cohesive (cf. Lott and Lott, 1965). The most important are as follows:

Physical proximity and frequency of interaction lead to friendship between pairs of people and the formation of groups among larger numbers. People working in the same room or area will tend to form a group, whether there is any connection between their work or not. A group whose members have worked together for some time tends to become cohesive, especially if it is fairly isolated from other people.

Same or similar work. Under traditional working arrangements a number of workers sit side-by-side doing identical or similar work – as in the Relay Assembly Test Room. This is a source of group formation since they are faced by the same problems and can help each other in many ways. Other conditions of work may stimulate group formation, such as sharing the same supervisor.

Homogeneity. Cohesiveness is greater in groups that are homogeneous in such things as race, age, social status, and in attitudes relevant to the work situation. If members are of unequal status, cohesiveness will be greatest when there is 'status congruence', i.e. those with high status in one respect (e.g. education or length of training) have high status in others (e.g. pay). Groups containing both skilled and less skilled members can be cohesive, if their skills are complementary, though there will usually be two sub-groups. The members do not need to have the same personality traits, but some combinations of personalities make for more cohesive groups than others – when there are not too many very dominant people, and when affiliative needs are strong. Certain personalities are disruptive

– schizoid and psychopathic ones are the worst. Sometimes conferences are started with parties or similar social occasions; this has the advantage of enabling a social system to be established and associating group membership with a rewarding experience.

The work-flow system affects cohesiveness. It is increased if the work-flow brings members together in a mutually rewarding or cooperative manner, rather than when it creates friction, frustration or competition. It will be greater if members can communicate easily with one another, less if distance or noise make communication difficult. Goldthorpe (1968) found that the technological conditions were unfavourable for the creation of work groups in the three Luton factories he studied. Overall 40 per cent reported that they talked a 'good deal' to their workmates; however, this was only so for 22 per cent of process workers. Relationships appeared to be superficial – 45 per cent had no close friends at work and 68 per cent said that they would not be bothered about being moved away from their present workmates. However this was a rather unusual sample of 'affluent' workers, and Goldthorpe recognizes that stronger groups form where there is team-work, as among miners, steelworkers, dockers, railwaymen, trawlermen, textile workers or printers.

The task or incentive system may be so organized as to generate *cooperative* behaviour in the group, which in turn results in cohesiveness. Individual incentive schemes can create bad relations between group members, if they are constantly competing to get the best jobs. A group bonus system, on the other hand, creates a shared group goal, so that the efforts of each member of the group will promote the interests of other members. However there may be very strong pressures on slow workers to keep up, if they are holding back the whole team, as in assembly-line working. Small assembly lines have been found to work faster than larger ones, partly for this reason and partly because slow workers are forced out of the group. Another example of cooperation based on common task and incentives is the small research team, whose members would all receive recognition and professional advancement from successful research results.

Cohesiveness develops if belonging to the group is *rewarding* in any of a variety of ways. A number of laboratory experiments have shown that members are more attracted to a group when it has been successful at a task in competition with other groups. In the work situation members are attracted to groups that are highly paid or enjoy high prestige for some reason.

The way in which the *leader* handles a group affects its cohesiveness. Democratic styles of leadership, encouraging group participation in decisions, increases it (p. 149f.). Also useful are leaders who improve synchronizing by integrating newcomers and isolated people, resolving conflicts, maximizing interpersonal satisfactions, and skilfully handling disruptive group members.

External threat has been found to increase cohesiveness, especially if cooperation is seen as the best means of dealing with it. This has been observed in groups who feel threatened by a new supervisor, or other groups in the organization.

Size. If a group is too large it will divide into two or more subgroups, usually based on differences of status, work, etc. Absenteeism is far higher in larger groups: in a British car factory it was found that the rate of voluntary absenteeism was four times as high in groups of 128 as in groups of 4 (Hewitt and Parfit, 1953).

Cohesiveness has certain definite effects on the social behaviour and standard of work of group members.

Social interaction. Members of cohesive groups interact with one another more, particularly on sociable matters irrelevant to the task; they interact more smoothly, they enjoy being in the group, and feel less tension at work. They get considerable social satisfaction and social support from their group, and thus are less likely to seek a personal relationship in other social contacts at work, for example, with customers or clients. They cooperate smoothly over the group's work, there is more division of labour, they help each other more, and there are reciprocated arrangements for helping. There is greater conformity to group norms, e.g. on output levels (Blau and Scott, 1963).

Labour turnover and absenteeism are lower in cohesive groups. A ratio of 3:1 in absence rates has been found between groups of different cohesiveness (Mann and Baumgartel, 1953). We can predict which members are most likely to leave from inspection of the sociogram – those who are isolated or rejected.

Productivity. A number of studies have shown that more cohesive groups get more work done. Van Zelst (1952), for example, put together cohesive teams of bricklayers on the basis of a sociometric survey and found that over an eleven-month period the cohesive groups achieved 12 per cent more output, with 16½ per cent reduction in costs on materials and a reduced labour turnover. However, in some studies a *curvilinear* relationship has been found between cohesiveness and productivity, with a fall in output under very high cohesiveness – probably because too much time and effort is now being devoted to social activities. The productivity of cohesive groups may also depend on whether the work *entails* social interaction and cooperation is necessary (as in bricklaying), *prevents* it (as in weaving sheds), or is *irrelevant* to it (as in side-by-side assembly work). Cohesiveness increases output when the work requires social interaction because it is socially motivated and a source of social satisfactions. Cohesiveness probably affects output most when helping is important. It was found that the foremen of 60 per cent of high-output sections in a heavy engineering factory said that their men were good at helping each other, compared with 41 per cent in low-output sections (Katz and Kahn, 1952). Cohesiveness also affects the amount of conformity to group standards of output, whether in the direction of restricting output or keeping up a high level of output, as was found by Seashore (1954) in a company manufacturing heavy machinery.

Attitude to other groups. Cohesiveness is associated with strong positive feelings towards other members and high evaluation of them, together with negative attitudes towards outsiders. The group has its own goals which others do not share, and its own norms to which others do not conform. This may produce hostility and lack of cooperation with people in other groups, especially if those groups are seen as a source of annoyance or competition. The more people like members of their in-group, the stronger their negative feelings are likely to be to members of out-groups. Sherif (1961) found that negative feelings towards another group of boys at a camp were produced simply by putting them in a different hut, and that when one group appeared to have eaten the other group's food, violence occurred. The salesgirls in a department store felt very hostile towards their customers, and placed them in stereotyped categories such as 'elderly frustrated females', 'peppery colonels', etc. (Woodward, 1960). This can be avoided by keeping up communication and interaction with other groups, by some individuals belonging to two groups, and by arranging things so that one group does not cause annoyance to another.

GROUP NORMS

One feature of all small social groups is that they develop *norms*, that is shared ways of behaving, shared attitudes and beliefs, and shared ways of feeling and perceiving, particularly in relation to their central task or activity. For a group to function effectively and smoothly there has to be a certain amount of agreement on how to do things; on the other hand, it is important for the group to adapt to changing conditions, and change is brought about by individuals deviating from the norms. It is now known that there are several different kinds of norm, all functioning rather differently; we shall discuss these separately as they occur in the setting of working groups.

Norms about the work. There are norms about the best and easiest methods of working. These represent collective solutions to problems connected with the job, and usually go beyond the instructions of supervisors. There are norms about how fast people should work, how hard and how long, what standard of workmanship should be attained, safety regulations, etc. These may all be kept down to a reasonable level to make life comfortable without management penalizing any individual. Roy (1955) describes the elaborate set of dodges and fiddles invented in a machine shop to outwit the time-study man, keep up earnings and keep them steady. Goffman (1961) maintains that in all 'total institutions' – and many work places are rather similar to these – the inmates resort to a variety of 'secondary adjustments', most of them infringing the regulations, in order to make life tolerable. Group norms include such secondary adjustments – the permissible limits of time-wasting, scrounging, cheating on incentive schemes, etc.; management is compelled to go along with these practices, condoning them, and attempting to manage them.

On the other hand, the group norms may sustain a high level of output. Military units are sometimes based on a cadre of experienced men who have worked together before and will pass on both working methods and standards of work. Groups of research workers have norms of high productivity in terms of number of publications, visits abroad, and so on. It has been found that productivity norms were set high in industrial working groups which were both cohesive and saw the company as providing a secure and supporting environment (Seashore, 1954). People who have received professional training – e.g. doctors, scientists or accountants – usually internalize certain standards of conduct, which are sustained in isolation from other members of the profession, often in the face of considerable social pressures. Conforming to such norms helps the individual to sustain his professional identity and contributes to the long-term position of his profession.

Attitudes and beliefs. Group members come to hold the same attitudes towards management and unions, and about how difficult or satisfying their work is; they hold the same beliefs about what management policy is, and about economic or technical matters. Shared attitudes to other people or groups are of course neither true nor false; they simply represent shared feelings. Beliefs, on the other hand, are often quite mistaken – they are myths on matters where information is lacking, on matters too complex to understand. Workers may have theories about how managers become managers, while managers may have theories about why workers are so idle, and how things were better in former years. These myths are mainly incorrect theories about the social behaviour of other people.

Interpersonal behaviour. Social behaviour connected with work has to be regulated; work becomes easier and also more effective if group members agree to proceed in a standard way. There are shared codes of non-verbal signalling, norms about helping and cooperating, about sharing tips or bonuses, and so on. There are also norms about social activities not directly connected with work – what is talked about at coffee time, where to go for lunch, the shared games and jokes that make work more enjoyable and knit the group together. Norms about interpersonal behaviour make life easier – the behaviour of others becomes predictable, orderly and satisfying, and shared routines can be enjoyed. They also resolve interpersonal problems and avoid conflicts over such matters as helping, division of rewards, and allocation of work.

Clothes, *etc*. Members of a group usually look alike, because of their norms about physical appearance. Physical appearance signals a person's identity, what kind of person he is, or thinks he is; groups bring pressures to bear on a member whose appearance is likely to project the wrong image of the group or bring it into disrepute.

Language. Social groups often adopt a private slang terminology, including technical terms related to the job, alternative expressions or 'argot' such as the nautical 'port' and 'starboard', nicknames for people and places, and sub-cultural styles of speech such as the obscenities of working-class work groups. This private language is adopted partly to make communication easier, but is probably also used to create group solidarity (Brown, 1954).

Norms begin as a kind of working consensus among the original members of the group, being joint solutions to the group's problems, both work and social. The more dominant members have the most influence over these solutions. The less influential members and most new members shift their behaviour towards this norm as the result of two main processes.

(1) In laboratory experiments it has been found that people deviating from the norm receive a lot of persuasion from majority members to conform; if they persist in deviating they become ignored and rejected. In field studies more serious punishments may be inflicted on deviates, since their deviation may constitute a serious threat to group goals. For example, a rate-buster (the other workers believe) may provoke a retiming of jobs so that everyone has to work harder to earn the same amount as before. Rate-busters in the Bank Wiring Observation Room were 'binged', i.e. given a sharp blow on the arm, symbolizing group disapproval (Roethlisberger and Dickson, 1939). Deviates are often rejected, 'sending to Coventry' being an extreme case. They receive no help when in difficulties, and may find that they get landed with the worst jobs, or that their work is interfered with, sometimes in ingenious ways.

(2) Group members may conform to norms because they think the majority view must be correct. This is likely when the other members are thought to be more expert or experienced, or have been found to be right before.

Acceptance of group norms commonly goes through two stages – compliance and internalization. In compliance a deviate conforms simply in order to avoid rejection by the group, but may behave quite differently when away from the group, or privately think the group is mistaken. After he has been a member of the group for some time, however, a slow change often comes about – he starts conforming whether the group is looking or not, he believes the group is right, and he starts bringing pressure to bear on deviates himself: he has now internalized the group norm.

The existence of group norms makes groups rather conservative – they create resistance to change and prevent their members from changing their behaviour or ideas. This is not the whole story however – groups also act as channels of communication through which new ideas can flow. If a member of the group has a new idea though, this will only be acceptable to the group under certain special conditions. Firstly, the originator has to be an informal leader, or regarded as the group expert on the topic in question (a case of role-differentiation). In either case his ideas have probably been found to work in the past, so that his behaviour is seen not as a failure to conform, but as a potentially valuable innovation. Secondly, the new idea must seem to be to the advantage of group members, such as making life easier or being financially advantageous: a skilled innovator can persuade other members of the group that this is so. Groups are linked to other groups principally by having overlapping members. Innovators often get their ideas from other groups, and it is through such networks of communication that groups act as channels for new ideas – though they have to be accepted by the group as a whole so that changes of behaviour are coordinated.

Often group norms restrict output or in some other way oppose management's plans. How can a supervisor deal with them? One way is through the manipulation of incentive systems (p. 85 f.) and productivity bargaining, where one side of the bargain is the abandonment of restrictive practices. Another method is the use of supervisory methods which encourage participation in decisions and use of 'group decision' techniques (p. 149 f.). A possible supervisory strategy is to make use of the informal hierarchy of the group; informal leaders are under less pressure to conform than those lower down and have some influence over norms and changes in norms.

It has been found that in nearly all kinds of primates, and in groups of primitive men, hierarchies of power or leadership develop; this can be regarded as part of the biology of groups, since it is very much to the advantage of all group members that there should be such a hierarchy. We can learn something about this from studying the conditions under which a leadership hierarchy appears most readily. These are, (1) when the group is large, (2) when decisions must be made quickly, (3) when the task is complex, and (4) when diverse persons or roles have to be coordinated. It looks as if a leader, or a series of leaders, is needed to organize and coordinate the group, both to perform its task functions and to integrate the different members socially. Group members probably arrive at this solution by trial and error; the family may provide a model which is copied in other groups; probably experience in one group affects behaviour in others.

A leadership hierarchy develops in groups, even when all members have identical formal status, and when official leaders are provided, for example the supervisors of work groups. There are certain differences between a formally appointed leader and an informal leader: (1) the relationship between the formal leader and the group is part of the social organization and does not need to be discovered afresh by the individuals concerned, (2) the formal leader is usually appointed by people outside the group, the informal leader by the group itself, and (3) the formal leader can use material rewards and punishments while an informal leader must rely on persuasion and the sanctions of approval and disapproval.

Informal leadership is a matter of degree – *all* group members exercise some influence, but some have more say than others. Although there may be a struggle for power between several members, there is a sense in which the group members want certain members to function as leaders – they realize that the group will be more likely to attain its internal and external goals if it has the best leaders.

The pattern of behaviour in informal hierarchies has been

studied in a number of investigations. In groups whose main activity is talking the more influential members talk more; when they talk they address the group as a whole whereas less important members address individuals, and when an influential person speaks the other members take more notice. In other kinds of group the leadership hierarchy can be seen in the frequency of attempts to influence other group members, by the success of such attempts, and by which member is turned to when difficulties have to be dealt with. In a working group the informal leader will have most say over decisions about matters such as the rate of work, methods of working, allocation of work between group members, and so on. There may be more than one informal leader, different people dealing with different spheres of activity, as will be described below.

So far we have been describing the informal hierarchy which is based on differences of power or leadership. A related dimension is that of *status* – the extent to which a person is esteemed or admired by other members of the group. Differences of status in working groups are mainly based on level of skill, or past achievement in relation to the work of the group. It was found in a government employment office that there were clear differences of status and that officials approached others of similar status to themselves when needing help; to have gone to someone of higher status would have involved loss of esteem – though they would have obtained better advice (Blau, 1955).

In some studies it has been found that two informal leaders of rather different types have appeared; one was a *powerful* person who exercised influence over matters connected with the group task, the other was a *popular* person who was more concerned with problems internal to the group – the welfare of members and relationships within a group. The work proper requires different skills, motivation and activities from the internal management of the group, and some studies suggest that it is impossible for an *informal* leader to perform both; however, it is essential that a *formal* leader should do both, and we discuss later how he can do this (p. 145).

Many investigations have been directed to finding out what

kind of personality traits informal leaders have, but only very small correlations have been found with traits such as intelligence and extroversion. The characteristics of people who become informal task leaders vary according to the group and the work; they are usually very good at the actual work. It also depends to some extent on their motivation to lead and ability to organize the members of a particular group. As we said above, *influence* is a function of skill at the task, *popularity* is a function of an individual's rewardingness to others.

There may be other kinds of role-differentiation in a working group as well as differences of power, status and popularity. This often exists already as a result of division of labour, but there are further unofficial kinds of role-differentiation as well. Informal task leadership may be divided between different experts in the group – one who knows about trade-union matters, another who knows about time-study procedures, and so on. Working groups may contain informal leaders who help the formal leader, and others who oppose him – leaders of the opposition. Unfortunately there is little systematic evidence about role-differentiation in working groups; research on other kinds of group, and industrial case-studies, suggests the following as possibly common roles: (1) assistant task-leader, (2) socio-emotional leader, most popular, (3) leader of the opposition, e.g. shop-steward, (4) isolate, and (5) deviate, e.g. rate-buster (Argyle, 1969).

THE OPTIMUM DESIGN FOR WORKING GROUPS

We have seen that when people work in small, cohesive teams, their productivity is 25 per cent or so higher mainly because they help each other and cooperate better; their job satisfaction is also higher, resulting in voluntary absenteeism and labour turnover rates of about one quarter or one third of that under other conditions. How can such teams be constructed?

(1) Some technological settings prevent group formation – for example, when men work alone, under very noisy conditions, or on assembly lines. Although automation abolishes

assembly lines, it sometimes produces isolation and communication difficulties. New systems under design should avoid this.

(2) As we have seen, the same technology can be managed in different ways, by constructing different kinds of group (p. 44). Ideally men should work in groups not larger than about eight and the group should cooperate over a joint task; all the necessary skills should be present in the group, but status differences should be kept small, and there should be some kind of group incentive. The work-flow should be planned so that people help each other by means of their complementary skills, and do not frustrate one another. All the people who need to communicate with one another should be able to do so easily. We have seen examples of reorganizing men into functional groups in which all the skills needed to complete a task are included in single groups. Long assembly lines can be restructured as smaller groups arranged in squares, creating groups that are smaller and more cohesive.

(3) The groups should be under the direction of a supervisor who understands the functioning of work groups, and who uses the optimum supervisory skills. We shall describe below the best social skills for handling working groups; these include encouraging group participation in decisions, being rewarding and supportive to individuals and maintaining harmony in the group. Likert's strategy (1961) for creating cohesive, high-output teams includes these skills and adds that of giving the group rapid feedback information on its rate of work.

We have concentrated so far in this chapter on groups engaged in some kind of manual work. We turn now to groups whose work consists of talking.

DECISION-TAKING, PROBLEM-SOLVING AND CREATIVE GROUPS

These groups do their work by talking; this makes them different from the groups we have discussed so far in a number of ways, though all groups do some talking and take some decisions.

Decision-taking groups, i.e. committees, are primarily concerned with coming to agreements over issues where individuals or groups may disagree. Committees also have to solve problems and think of new ideas, indeed this is often needed to find a solution to a problem which is acceptable to most members; particular bits of problem-solving are often delegated to sub-committees. *Problem-solving groups*, such as sub-committees and working parties, have some resemblance to other work groups, in that intellectual work is performed: they may have to collect information, study reports, and consider alternative solutions. *Creative groups* include research workers, advertising men, film producers, etc. The groups do other things besides talking, but there are usually meetings at which it is hoped new ideas will appear. The same is true of problem-solving groups and, to a much lesser extent, committees.

One of the most striking differences between all these groups and the other kinds of working group is that the work of talking groups could be done by an individual. What is gained by using groups? In the case of decision-taking the main advantage is that decisions are taken which are acceptable to most of the individuals and bodies concerned; those who take part in decisions are also committed to those decisions and will implement them with greater willingness. Many studies have shown the importance of participation, but little is known about the group procedures which maximize this feeling; it is certainly increased by democratic, participatory styles of chairmanship, and is probably greater in smaller groups.

It is assumed that better solutions will be arrived at in groups. More man-hours are obviously used, and it takes longer to solve problems in groups, but are the solutions better? There appear to be three processes which can produce superior solutions. One, if the problem can be divided up and members possess different and complementary skills or knowledge, the group does better than any individual, for example, a psychological research group might need a statistician, a sociologist, etc.

Two, interaction between members can result in the correction of errors, and ideas produced by one member may stimulate further thoughts in the minds of others. Three, as in other groups there is greater arousal; members formulate their suggestions more carefully than if they were alone. Although these processes all occur, it is only the first which has consistently been found to give groups an advantage over individual problem-solvers (cf. Kelley and Thibaut, 1969), i.e. groups have a clear advantage over individuals when a wide range of information or different skills are required. The same applies to creative groups. There has been a fashion for these groups in some circles such as advertising, and special techniques like 'brain-storming' have been devised, in which critical judgement is suspended and members are encouraged to throw out ideas and develop one another's suggestions, leaving evaluation until later. When brain-storming groups have been compared with individuals, however, they have usually been found to be inferior (e.g. Taylor, Berry and Block, 1958). Individuals are better at generating ideas – group discussion is more useful for evaluating ideas than for thinking of them (Vroom *et al.*, 1969).

We shall now describe the interaction processes that occur in talking groups, and go on to specify the conditions under which they are most effective. Like other work groups, talking groups have a definite membership, a task and an appointed leader. There are often other formal roles in committees – secretary, treasurer, etc., and people who have been elected to represent a certain group or point of view. The procedure of committees is extremely formal: there is an agenda and elaborate rules of procedure – all remarks must be addressed to the chairman, voting on an amendment is taken before voting on the original motion, etc.; in addition, particular committees often have rules of their own, for example about how and when the chairman is elected, and when meetings shall end. These arrangements result in a restrained orderliness which is very different from spontaneous conversation. Problem-solving and creative groups are less formal, but the leader often specifies the procedure to be followed.

In talking groups members make carefully delivered

utterances, asking questions, conveying information, making suggestions, commenting on what has been said, agreeing and disagreeing. Discussion often goes through a standard sequence – stating and identifying the problem, putting forward information and suggestions, examining these and deciding on one solution. Use is made of a rather limited range of non-verbal signals, such as tone of voice, facial expression and direction of gaze, to establish and sustain coalitions and other relationships. These signals are also used to provide feedback to the speaker, or comments to others on what is being said, and to negotiate who shall speak and for how long. There is almost no pure sociable activity during committee meetings, though this may occur immediately before or after the meeting. Relations between members often arise directly out of the matters being discussed; any permanent bonds and sub-groups are often weak, and a person may find himself in quite different temporary coalitions for different items on the agenda.

Talking groups form norms on a wide range of topics, for example, the general policies to be followed. There is also something like norm-formation in miniature as the group deals with specific problems: there tends to be a fairly rapid convergence of views. When the majority view is correct some convergence helps to eliminate incorrect ideas; there may however be premature convergence on one solution before other alternatives have been properly examined, and the existence of conformity pressures can inhibit members from bringing forward unusual ideas, and thus reduces creativity. Talking groups have informal leadership hierarchies in which more time is spent on the ideas of important members, while less important people may have difficulty in making themselves heard. If the informal leaders are more expert or experienced in the matter being dealt with, paying more attention to their views is useful and will help the group to produce a better solution. If, on the other hand, an informal leader knows less than other people, which can certainly happen, then the normal pattern of interaction in a hierarchy will hinder the group.

The work of committees can be looked at in terms of risk-taking, in that some possible decisions are riskier than others.

It has often been thought that committees are 'safer' than individuals and take fewer risks. A large number of experiments have however now demonstrated that this is not so; when subjects make individual decisions and later reconsider their decisions in groups there is often a so-called 'risky shift' to a less safe decision. It is not yet known why this happens; one view is that there is diffusion of responsibility, so that members do not feel individually responsible for what happens; another is that there is a cultural norm in favour of risk-taking rather than playing safe on many issues, so that people in groups hesitate to express cautious views (Kogan and Wallach, 1967). Whatever its causes the risky shift is clearly a source of unwise decisions in groups. Chairmen should be aware of this and perhaps take the side of caution.

We can now specify the conditions under which committees and other talking groups will be most effective.

Composition of group. Talking groups should not be too large; five is the size people prefer, and three to six is found to work well, though groups are often rather larger (Thomas and Fink, 1963). With six members there is enough variety of knowledge or expertise for most purposes. Problem-solving groups should be varied in skills, but homogeneous in other respects, so that cohesiveness can develop easily. Creative groups, however, produce better ideas if there is initial disagreement, despite the difficulties of interacting. But if there are large differences in age, seniority or status a steep informal hierarchy will be formed, which generally inhibits discussion.

Leadership skills. The inhibiting effects of premature conformity can be avoided by getting the group to consider two possible solutions. The effects of the informal hierarchy can be counteracted by making sure that minority views are expressed and considered. The work should be divided up and each problem given to the person who is best fitted to deal with it. Ideas should be developed by individuals alone and discussed later in the group. These techniques have been found by N. R. F. Maier to lead to better group solutions. Other techniques he

133

suggests are to identify the problem and ask each member for his views, to focus on disagreement in the group and try to arrive at a creative solution, to evaluate each solution in relation to agreed criteria, and to ask stimulating questions to make the group question its approach (Hoffman, 1965). Special techniques such as brain-storming are sometimes used in creative groups but, as we said above, they do not seem to be very effective. Skills of chairmanship are discussed further on p. 167f.

CHAPTER 7

SOCIAL SKILLS AND WORK

The importance of social skills – the nature of social skills – supervision – management – some specific social skills – methods of social skills training.

THE IMPORTANCE OF SOCIAL SKILLS

ELTON MAYO, one of the founders of the Human Relations movement, maintained that all that was needed to improve the effectiveness and happiness of working organizations was to improve the social skills of those who ran them, particularly supervisory skills. The same assumption may be found in the writings of later workers in this tradition. Likert (1961) for example describes how organizational structures can be changed by changing the social relationships in the hierarchy. While fully accepting the importance of social skills at work, we would argue for a broader approach that includes the possibility of other kinds of organizational change, for example of the span of control and the number of levels in the hierarchy, of changes in technology and the work-flow system, and of changes in incentives.

For many years industrial psychologists concentrated their attention on the performance of manual skills, and devised improved methods of working and training. No interest was taken in the more responsible and highly paid supervisors and managers, who had to learn *their* skills as best they could, on the job. It is not only supervisors and managers who have to deal with people as part of their work: everyone has to. Research men work in teams, manual workers work in groups; both have to deal with immediate co-workers, and have to collaborate with a variety of other people such as their immediate superiors, shop-stewards, the personnel department, inspectors, and others. For everyone work involves both dealing with people and dealing with physical objects, papers or ideas.

But how important are social skills? No one disputes that they have some effect, but the question is how much. Similarly there is little doubt that, for example, a supervisor with the worst style of supervision conceivable would have a bad effect on output, job satisfaction, etc.; exceptionally bad social skills in fact constitute a special problem, which will be discussed later. It is more useful, however, to consider variations within the normal range of social performance which is commonly found in working organizations.

The best way of finding out what effects different social skills have is to compare the effectiveness of people with different styles of social behaviour.

The effects of supervisory skills on work groups. (a) Output. The effect of supervision on output varies greatly under different conditions. Likert (1961) reports a number of studies showing large differences in the productivity of similar departments whose supervisors used different styles of supervision, e.g. democratic–autocratic. In one of these studies the productivities of different clusters of departments were 6, 40, 46 and 71 respectively; however the first cluster consisted of two departments which were very hostile towards their supervisors; but the ratio of 40:71, or a 78 per cent increase is still rather greater than has been found in most studies. The effects of supervision are much less than this where work is machine-paced (Argyle *et al.*, 1958).

(b) Absenteeism. There is a rather closer relation between absenteeism and supervisory behaviour. In the famous Relay Assembly Room at the Western Electric Company, absenteeism dropped to one fifth of what it was before the girls were moved into the test room (one third the rate for the rest of the factory), as did amount of illness and lateness (Roethlisberger and Dickson, 1939). Other studies have obtained similar results.

(c) Labour turnover. Fleishman and Harris (1962) found a ratio of about 4:1 between turnover rates in departments whose

supervisors differed in styles of supervision. However the effect became marked only for the very worst supervisors – things have to get pretty bad before people go as far as leaving (Figure 12).

(*d*) *Job satisfaction.* In the same study there was a ratio of about 8:1 in number of complaints, and this was not just for the worst supervisors.

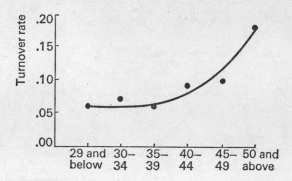

Figure 12(*a*). Initiating structure

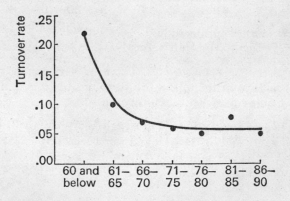

Figure 12(*b*). Consideration
(From Fleishman and Harris, 1962)

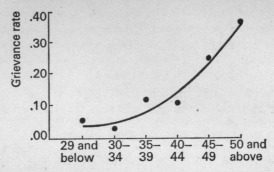

Figure 12(*c*). Initiating structure

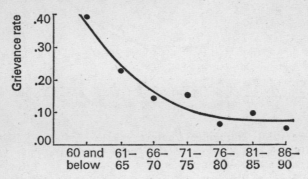

Figure 12(*d*). Consideration
(From Fleishman and Harris, 1962)

The effects of other social skills. There is a very wide variety of social skills to be found in work situations but it is difficult to measure the effectiveness of most of them.

(*a*) *Selling.* Argyle, Lalljee and Lydall (in Argyle, 1978) studied the amounts sold by the best and worst salesmen and salesgirls behind the same counters in department stores. Averaged over a period it was quite common for there to be a ratio of 4:1 in the amounts sold.

(*b*) *Selection interviewing.* (This involves skills of controlling the candidate and asking the right questions, and also skills of assessing him correctly.) The best index of the effectiveness of an interviewer is how much he can increase the accuracy of prediction over that made on the basis of application form, tests, etc. (p. 76). While some can raise it from about 0·4 to about 0·7, others *reduce* it to below that of the dossiers. They also vary in their power to attract people to the organization; it is commonly reported that the numbers of candidates accepting invitations to second interviews in the same organization varies from 25 to 75 per cent for different interviewers.

(*c*) *Persuasion and presentation.* Many studies have been made of the effectiveness of different people and different techniques in changing the attitudes or influencing the behaviour of the people they are addressing (McGuire, 1969). Some speakers are extremely effective, while others create a 'boomerang effect', i.e. the attitudes of their hearers may shift in the opposite direction to that desired. There are some Oxford dons who regularly make speeches about University business and it is estimated by experienced observers that they are worth twenty-five or fifty votes for the other side.

*

The current situation in British and American industry is that there is a very great demand for social skills training. This is perhaps partly due to a delayed acceptance of the Elton Mayo and Human Relations position, partly through T-groups and other widely publicized methods becoming fashionable. There also appears to be a need to understand social behaviour and social phenomena, and perhaps for self-insight, on the part of managers. What is rather surprising is that these new ideas and training methods have been accepted so uncritically, regardless of any follow-up data about the value of the methods in question. Later in this chapter we shall take a critical look at the follow-up evidence now available for different kinds of training.

THE NATURE OF SOCIAL SKILLS

Research carried out during the past few years has given greatly increased understanding of the nature of social skills. A detailed account of this research can be found elsewhere (Argyle, 1978; 1969), so I will only give a summary of the main points here.

Social performance consists of the use of closely coordinated verbal and non-verbal signals. The *verbal signals* are used mainly to ask questions, convey information and give instructions; the non-verbal signals are used mainly to manage the immediate social situation, and to support verbal signals in several ways. Social skills are in certain respects similar to motor skills, like cycling or driving a car. In each case the performer is trying to influence events in the outside world, either a machine, or other persons. In order to do so he performs a continuous sequence of motor responses, of hands and feet in one case, so that if earlier responses are not wholly effective they are modified to get better results, for example, steering a car in the right direction. An example of such corrective action for a social skill is dealing with a person who talks too little: the structure of utterances can be changed towards easy, open-ended questions, and any replies can be rewarded by eye-contact, smiles, head-nods, or encouraging noises. Both motor and social skills have a hierarchical structure – the smaller units become integrated into habitual, automatic sequences, each with their own feedback loops – a cyclist does not have to think about each turn of the pedals. The larger units are less habitual, more under conscious control, and subject to deliberate plans of action and the rules governing behaviour. Any particular motor or social skill consists of a coordinated sequence of responses, the collection of feedback, and learned sequences of corrective action.

For social skills to work there have to be a number of shorter stimulus–response sequences, whereby an act of A's influences the next act of B's. There are verbal–verbal links, for example a question leads to an answer and an open-ended question to a longer answer; the verbal sequence has to make sense in this kind of way. There are verbal–non-verbal links: if A rewards an act of B's, B will do it again. For example if A nods his head or smiles whenever B talks about himself, B will talk about this subject more. It is interesting that people appear to be influenced in this way very rapidly, and without realizing what is happening – furthermore the rewards (and punishments) are given without the sender being aware that he is sending them. Interactors are continuously influencing and being influenced, without realizing it; each person gets the others to behave as he would like them to, to some extent. Another sequence is imitation; if A makes long utterances, interrupts, laughs, nods his head, smiles, or adopts a particular posture, B is likely to do the same, again without realizing the reason for his behaviour. The main non-verbal signals are bodily contact, proximity, orientation, physical appearance, posture, facial expression, direction of gaze, head-nods, and gestures. Each of these functions in a special way, or in several ways. For example, a gaze at another person is used to collect feedback, to indicate attitudes towards him, and to synchronize speech. Verbal signals can be classified into questions, information and instructions, also into formal and informal, latent and manifest messages, and in other ways. The main kinds of messages used in working groups are listed on page 112f.

Non-verbal signals play several important roles in social behaviour.

Managing the immediate social relationship.
(*a*) Interpersonal attitudes such as friendly–hostile, inferior–superior, and sexual attraction are mainly signalled non-verbally. In laboratory experiments at Oxford it was found that non-verbal signals for interpersonal attitudes had about five times as much effect as equivalent verbal signals; different verbal messages were delivered in different non-verbal styles by speakers who were seen on a television screen from videotapes and rated by viewers (Argyle *et al.*, 1970). Non-verbal signals are also used to take corrective action and alter a relationship: if a person wants to be more dominant he may adopt a more erect posture, tilt his head back, look less pleasant, speak more loudly, and in a more resonant tone of voice.

(*b*) Emotional states are similarly communicated by non-verbal cues, such as facial expression and tone of voice, rather than verbally.

(c) Self-presentation, i.e. sending messages about the self, about how an interactor sees himself, and how he would like to be treated, is mainly done non-verbally. He might indicate that he is a manager, or a research worker. The main signals used are clothes, tone of voice, and general manner – there is a taboo in many parts of the world on direct verbal self-presentation.

Supporting verbal messages

(a) A speaker needs feedback on how his utterances are being received. This is obtained from careful scrutiny of eyebrows and other parts of the other's face, showing puzzlement, surprise, displeasure, agreement, etc.

(b) Two or more speakers have to synchronize their utterances – this is achieved by signals such as head-nods, shifts of gaze and grunts. For example, at a grammatical break in a long utterance a speaker will look up to see if the others are willing for him to carry on talking – if they are willing they will nod and grunt.

(c) Interactors have to provide continuous evidence of their interest in and attentiveness to the particular encounter. This is signalled by the use of appropriate proximity and orientation, intermittent looking at the others, and coordination of bodily position and gestures with those of the others.

Replacing verbal messages. In noisy factories and in other situations where speech is impossible it is replaced by non-verbal signals, and special gesture languages are built up to communicate the necessary kinds of information.

*

So far social skills have been considered from the point of view of one interactor only. However, no useful social interaction will take place at all if, for example, both talk all the time, or only ask questions, or in some other way fail to coordinate or synchronize their behaviour. We have discussed the timing of speech – there usually has to be some accommodation by one person or both, before a smooth sequence of utterances is achieved. There has to be synchronizing in several other areas too. They must agree about: the activity engaged in, or the topic talked about; the role relations between them, e.g. interviewer–interviewee or two friends chatting; the status relations; the degree of intimacy; the emotional tone of the encounter. When two or more people meet, it is unlikely that their habitually preferred styles of behaviour will form a smoothly meshing system. It takes a period of joint problem-solving, in which relationships are gradually worked out, mainly by means of minor non-verbal cues. For some combinations of people such accommodation can be achieved only at the cost of adopting unacceptable patterns of behaviour, so that a stable relationship is not possible.

Interactors are not only trying to manipulate each other as if the others were machines; they find themselves imagining how the other is feeling or perceiving the situation – they 'take the role of the other'. This is done whenever another person is spoken to, since the style of speech used is found to vary according to the knowledge or sophistication of the listener – except in such rural road directions as 'you go down to where Farmer George's horse died last year. . .'. People who are being interviewed or otherwise assessed tend to see the situation primarily from the other person's point of view – they are concerned with seeing how they are being assessed, rather than with assessing the other. In experiments at Oxford it was found that people take the role of the 'observed' rather than of the 'observer' in such situations (Argyle and Williams, 1969). Experiments have shown that people who are good at social skills are good at taking the role of the other.

To be effective at a social skill one should be aware of the elaborate set of rules governing them. For example, an interviewer should be aware of the conventions of the interview – that personal questions may be asked if they are relevant to the selection, that the interviewer can take notes, etc. Training courses on dealing with people from other cultures or social classes include information about the relevant customs and conventions, for example of buying and selling to Arabs. You do not have to comply with all the rules, but a socially skilled performer should be aware of them, since they show what other people expect will happen. Particular verbal or non-verbal signals have special meanings within given cultural settings, and one must know what these are. This is seen strikingly in cross-cultural encounters: when an Arab adopts a proximity of eighteen inches this does not indicate a great desire for intimacy; when he asks a grossly inflated price for an object being sold, this does not mean that he expects to get this price.

SUPERVISION

Supervision of groups is one of the central social skills connected with work. We traced earlier the changing relationships between supervisors and working groups in different historical periods. We are now entering a new historical period in which one of the main causes of change is research into the most effective styles of social behaviour. The supervisor has two main tasks – one, to see that the work is done properly, i.e. to keep up productivity, and two, to look after the welfare of the group members – i.e. to keep up job satisfaction. A supervisor is different from an informal leader in that normally he is not elected by the group but is imposed from outside, and in that he has power to deliver various forms of reward and punishment. In modern industry some of the work of traditional supervisors is done for them by impersonal mechanisms of control, such as automated and machine-paced equipment, and incentive schemes. However supervisors are still needed because of unforeseen contingencies, changing environmental conditions, and the various problems of individuals that have to be dealt with.

Sociologists say that there are two main ways in which a supervisor can influence his subordinates. One, he can make use of *power* based on sanctions of reward or punishment. Two, he may have *legitimated authority*, based on his subordinates' respect for authority or for his expertise (cf. Fox, 1971). Research by social psychologists suggests the importance of a third factor – social skills, though the way these are exercised certainly depends on the two factors just mentioned.

Two dimensions of supervisory behaviour have been identified in studies of industrial and military groups. *Initiating structure*, i.e. concern with the group task, and *consideration*, i.e. looking after the group members (Halpin and Winer, 1952). A third dimension has been identified in other studies – the use of *democratic–persuasive skills*. This third factor provides the missing key to the first two: leaders who concentrate primarily on production tend to upset their group, unless they use a particular set of social skills; if they use participation and persuasion they can deal with both task and group at the same time.

There are certain problems about research in this area. One method is to compare a number of supervisors in the same or similar organizations and see if there is any correlation between their style of supervision and their effectiveness. The difficulty with this method is that the direction of causation is not clear: if there is a correlation between output and consideration this might be because supervisors become more rewarding when their men work hard, or it could be because some third factor affects both output and supervisory behaviour. Another research method avoids this problem: experimental changes are introduced, either by shifting supervisors round, or by retraining some of them. Now another problem arises, that any changes that appear may be due to 'Hawthorne effects', i.e. are the result of there being an experiment and special attention being paid to those involved. The results of field experiments are only fully satisfactory if two or more different *experimental* conditions generate quite different effects in terms of productivity, etc. Difficulties also arise in assessing the different styles of supervisory behaviour. It is rarely possible actually to observe this behaviour; reports by subordinates are liable to be biased and may also produce spurious correlations with questionnaire measures of job satisfaction; for example, subordinates may ascribe supposedly good practices to their supervisors, but this is not necessarily a valid measure of supervisory behaviour, because of subordinates giving socially desirable answers. A questionnaire measure of. Initiating structure and Consideration has been devised and has been widely used for research in this area (Halpin and Winer, 1952). Another method is to get ratings from colleagues or personnel managers.

We shall now consider the effects of the three dimensions of supervision on one, productivity, and two, job satisfaction, absenteeism and labour turnover.

Initiating structure. There are a number of definite jobs which the foreman should do which are directly related to the task; these aspects of behaviour have been found to correlate together, and have been named 'initiating structure'. The jobs include planning and scheduling the work to be done, and making sure supplies are available; instructing and training subordinates in how to do their work; checking and correcting the work that has been done; giving subordinates feedback on how well they are doing; and motivating them to work effectively. In a series of studies in different industrial settings by the Michigan group it was found that productivity of work groups was higher when supervisors spent most of their time on these supervisory tasks, as opposed to working with the men, or doing routine jobs which could be delegated (Likert, 1961). On the other hand, output was usually higher under general than under close supervision, and it looks as if too much initiating structure leads to a drop in output – it also leads to a drop in job satisfaction and labour turnover, i.e. people do not like too much bossing and interfering. Fleishman and Harris's results' (1962) are shown in Figure 14. There is probably an optimum amount of guidance for any particular work group and type of task. The more highly skilled the subordinates, the less direction they need (as suggested by the Jaques time-span measure, p. 89f.). It may not be very clear just how much guidance is in fact given: Pelz (1957) found that the productivity of research workers was highest when they ostensibly had most freedom to do their own work, *but* saw the group supervisor every day. He writes:

What goes on in these daily encounters? We aren't sure, exactly; this is one of the areas that we are pushing further in our current studies. In all probability, the chief – by frequent enquiries, shows his interest in and enthusiasm for the work, and this is something on which a young scientist thrives. The chief may offer hints as to methods; he may refer to relevant articles; he may simply express his confidence in the progress that is being made. His very presence may serve as a motivating factor, causing the young scientist to push ahead as rapidly as he can, knowing that the chief will take pleasure in the results.

We are becoming more and more convinced that this active interest in the ongoing work, combined with a hands-off policy concerning its direction, is one of the most fruitful things a research chief can do.

There are special social skills associated with different parts of Initiating Structure, such as setting targets, and appraising the results of work done. These skills will be discussed later.

A supervisor's work depends on the range of men and equipment he is supervising, and on the amount of authority and responsibility he has. Supervision is an integral part of the socio-technical system. A field experiment was carried out in a military organization for repairing and testing aircraft. Some supervisors were given responsibility for all aspects of the operation being supervised, including quality control in some cases. This involved regrouping men and equipment, and resulted in supervisors spending their time differently – more time on inspection, talking to their men about production, and reporting to their own supervisors. Supervisors treated their men as a team, delegated responsibility for checking to craftsmen, rotated men between jobs, and encouraged communication between section members. The result was an increase in quality, a reduction of costs, supervisors felt more autonomous and satisfied, and their men were more satisfied with their jobs (Davis and Valfer, 1966).

Consideration (or 'employee-centredness'). The supervisor also has to look after the members of his group. This consists of consideration of the needs of subordinates, helping them to attain rewards and avoid punishment, establishing a warm and friendly supportive relationship with them and taking a personal interest in individuals, being understanding about mistakes, and dealing with interpersonal problems in the group.

Consideration is not the opposite of production-centred behaviour, as was once supposed, but is independent of it (Halpin and Winer, op. cit.).

A number of studies have found a correlation between consideration and productivity. This was found by Katz and others (1951) for railway maintenance groups, by Argyle and others (1958) for British electrical engineering workers, and in a variety of other settings. However, the size and also the direction of this relationship has been quite different in different studies, and it is not clear what the conditions are under which consideration affects output. Bass (1965) suggests that the crucial variable is not how much reward is given, but whether rewards are made conditional on output. Rather limited support was obtained for this hypothesis in a study which found that supervisory behaviour had only a small effect on the extent to which men saw rewards as being conditional on output (Evans, 1970). A further problem is that the direction of causation may be the reverse of that assumed so far, i.e. supervisors may become more considerate when their groups work well. This is, however, opposed by one or two field experiments in which supervisors have been switched round – with the effect that output in each department changed too (e.g. Feldman, 1937).

A number of studies have shown that there is a strong relationship between consideration and job satisfaction, absenteeism and labour turnover. The effect on the last two variables is of the order of 4:1 for supervisors at the upper and lower ends of consideration (Figure 14). However, it is not enough for a supervisor to have good intentions, he must be sufficiently powerful to deliver rewards; it is found that there is a correlation between consideration and job satisfaction only for supervisors who are influential with their own superiors (Pelz, 1952).

Democratic-persuasive social skills. Effective supervisors are found to use a set of social skills which are not covered by the two dimensions considered so far, but which are necessary in order to combine them successfully. There are three main components: motivating people by explanation and persuasion rather than just giving orders, allowing individual subordinates to participate in decisions that affect them, and using techniques of group discussion and group decision. By these skills the supervisor succeeds in getting the group to set high targets, and to internalize the motivation to reach them, without exerting pressure himself. The democratic-persuasive style is totally different from *laissez-faire*. The democratic leader really does lead, and sees that decisions are taken and carried out – but he involves the group in these decisions. Lippitt (1940) in his study of democratic and autocratic boys' clubs found that the democratic groups worked just as hard when the leader was out of the room, while the autocratic ones stopped work.

The effects of formal arrangements for participation in decision-making are reviewed later (p. 203 f), where we see that this participation makes people more cooperative and increases output and job satisfaction. We are concerned here with variations in supervisory behaviour. Numerous studies have found that when workers under piecework conditions are consulted, they often set higher targets and enjoy the work more, and labour turnover is less. Strauss (in Whyte, 1955) reports an increase of 30–50 per cent in rate of work by a group of girls, on a group bonus, who were allowed to control the pace of their assembly-line belt. Increased output has been consistently found to be related to the use of democratic and participatory skills in other settings as well. It is interesting that participation in decisions affects productivity not only in the U.S.A. but also in Britain (Argyle *et al.*, 1958) and Japan (Misumi, 1959). Democratic skills are even effective in the army. Selvin (1960) found that authoritarian leaders in the American Army led to a high rate of AWOL, eating between meals, drunkenness, seeing the chaplain, blowing one's top, fighting and sexual intercourse.*

Allowing a group to participate in decisions involves the use of special group decision techniques. It has long been realized that when a supervisor is dealing with the members of a cohesive group, he is no longer dealing with a series of individuals –

* For reviews of the literature on the effects of participation, see Vroom, 1964, and Blumberg, 1968.

because the group has a greater influence on each person than he has. The supervisor must therefore deal with the group as a whole. The group decision technique has three stages: (1) general discussion, intended to loosen the existing norm on a particular topic and bring out the diverse opinions held in the group, (2) persuasion by the leader, in the direction of a revised norm, and (3) trying to bring the group to decide in favour of the new goal, method, etc. Both laboratory and field experiments have shown the effectiveness of this technique, though it varies between different leaders. In an experimental analysis of the procedure it was found that the most important factors were the making of a group decision and the perception of unanimity in the group (Bennett, 1955). Other experiments show that group discussion is not effective unless accompanied by decision-taking. Of course, there are definite limits to what a particular group can decide about. It *can* decide about arrangements internal to the group, including allocation of jobs, training procedures, holidays, etc. It probably *cannot* decide about rates of pay or the technology – though it could certainly put forward suggestions on such matters.

Why do democratic-persuasive skills increase productivity? There are a number of reasons: one, participation leads to better decisions being made (p. 130f.); two, those who take part in decision-taking become committed to the plan of action decided on, and internalize the motivation to carry it out; three, if people take part in decisions they understand them better; and four, discussion in the group develops group cohesion, and establishes norms, so that there are group pressures to carry out decisions.

If the democratic-persuasive style is so successful, why do so many leaders continue to be authoritarian, and believe this to be the best style? Likert (1961) suggests that many supervisors may have realized that there is no correlation between productivity and job satisfaction, and have therefore put all their efforts into production, not bothering about their relationship with the men. And, of course, authoritarian supervisors *can* be effective, if combined with sufficiently heavy sanctions and efficient inspection – but at the cost of unhappy and unwilling workers, absenteeism and turnover, wastage of materials, and a complete lack of everyday helpfulness and cooperation. During the Industrial Revolution this was the normal state of affairs.

Although subordinates expect to be treated better nowadays, they do not always have the social skills and attitudes to authority that go with participating in decision-taking; they need to adopt the style of behaviour which goes with the recommended supervisory style. There is a case for training subordinates as well as leaders, at all levels; this would have the further advantage of preparing people for promotion.

Democratic-persuasive skills also affect job satisfaction, labour turnover and absenteeism. For example, Coch and French (1948) found no labour turnover in their participation group, compared with 17 per cent in the others.

Blake and Mouton (1964) introduced a two-dimensional 'managerial grid' in which managers are given scores from one to nine on their concern for production and their concern for people, which can be assessed by questionnaire. They believe that the two dimensions can be combined by integrating the two concerns in team management. However, the evidence suggests that there is a third dimension – democratic *v.* authoritarian social skills, and that it is by the use of democratic-persuasive skills that the other two dimensions can be integrated. Further research shows that the optimum style of supervision varies according to the work and the nature of the group, and that the democratic-persuasive style is not always the most effective (see below). Blake and Mouton have built a system of training and organizational change round their dimensions; this is discussed on p. 202f.

Dealing with individuals. Most of the work of a leader consists of dealing with the different individuals in his care. They all need to be handled differently, depending on their personalities. For example, more intelligent people can be talked to more rapidly, with longer words; more neurotic individuals should be handled gently, and protected from stress and strain; more authoritarian subordinates prefer firm direction, while non-authoritarians like to take an active part in decision-taking

(Vroom, 1960); different needs and goals can be appealed to in order to motivate different people – some want to achieve great things, others prefer a quiet life. A leader needs to be aware of these aspects of personality in his subordinates and vary his style of handling accordingly.

He may use a number of different techniques for dealing with individuals. First, he may deal with individuals directly. This is done when giving out and checking work, in appraisal and selection interviews, and in the continual attempt to sustain motivation and keep up job satisfaction.

Alternatively, he may deal with the group. The problem of handling individuals is complicated by the fact that they are members of a group and their relationship with the other members has to be considered. They will be affected by the norms of their group – for most people the group is a more powerful influence than the leader so that it is no good asking an individual to deviate from a group norm, e.g. an output restriction norm. Norms can be influenced through group decision techniques. The leader can also deal with the group as a whole by administrative methods – inventing rules that will apply to all equally, though his intention is to deal with certain difficult individuals.

The leader may choose to work through the group structure. Individuals belong to an informal influence or leadership hierarchy. The junior members of this hierarchy want to be accepted by the group and will do what the most powerful members say; the more influential members, on the other hand, are more independent of group pressures, and the official leader can elicit their cooperation and influence the group through them. Group members also belong to a friendship structure, consisting of sub-groups, chains, etc. The individual can be influenced via the other members of his sub-group, he can be moved to a different sub-group, or sub-groups can be disbanded.

A leader's skills may be taxed by various kinds of difficult subordinates. Those who are hostile to people in authority are better handled by impersonal administrative techniques, and by the other group members: direct confrontation should be avoided. Quarrelsome and psychopathic individuals are extremely difficult to handle. Their behaviour may improve if the causes of their annoyance are removed, and sometimes individuals or sub-groups can help to contain them. However, in these and other cases the leader should keep to the general style of supervision described earlier – consideration for the welfare of those concerned, attention to structuring the job, and the use of the democratic style of leadership.

Variation of supervisory style in different situations. It has come to be generally recognized that the most effective style of supervision may be different under different conditions. Fiedler (1967) has put forward the most extensive formulation and stimulated the most research on this problem. He has worked with the Least Preferred Co-worker (LPC) score, in which a high score means that the least preferred co-worker is described in favourable terms, and is taken to mean that the supervisor is relationship-oriented (i.e. high on consideration) rather than task-oriented (i.e. high on initiating structure). Fiedler's theory is that consideration-oriented leaders are most effective under conditions that are moderately favourable, but that task-oriented leaders will do better both when things are very favourable, and when they are very unfavourable. A situation is said to be unfavourable when (*a*) the group rejects the leader, (*b*) the task is nebulous and unstructured, or (*c*) the supervisor has little power. Fiedler's original studies found correlations between LPC scores and effectivess of − 0·58 to 0·47 for different combinations of these variables, and this pattern has been on the whole confirmed by later studies (Fiedler, 1970). It is unfortunate that a rather obscure measure (LPC) should have been used in these studies.

The second variable is of some interest – the degree of task structure. When the task is highly structured all the leader has to do is to see that it is properly done, which is more a question of surveillance than leadership proper. As Fiedler points out, a leader might need to use different leadership styles at different phases of a group's work.

Other studies have shown that the value of democratic-persuasive skills varies considerably from one set of conditions to another. Not everyone wants to take part in decisions: some would rather be told what to do. In a study of the participation of supervisors in higher decisions it was found that participation led to job satisfaction only for those who valued independence and were not authoritarian. Similar findings were obtained for measures of their level of performance (Vroom, 1960). When rapid decisions have to be taken, as in military or surgical operations, there is no time for discussion, though there can be participation in general planning. When a group is large, participation becomes more difficult, the need for centralized control is greater, and such direction more acceptable.

The most effective style of supervision probably varies according to the technology. Certainly the supervisor's job is quite different under different technologies. We saw earlier how in assembly-line work groups are large, men are controlled by machine-pacing, and there is little contact with supervisors. With individual piecework without machine-pacing, on the other hand, there may be constant conflict with the supervisor over the timing of the work and the allocation of the best jobs.

The supervisor's relations with those above and below. Anyone in an administrative hierarchy is a 'man-in-the-middle', and experiences a special kind of role-conflict. He is under pressure from above to pass on and explain management directives, and is expected to act as spokesman and protector by those below. He is expected to concentrate on initiating structure by those above, but on consideration by those below. This requires considerable skill, keeping both sides happy, negotiating compromises, care over taking decisions since any decision will annoy one side or the other, and not becoming completely committed to ideas or individuals (Bass, 1965). The conflict is particularly acute for the supervisors (foremen), since their subordinates are least likely to identify with the organization, may not be satisfied with their jobs, and are likely to combine together in defence against management. Their position can be undermined by worker representation through the unions or through consultative committees. It has been found that it was important for such supervisors to have sufficient influence with their superiors – only for influential supervisors did consideration lead to job satisfaction (Pelz, 1952). In a study of insurance office supervisors it was found that productivity was higher under men who identified with employees, and liked to share the same dining-room (Katz, Maccoby and Morse, 1950). On the other hand a number of studies show that a supervisor should be somewhat detached from his men, in the sense of not being dependent on them, and of performing a quite different role. We turn now from first-line supervisors to more senior leaders and managers.

MANAGEMENT

Above the first-line supervisors come second-line leaders, who can be called 'managers', though they are given different titles in educational, military, religious and other organizations. The manager's job is different from that of the first-line leader, and requires extra social skills – though managers also have to deal with groups composed of their immediate subordinates.

Rosemary Stewart (1967) asked 160 industrial managers to keep diaries of how they spent their time. The results are summarized in Table 2 on p. 156. In this same study it was found that there were several different kinds of manager, with different patterns of activity: emissaries (who had a lot of outside contacts), writers, discussers, trouble-shooters, and committee men.

It is clear that although managers have to think and plan they spend a great deal of their time with people – about two thirds on average. Although much of this discussion is technical in content, social skills are needed to manage the social situations involved. Managers also need more complex social skills in addition to those of handling immediate subordinates.

There have been a number of studies of the effects of the different supervisory styles of second-line leaders on productivity

Table 2

How managers spend their time (%)

alone	34	paperwork	36
with one other person	32	inspection	6
with two or more others	34	informal discussion	43
with subordinates	26	committees	7
with boss	8	telephone	6
with colleagues	12	social activities	4
with fellow specialists	8		
other internal contacts	5		
external contacts	11		

and job satisfaction. These show that they have a greater influence on productivity and satisfaction than first-line leaders (Nealey and Fiedler, 1968). A number of studies have shown that delegation and the use of participatory methods of leadership are effective at both levels. On the other hand, it was found that while first-line leaders in a nursing hierarchy should be *high* in initiating structure, second-line leaders should be *low* (Nealey and Blood, 1968).

Managers are often unwilling to delegate responsibility, and they resist the introduction of democratic methods. Some may be afraid that if their subordinates participate freely in decisions they might turn out to be more knowledgeable and competent. Greater delegation of responsibility might also result in some managers becoming partly or wholly redundant, since there would be less work for them to do, and each manager could deal with a larger number of subordinates.

'Management by objectives' is the name for a set of social techniques for handling subordinate leaders (though it can be applied lower in the hierarchy too). A company adviser helps managers to clarify the objectives of the units under their control; a *key results analysis* is prepared for each of their subordinates, listing their key tasks, the levels they should aim at for each task, the criteria to be used for evaluating their success, and any suggestions. Those concerned participate fully in the discussion of these analyses, and try to improve arrangements for each job; work proceeds for a period of time, perhaps three months, and performance is reviewed. Although no specific follow-up studies have been made of this approach a number of large firms have introduced the scheme and report favourable results, such as more production suggestions, organizational changes, improved morale, and better forward planning (Humble, 1968).

McGregor (1960) described a style of personnel management in which an attempt is made to show workers how their own needs will be met by pursuing organizational goals. Supervisors discuss each person's work with him, find out what his motivations are, and help him to set targets which will meet both his needs and the goals of the organization. Similar principles are applied in appraisal and personnel interviews, as described later. For the majority of workers the two sets of goals are fairly compatible, in that hard work will le id to promotion and better pay. It is more difficult if a person's main goal is promotion, and there are no prospects of promotion, or if his main goal is increased pay and there is a fixed hourly rate.

Managers do not need technical expertise in the work of all the sections they handle, since they can depend to some extent on lower leaders and staff experts for guidance, though they should be familiar with the work of each section. They must, however, possess the skills of managing organizations: of designing the best work-flow systems, administrative hierarchies and committee structures. They must be sensitive to pressure from individuals or groups in their departments, and be able to keep them working together cooperatively. They must be sensitive to sources of job dissatisfaction. Managers also need to understand the total picture of how their department fits into the rest of the organization, and what area of freedom they have to operate in.

One of the main ways in which a manager can influence his department is by selecting and training subordinates. These are specialized social skills of great importance for the effectiveness and happiness of the organization. In addition, he should keep a continuous eye on the career development of his subordinates, though this may be discussed formally with them only at periodical appraisal interviews. His subordinates will be deeply concerned with this themselves, and about their prospects in relation to each other, so great skill must be exercised here.

The selection interview. Millions of interviews for jobs take place each year, and the selection interview is a familiar social situation with established rules and conventions. It is usually expected that it should last between ten and forty minutes, that the interviewer (I) will ask most of the questions, and take notes, though the candidate (C) will be able to ask questions later, and that it is a formal occasion where both will be properly dressed and behave politely. It is often expected that I and C will face each other across a desk, but this convention is changing in favour of a 90° orientation with a low coffee table or no table at all. If any of these rules is broken some explanation should be given to C, or his permission asked, e.g. if a trainee interviewer is to be present to observe the interview.

Part of the skill consists in establishing the right relationship – one where C trusts I sufficiently to feel that he will be properly assessed and is prepared to talk truthfully about his past experience. I should convey his interest and sympathy with C by appropriate non-verbal signals and should try to understand C; however he should not take the role of C to the extent of trying to get C the job – because there are other Cs to be considered; I should remain somewhat detached while at the same time being genuinely sympathetic. While I's role is to carry out selection rather than vocational guidance, he may give some vocational advice if it is asked for. The interview should be a rewarding experience for C, and he should feel that he has been properly and fairly assessed.

The selection interview has four main phases: welcome, in which the procedure is explained, C is put at ease, and encouraged to talk freely – I and C may chat briefly on safe topics of mutual interest; gathering information, in which I goes over C's record, with the aid of the dossier, and tries to assess C on a number of traits; supplying information, in which C is invited to ask any questions he may have; conclusion, in which it is explained what happens next. There may also be a phase of negotiation, in which C is offered the job, which requires further social skills.

There are special skills in asking questions. Each topic is usually introduced with an open-ended question, followed by a series of follow-up questions (e.g. 'What did you do for your third-year project?'). I's questions should be responsive to what C has just said, so that there is a proper dialogue, or flow of conversation. The questions on a given topic can be designed to obtain information about different aspects of C's abilities or personality. For example, leisure activities can be pursued to find out about social skills, creativity or emotional stability. Some areas need carefully phrased questions to elicit relevant answers; for example, judgement can be assessed from questions about C's opinions on complex and controversial social issues with which he is acquainted. Special care is needed when inquiring about areas such as physical disabilities, failure, or other potentially embarrassing topics; questions on these areas should be given in a friendly and objective manner, showing sympathy and avoiding loss of face by C.

I should try to assess a number of abilities and personality traits that are thought to be most relevant to the job. Some of the dimensions which are commonly assessed at selection interviews are intelligence, judgement, creativity, social skills, attitudes to authority, stability, self-image and achievement motivation.

Each of these dimensions can be assessed from the answers to suitable questions. For example, attitudes to authority can be assessed by asking questions about past relationships with others of higher or lower status, and attitudes towards traditionally respected groups and institutions, and towards commonly despised social groups. In each area several different questions should be asked, in order to sample the dimension in question.

A strategy commonly adopted by interviewers is one of looking for weak points in the C, i.e. looking for reasons to reject him. This is partly justified by the C's use of the complementary strategy, i.e. of covering up his weak points. Nevertheless, it would be useful for Is to be on the look out for exceptionally strong points in Cs as well. It has been found that Is are often influenced by their early impressions of Cs based on their application forms, clothes, accents, etc.; these impressions should be checked carefully by collecting further detailed information in relevant areas (Webster, 1964).

The main problem with the selection interview is the proneness of Is to make a number of different kinds of error. These errors can be reduced by the use of five-point rating scales, where the dimensions are clearly understood by Is. An example of such a scale is:

Social Skills

low	below average	average	above average	high

Five points are as many as an interviewer can use efficiently; he should distribute his judgements on each scale so that about 10, 25, 30, 25 and 10 per cent of Cs fall at the different points; and he should discover through training, experience and comparing notes with other interviewers what the average level is for the Cs seen.

The main errors made by interviewers are:

Errors of 'level' – a tendency to rate all Cs on average too high or too low.

Errors of 'spread' – using too large or too small a scatter of ratings.

Stereotyped judgements based on the social class, race, sex, etc. of Cs.

Search for consistency, failing to recognize that a C may be clever but lazy, etc.

Implicit theories about personality – Is have private theories, implicit or explicit, about which traits should correlate together.

The behaviour of a C during interview cannot be regarded as a typical sample of his performance from which a prediction can be made; the interviewer should try to get the C to talk about what he did in situations resembling the future work situation, from which predictions can be made. Thus an estimate of a C's creativity can be obtained by asking him to describe situations in which he might have displayed originality.

Part of the skill of interviewing consists of being able to deal with awkward Cs. There are a number of types of awkward Cs: Some talk too much, others too little; some are very nervous; some play the wrong role and try to ask all the questions or get free vocational guidance. Some are not interested in the job; there are the glamorous females – Is enjoy interviewing them, but often fail to ask demanding questions or establish whether the C has the necessary abilities for the job; others are of a different class or culture from the I.

There are special ways of dealing with each of these problems. For example, the C who talks too little can be dealt with by asking easy, open-ended questions, by using reinforcement techniques (smiles, nods, eye-contact, and encouraging noises), and by I not talking too much. (Details about how to assess the traits mentioned and deal with the awkward Cs are given in Sidney and Argyle, 1969.)

The appraisal interview. In many organizations supervisors and managers hold an appraisal interview every six, twelve or eighteen months with their immediate subordinates. This may be closely linked to other personnel practices – career structure, salaries and promotion, and job analysis. Where there is no formal scheme, supervisors still have to find out from time to time how their subordinates are getting on, give them feedback on progress and discuss their career prospects, and motivate them by giving fresh targets. This kind of interview is an integral part of supervisory skill, and the way in which it is carried out is very important for the relationship with subordinates and the effectiveness of a working group.

The supervisor's manner in an appraisal interview should be warm, positive and sympathetic, indicating that he is on the subordinate's side in the sense that they belong to the same group and are pursuing the same goals, and that he has a personal concern for the subordinate's welfare, and is trying to understand and sympathize with his problems. At the same time, the supervisor must remain detached in the sense that he is applying objective standards of assessment to the subordinate's performance, providing realistic information on his career prospects, and is concerned with the effectiveness of his group.

There are three main aims for appraisal interviews, which require somewhat different social techniques (Maier, 1958).

(1) *Evaluation.* The aim here is to obtain further information about someone's progress in addition to what is known already. This may be done as part of a general system of periodic appraisal by managers or personnel departments, or when a subordinate's work is not entirely visible to his immediate superior. This is rather similar to a selection interview; detailed information should be sought under a number of headings, and ratings made. In addition to the interview, objective data on work performance should be obtained. It is essential that more than one person should make the ratings, either by having a board interview, or preferably by having several individual interviews; this enables some of the unreliability of these judgements to be overcome, while discussion between the interviewers can lead all of them to a more accurate appraisal.

(2) *Providing information on progress.* People want to know how they are getting on and like to be able to discuss their career prospects with someone in a position to know about them; on the other hand, they are often very defensive and resistant to this kind of information, are liable to quarrel and refuse to accept criticisms. It has been shown that appraisal interviews can result in lowered self-esteem and deterioration in work (Kay, Meyer and French, 1965). Sofer, in an unpublished study, has found that interviewers often say they

discussed a particular topic with a subordinate, but that often the latter cannot remember this topic having been brought up, presumably because it was not emphasized enough. McGregor (1960) suggested that supervisors and subordinates plan together the targets for the next six months, and then meet to discuss progress. It is useful to start by asking for the subordinate's views about his standard of work, though these are not always very realistic. The supervisor should then mention positive aspects of the subordinate's work, before going on to any specific criticisms; these should be given in an objective and constructive manner, avoiding conflict, avoiding damaging his self-esteem, and discussing the matter on the assumption that the two of them are cooperating over a piece of joint problem-solving, to see how things could be improved. Careful attention should be paid to the subordinate's side of the story, as in the personnel interview. Sometimes a subordinate has to be redirected towards alternative goals or a different career – 'cooling the mark out' – which requires particular tact and sympathy, finding out what the best plan for him would be, and showing its advantages for him.

(3) *Setting targets and arousing motivation.* McGregor (1960) stressed the importance of participation in target-setting, which was discussed above. The key technique here is aligning the individual's motivations with the needs of the organization. The supervisor should find out which kinds of motivation can be appealed to in a subordinate, and then show him how these needs can be satisfied by pursuing organizational goals, e.g. if he works better he will be paid more or promoted. An appraisal interview can also show the subordinate how to improve himself, by getting appropriate training, to prepare himself for a better job.

A follow-up study was carried out of fifty managers who were given thirty hours of training in the appraisal interview by means of role-playing exercises. It was found that 70 per cent of subordinates felt that their supervisors had a better understanding of how they performed their jobs, 67 per cent thought their supervisors understood them better as individuals and 65 per cent had a better idea of what was expected of them (Moon and Hariton, 1958).

The personnel interview. This kind of interview is really part of the supervision of work groups. It includes dealing with an employee whose behaviour has been unsatisfactory, as well as the inspection and evaluation of work. In other settings it includes rather similar interviews between tutors and students, and between parents and adolescent children. This is a very difficult kind of interview to do: it is feared and resented by the interviewees, and is often funked by those who ought to carry it out. Research on supervision has suggested a totally new approach to it, which can make it a pleasanter and more effective occasion. What is recommended is something like the strategy that follows.

(1) The supervisor (S) finds out as much as he can about the performance and relevant circumstances of the client (C). He also decides on a strategy, what goals he will try to achieve, and what kinds of persuasion he will use. This strategy is provisional, as new facts may come to light during the interview.

(2) S establishes rapport with C, who may be very nervous about the interview. This will be easier if S maintains good day-to-day contacts with C. They might chat briefly about common interests, so that status barriers are reduced, and C is ready to talk freely. It can be enough for S to create an easy relationship by non-verbal signals.

(3) It may be necessary for S to explain that there is a problem – C has been persistently late so that production has fallen, C has been getting very low marks, etc. This should be done by stating objective facts, not by passing judgement, and should be done in a manner that is pleasant rather than cross.

(4) S now invites C to say what he thinks about the situation, what he thinks the reason for it is. This may involve a certain amount of probing for fuller information, if C is reluctant to open up. S is sympathetic, and shows that he wants to understand C's position. S may ask C whether he thinks the situation is satisfactory; in an evaluation interview he can ask C to evaluate his own performance.

(5) There now follows a period of joint problem-solving, in which C and S try between them to work out a solution to the problem. This may involve action on S's side as well as on C's – such as giving C a different job, or making some other change in the situation. It may involve a trial period after which S and C will meet again to review the situation.

(6) If some change of behaviour on C's part is indicated, and if C proves uncooperative, further steps may be necessary. The first of these is persuasion. S may be able to point out that C will not reach his own goals by his present line of action – as with a student who will fail his exams if he does not work harder. Such social influence is a subtle skill in itself, and depends on being able to appeal realistically to the right needs in a particular individual.

(7) If this fails, and if further interviews become necessary, sterner means of influence may have to be resorted to. Most Ss are in a position to control material sanctions, such as bonuses, promotions, and finally dismissal. S will not usually want to sack C – what he wants is to keep him but get him to behave differently. The possible use of such sanctions should first be mentioned reluctantly as a rather remote possibility – for example by the quite objective statement 'there are several other people who would like this job', or 'I may have to tell the people who pay your grant about your progress'.

(8) The interview should end with a review of what has been agreed, the constructive steps that have been decided upon, when S and C will meet again to discuss progress, and so on. The meeting should end on as friendly a note as possible (Argyle, 1978).

Presenting material to an audience. It is often necessary at work to present ideas or findings to groups of people, large or small, with the intention of conveying information, changing their attitudes or influencing their behaviour. This is often done very ineffectively, because the speaker is inaudible, boring, unconvincing, nervous, cannot handle an audience or presents the material badly. The manner of a speaker is very important. He will be more effective if he is seen to be an expert on his subject, and is well intentioned towards his listeners; this can be indicated by the appropriate non-verbal signals of dress and general demeanour, especially perhaps tone of voice. He should be seen as an expert, but also as a member of the group on equal terms with the audience. He should have a friendly, agreeable and lively manner, and make the presentation interesting and enjoyable throughout. He should have 'poise', i.e. confidence and lack of anxiety, and 'presence', i.e. be in constant contact with and control of the audience.

A lecture or other presentation may have a number of phases. For a persuasive message, the following order is most effective (McGuire, 1969):

(1) *Opening*. The speaker makes contact with the audience, secures their attention, puts them in the right mood, mentions his links with the audience or does other self-presenting, and explains what he is going to talk about and why. He should arouse interest and create the expectation that he is going to solve important problems or show how to satisfy important needs.

(2) *Positive arguments*. The positive case is put forward with the support of sound and compelling arguments, clear evidence, good illustrations and clear visual aids. This should be clearly structured, and the materials used should be intrinsically interesting. When unfamiliar ideas are being put forward it is necessary to use striking examples to jolt the audience out of old ways of thinking.

(3) *Dealing with objections*. It is useful to deal with objections, especially when the audience is intelligent or would be expected to see them.

(4) *Drawing conclusions*. At the end the most important conclusions should be explicitly drawn, especially conclusions for action.

A number of subsidiary social skills are involved in presenting. One, the speaker should choose arguments and illustrations that will appeal to the audience. To make his case persuasive he should show how it will meet the needs of the listeners. To make it interesting he should use examples which are familiar to them. Two, he must be continuously responsive to his hearers' reactions, and keep control of the audience. This is done by being in almost continual visual contact, studying their reactions to what is said, and taking rapid corrective action, e.g. by speaking louder, explaining points that were not understood, arousing more interest, or quietening them down. Three, a speaker should speak loudly and distinctly, 'project' his voice to all corners of the audience, keep his voice quality under control, and vary pace and tone enough to make it interesting. He should not sound superior, nervous or boring, and the delivery should be appropriate to the size of the audience. Four, a speaker should control his anxiety – this will disrupt his performance and distract the audience. He should concentrate on performing the task in hand competently, and focus his attention on relevant aspects of audience reaction, i.e. whether they are understanding him, not whether they like him. Careful preparation of the material to be presented will increase his confidence. Five, slides and other audio-visual aids should be carefully prepared, and make their points clearly. The stage should be arranged skilfully so that the performer does not get in the way or lose visual contact with the audience. Six, during the discussion the contributions of the audience should be taken seriously and sympathetically, and an effort made to see the points of view expressed. The speaker should not merely 'deal with' the points made, but try to work out the best solutions with the audience's help. He should avoid any confrontation with the audience.

Committee chairmanship. The task of committees and other discussion groups is to solve problems and take decisions in a way that is acceptable to those present, and to those they represent. In some cases the emphasis is on problem-solving and creativity, in others the emphasis is on obtaining consensus. Such groups usually have a chairman, unless there are only three or four people present. The chairman has a generally accepted social role of controlling discussion and helping the group make decisions. His position is often more temporary than that of other group leaders, and the chairmanship may be rotated so that other committee members take it in turns. Being chairman carries a certain amount of power, but it has to be used with skill. A chairman should see that all members are able to express their views, and that the decisions arrived at are agreeable to as many of them as possible. He should be able to keep control with a light touch, and keep people in order without upsetting them.

At the beginning of the meeting the chairman should create the right atmosphere, by the use of appropriate non-verbal signals. There are several phases to the discussion of each item on the agenda. First, the chairman introduces the item by outlining the problem to be discussed, summarizing briefly the main background factors, the arguments on each side, and so on. Then the committee is invited to discuss the problem; enough time should be allowed for different views to be expressed, and the chairman should try to keep the discussion orderly, so that different points are dealt with in turn. Now the chairman can help the group to come to a decision, by focusing on disagreements among them and trying to arrive at a creative solution, evaluating different solutions in relation to criteria if these can be agreed, considering sub-problems in turn, or asking the committee to consider two possible solutions. Finally, an attempt is made to secure the group's support for a particular solution. If this is impossible it may be necessary to take a vote; this is unsatisfactory, since it means that some members are not happy about the decision, and will not support it very enthusiastically.

A chairman should be aware of the main processes of behaviour in groups, and be able to prevent these processes interfering with the effective working of the committee. The formation of a status hierarchy will inhibit low-status members from contributing: they should be encouraged to speak. Conformity pressures may produce over-rapid acceptance of the first solution offered: this can be prevented by asking the group to consider a second solution. The 'risky-shift' phenomenon may lead committees to adopt risky solutions to problems, and the chairman should be on the watch for this.

There are a number of subsidiary social skills involved in being a chairman. He should study the agenda carefully beforehand, and prepare his introduction to the different items. He should be able to anticipate the items which will cause difficulty of some kind. He should be familiar with the rules and procedure of the committee, and be able to explain what should happen when the voting is equal, what to do if there is no quorum, and so on. It is often useful to appoint a sub-committee or working party to deal with problems involving fact-finding or drafting. The composition of sub-committees is important: they should be small but contain the right combination of skills or experience. There may be problems about dealing with awkward members of a committee. The chairman should avoid direct confrontation, or the use of naked power. It is better if he can apply impersonal rules, or leave it to the rest of the committee to deal with difficult individuals. People who want to talk too much can be gently discouraged by the use of non-verbal signals. Members who put forward preposterous ideas can be firmly out-voted (see Hoffman, 1965).

METHODS OF SOCIAL SKILLS TRAINING

We have shown that social skills are extremely important at work. During recent years a bewildering variety of methods of social skills training have sprung up, some of them solidly based on interaction research, others of much more dubious value. We shall describe here the main varieties of training, and review the evidence of their success as shown by follow-up studies.

Because there is a widely practised method of training, and because those who experience it enjoy it and are enthusiastic about its benefits, it does not follow that the training does any good. Early methods of supervisory training, based on lectures and discussion, were found to have no effect on supervisory skills (Argyle *et al.*, 1962). It is necessary to show that there have been changes from before the training to after it, and that such changes are greater than those in a comparable untrained control group (to eliminate the effects of the passage of time and taking tests). The assessment should not consist of questionnaires, since the course may affect verbal responses but not other aspects of behaviour. When ratings by colleagues are used, these should be made 'blind', i.e. the raters should not know who has been trained, or their attitudes to the training may affect their ratings. The best criteria are objective measures of output, sales, etc., where these are available.

Learning on the job. In the past the commonest way of acquiring social skills was on the job – by trial and error, by imitation of others, occasionally helped by comments and suggestions from colleagues. However, it is not very successful. Fiedler (1970) actually found a negative correlation (-0.12) between the effectiveness of leaders and years of experience, i.e. the more experienced were slightly worse. It has been found that some supervisors seem to have learned the wrong social skills through experience, e.g. they use close, punitive and authoritarian methods (Argyle *et al.*, 1958). Salesgirls *on average* slowly increased their volume of sales with time, but some stayed unchanged, while others became worse (Argyle, Lalljee and Lydall in Argyle, 1967). Experience with training interviewers has shown that after years of experience interviewers may not have acquired quite simple and basic social techniques – such as how to make a candidate talk more – which can be taught in a few minutes.

However, a number of studies suggest that learning can take place on the job if the right conditions for it are created. Clear feedback must be given on what the trainee is doing wrong. Some 3,900 schoolchildren were asked to fill in rating scales to describe their ideal teacher and how their actual teachers behaved; the results were shown to half of the teachers, who subsequently improved on ten of the twelve scales (Gage *et al.*, 1960). However, in most work situations this kind of feedback is not available. In order to improve performance, new social techniques must be found. The best way of generating new responses is for an expert to suggest and demonstrate them. Learning on the job can be speeded up by imitating successful practitioners, but it may not be clear exactly what they are doing. Learning on the job will occur if there is a trainer on the spot who frequently sees the trainee in action, and holds regular feedback and coaching sessions. The trainer should be an expert performer of the skill himself and sensitive to the elements and processes of social interaction. The success of such coaching depends on there being a good relationship between the trainee and the supervisor.

There is one great advantage of learning on the job over all other forms of training – there is no problem of transferring to the job skills which have been learned in a training situation.

Role-playing. Here the trainee practises the skills in a laboratory mock-up of the real situation, with other trainees or stooges playing the other parts. This is one of the main forms of laboratory training in social skills. Though the method has been known for some time, recent developments in techniques and equipment have changed it considerably in recent years. Before any useful role-playing can be done trainers should find out the main problem situations likely to be faced by trainees, and what would be the best social techniques for dealing with them. There may be research material available on the skill in question, and use can be made of general principles of social interaction; otherwise reliance must be placed on the advice of experienced practitioners – though this is not always reliable, as we showed above. There are three phases to role-playing:

First, there is a lecture, discussion, demonstration, or film about a particular aspect of the skill needed in the particular role. Second, a problem situation is defined, e.g. interviewing the main types of awkward candidate, and stooges are produced for trainees to role-play with, for seven to fifteen minutes each. The background to the situation may be filled in with written materials, such as the application forms of a candidate for interview, or background information about a personnel problem; the stooges may be carefully trained beforehand to provide various problems, such as talking too much, or having elaborate and plausible excuses. Finally, there is a feedback session, consisting of verbal comments by the trainer, discussion with the other trainees, and playback of audio- or video-tapes. The verbal feedback is used to draw attention, constructively and tactfully, to what the trainee was doing wrong, and to suggest alternative styles of behaviour. The tape-recordings provide clear evidence for the accuracy of what is being said.

A series of sessions of this kind is usually held, covering the main problem areas or sub-sections of the social skill. There may be from three to twelve such sessions of one to three hours each.

Role-playing can be conducted without any specialized equipment, but it is much better if certain simple laboratory arrangements are available. An ideal set-up for interviewer training is shown in Figure 13.

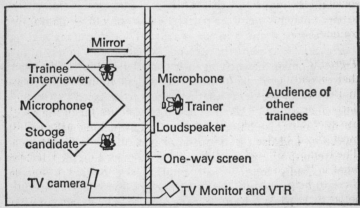

Figure 13. Laboratory arrangements for interviewing training (from Argyle, 1969).

The role-playing takes place on one side of a one-way screen, and is observed by the trainer and other trainees. A video-tape is taken of the role-playing, the mirror being used to film both people simultaneously. The trainer is able to communicate with the role-player through an ear-microphone. Alternatives to a mirror are a wide-angle lens or two cameras and a video-mixer.

A number of follow-up studies have been carried out of the effects of role-playing on industrial supervisors, and others. There is little doubt that the method is very effective in teaching specific social techniques, that feedback is important, and that video-tape playback is very useful (Argyle *et al.*, 1962; Haines and Eachus, 1965). One difficulty is that trainees may think it is silly or may over-dramatize their performances. The trainer should introduce the sessions carefully, and create the appropriate attitude to them. Another problem is that trainees have to apply what is learned to a different and real-life situation. This can be met by having periodic sessions, so that trainees can report progress in the work situation, and mock-ups of real problem situations can be created in the laboratory. It is very important that the trainer should be good at the skill being taught, sensitive to non-verbal cues and processes of social interaction, and have the further social skill of being able to give feedback firmly and kindly enough for it to change the trainees' behaviour.

T-groups. T(training)-groups have grown in popularity since their invention in 1947 at the National Training Laboratories in Bethel, Maine. There are now a number of varieties and derivatives, though the whole process has been the object of considerable criticism. The basic procedure is for a trainer to meet about twelve trainees for a series of two-hour sessions. The trainees are told that their sole task is to study and discuss what is happening in the group itself, and that the trainer is there to help them do this. The group may start slowly, with some member asking who is in charge, whereupon another member comments on the behaviour of the first, and so on. There is a lot of direct comment on the behaviour of individual members; the trainer may intervene to provide such comments himself, or to explain what he thinks is happening in the group. In addition, there may be a number of ancillary exercises such as role-playing and lectures. This all provides a very unusual experience which is commonly found to be fascinating and sometimes unpleasant. The goals of this kind of training are ambitious: to increase sensitivity to interpersonal behaviour, to show trainees how they are seen by others, and to improve their general social skills in the work situation.

There have been a number of extensive and careful follow-up studies (Bradford *et al.*, 1964) with control groups, and before-and-after analysis of behaviour on the job. Typical findings are that 30–40 per cent of trainees do improve to some extent in the three ways listed above, compared with 10–20 per cent of the control groups (Campbell and Dunnette, 1968). However, the improvement may not have been due to the T-group training itself, since in all the courses followed up there were other kinds of training as well, such as role-playing. Furthermore, these follow-up studies used ratings by colleagues, which were not made blind, so that it is possible that the results were affected by their attitudes to the training.

The main problem, however, is that different trainees respond very differently to this form of training. In addition to the 30–40 per cent who benefit from it a majority are unaffected, and others are upset by it and are found to be *less* effective after the training than before. One study found that for every two that became more effective, one became less so (Underwood, 1965). In addition, there is a rather smaller group who are seriously disturbed by T-groups and need psychiatric treatment. One solution to this problem is to do more careful screening of those going on T-groups or for trainers to be more watchful for signs of distress; however part of the point of T-groups is to do something about authoritarian or other awkward characters in organizations – just the people who would be screened out. Another solution would be to reduce the level of emotional stress – some T-group practitioners do this, but others believe that the emotional arousal is necessary – 'it is a matter of what you are prepared to pay for psychically'.

The present T-group scene is wild and chaotic. There are also different kinds of 'encounter groups', and training groups with very peculiar exercises. There are all kinds of trainers, some of whom appear to be skilled, kind and therapeutic, and others who do not. In my view, the benefits to be obtained from T-groups can be obtained more painlessly and less dangerously in other ways. However, if there is an insatiable demand for this kind of experience, a rather conservative type of procedure should be followed, in which the following conditions are observed:

(1) Screening of trainees likely to be upset.
(2) Lowering of the emotional stress.
(3) Learning of specific social skills by role-playing or other exercises.
(4) Trainers who are extremely socially skilled and therapeutic.

Training and treatment for extreme social incompetence. We saw that the effects of social skills on work performance are most marked in cases of extreme social incompetence (p. 137f.). Part of the reason for the popularity of T-groups is that it is hoped that they will have some effect on highly authoritarian or otherwise difficult members of organizations. Indeed a lot of the interest in psychology and social science probably stems from the everyday experience of having to deal with difficult people.

A considerable proportion of the members of any organization are difficult in one way or another – about 8 per cent are neurotic, 1 per cent are psychotic, and there are the lower 10 per cent (say) on measures of social competence, and the upper 10 per cent (say) on authoritarianism (Argyle, 1969). There will be some overlap between these categories, and some of them will make a person less likely to rise to a position of much responsibility. One solution is simply to dismiss those concerned; this may be the only solution in some cases, e.g. the psychotics, but it is otherwise resisted both on humanitarian grounds and because the people concerned may be very able in other respects. Another solution is to move them to jobs where the social demands are fewer, or where they can do less damage; however there are only a few such jobs in any organization. What we recommend are various methods of specialized training and treatment.

Authoritarians. This used to be a serious problem in British industry, due to the survivors from a more authoritarian era, and a large number of ex-army officers. However, some organizations

have made great efforts, through both selection and training, to deal with this problem. It is doubtful whether T-groups
are very successful with authoritarians, though T-groups make
them aware for the first time of what younger people think of
them. A variety of role-playing which has been used is to give
trainees the experience of serving under authoritarian and other
kinds of leaders – a kind of 'role reversal' (Blake and Mouton,
1961). It must be admitted, however, that authoritarians are
very difficult to retrain, partly because they are convinced that
everyone else is wrong and also because they have no respect
for either trainers or psychologists.

Social anxiety. Some people experience acute social anxiety,
either in all social situations or specific ones, such as public
speaking, taking the chair or seeing superiors. This leads to
their avoiding these situations and makes them ineffective at
their job. One solution is psychotherapy, but this is extremely
slow and expensive and does not work for everyone. Recent
studies show that behaviour therapy is more effective. The
relevant form of treatment is 'desensitization': the patient is
helped to work out a 'gradient' of related situations, from the
most to the least disturbing. He is then taught to relax his
whole body, and imagine the least disturbing situation. He then
stops imagining, relaxes again, and imagines the next most
disturbing, and so on (Wolpe, 1958). It was found in a study of
the treatment of public speaking anxiety that this method was
more successful than psychotherapy (Paul, 1966).

Inadequate social skills. There is another group of people who
simply fail to cope with social situations at work. They may be
always quarrelling instead of cooperating, they may be very
unpopular and generally avoided, they may be unable to
deal with certain categories of people – superiors, subordinates,
other social classes, women, etc., or they may be very ineffective on committees or other kinds of encounter at work. Such
inabilities commonly stand in the way of them being promoted,
and may lead to dismissal, but they can be modified by appropriate training. I have been treating neurotic patients and

others with acute interpersonal difficulties for some years by means of role-playing and other exercises. The trainee is interviewed at length and observed in laboratory encounters, in order to build up a picture of what he is doing wrong. Then a series of exercises is devised to meet his particular needs. These include role-playing of appropriate problem situations, with suitable stooges, exercises in non-verbal communication and basic social interaction skills, exercises in perception of other people, and tutorials on relevant aspects of social behaviour (Trower, Bryant and Argyle, 1978).

Industrial psychologists recognized the importance of manual skills, devised the best ways of performing them, and instituted training schemes in the early years of this century. It was not until the 1950s that the importance of *social* skills was recognized. We now understand how supervisory and other social skills work, what the most effective skills are, and how they can be trained.

CHAPTER 8

WORKING IN ORGANIZATIONS

*The growth of organizations – different kinds of organiza-
tion – ideas about organization – roles and role conflict –
communication in organizations – conflict between groups
– the optimum design of working organizations – producing
organizational change. Appendix A : Industrial democracy
– Appendix B : Work in Israel, Yugoslavia and Japan.*

FROM early times men have worked not only in small social
groups but also in organized social groups. For example, working groups with leaders based on kinship structures, the Roman
ergasterions, the feudal system, the domestic system – these
were all different kinds of work organization (Chapter 2). In an
organized group the pattern of relationships is fixed, having
been worked out by earlier members of similar groups. The
behaviour of the present members is therefore to a considerable degree *preprogrammed*. Each person occupies a position –
such as slave, feudal lord of the manor, merchant capitalist,
shop-steward; and associated with each position is a standard
pattern of behaviour, or *role*. These roles *interlock* – for
example, there was a standard pattern of interaction between a
feudal serf and his lord of the manor, which was quite different
from that of subordinates and supervisors today.

The tendency to form social organizations is probably not
innate, but rather the result of slow cultural growth, partly to
deal with the increasing size of human groupings, partly in
response to the development of more elaborate technology. All
advanced civilizations have produced large-scale organizations
for industrial, military, governmental, educational, religious
and other purposes. The pattern of these structures has
changed historically, and ideas have developed about how
work should be organized, culminating in contemporary

theories of management. However, we have now moved into a new historical phase, in which social scientists are able to examine social organizations, compare the efficiency of different designs, and see which ones make their occupants happiest. It is clear that working organizations as we know them today are far from satisfactory, and their shortcomings will be discussed below. We shall be looking at some alternative forms of working organization found in other countries (Appendix B), and we shall consider some new kinds of design which are being tried in the West.

THE GROWTH OF ORGANIZATIONS

Organizations develop gradually out of small social groups. Informal leaders become formal leaders, role-differentiation becomes division of labour, and norms become rules.

Leadership and hierarchical structure. We saw in Chapter 6 how small social groups spontaneously develop a hierarchical structure. It has been found that when a group develops a clear leadership hierarchy it is better at problem-solving (Heinecke and Bales, 1953). In the most primitive communities work leadership was based on the status system of the community, itself usually a matter of kinship. It looks as though working groups usually develop a hierarchical structure, and this is useful for organizing the work.

When a group gets larger it tends to split into sub-groups, indeed this happens by the time a group reaches ten in size. Each sub-group then has a leader, and these leaders have to coordinate the activities of their sub-groups, so that with increasing size a second line of leadership may emerge of men whose job it is to coordinate and direct the first-line leaders. Very large organizations often become very bureaucratic, with ten or more levels in the hierarchy – a source of great discontent for those at the lower levels, and also a cause of enormous communication difficulties (p. 192 f.). In small groups the hierarchy is based on different degrees of expertise at the group task. In traditional organizations it is based on family relationships.

In modern working organizations it is based largely on competence at the administrative tasks to be performed at higher levels – the managing director of an oil company is not necessarily better at drilling holes than the others, but he must be an expert at administering large-scale organizations; those who want to be promoted must abandon their speciality.

Some degree of hierarchy seems to be unavoidable but attitudes to authority vary greatly in different cultures, and the kind of hierarchy that is acceptable varies accordingly. The Japanese tradition of feudal social structures has made this kind of organization perfectly acceptable in Japanese industry (see p. 217f.) In the U.S.A. there is a much more egalitarian tradition, and there are demands for participation and the levelling of hierarchies. In Britain at the present time subordinates appear to be acquiescent but without much respect for authority (Fox, 1971). There is a considerable range of individual differences in attitudes to authority, varying from nervous dependence to militant rebellion.

Role-differentiation and division of labour. Role-differentiation appears in small social groups, as division of labour appeared in the earliest human communities – different people specializing in farming, looking after animals, crafts, trade, etc. The larger the group and the more complex the technology the more division of labour there is. In a modern factory there may be hundreds of distinct jobs, each with its own special skills, for which selection and training are needed. In addition to a large number of different kinds of manual work there are also many kinds of non-manual work – accounting, computing, clerical, managerial and research work, inspection, time-study, and the work of foremen, shop-stewards, management services specialists, financial and legal experts, and many others: all are 'working' in the organization and contribute to its effectiveness.

Incentives. In small social groups the members often gain directly through their work. In primitive societies families farm to produce their own food, or to barter it for household goods, make houses for themselves or neighbours, and so on.

In more advanced societies, with more elaborate technologies, workers are not able to consume the products of their work so directly and they have to be motivated in other ways. Slaves were coerced, feudal tenants had a sworn obligation to render services, and more recently workers have been motivated by economic incentives. Some people to some extent are also affected by *intrinsic* motivation – they work because they believe that the work is worth doing and that the products of their work are important. Working organizations have moved away from coercion and obligation towards economic incentives in the course of history; perhaps the next stage is to move to intrinsic motivation.

Norms and rules. Small social groups develop norms, both about how tasks shall be performed and about how interpersonal relations within the group shall be regulated. Norms represent group solutions to the external and internal problems that confront the group. Friction and disorder is created by deviation, so pressures are used to maintain conformity in the group. The same is true of social organizations, except that norms become formalized into rules, e.g. about promotion and discipline, which are used to administer the activities of the organization. As organizations become larger increasing use is made of rules as an administrative device to coordinate and control a large and often heterogeneous body of people (Rushing, 1966). Newcomers often resent regulations, since they played no part in drafting them, and they often fail to see the purposes of the rules; the solution to this is better communication and the participation of members of the organization at all levels in running it.

Channels of communication. Even in a group as small as five, an 'all-channel' structure where anyone can talk to anyone is less effective for a number of purposes than a structure where only some channels may be used (Glanzer and Glaser, 1961). In much larger groups it is essential that there should be recognized channels of communication. These include, (1) the leadership hierarchy, (2) personnel, work study, and other staff departments, in an advisory relationship, and (3) arrangements for joint consultation, etc. In addition to these formal lines of communication, 'informal' channels are created and those play an important part in the running of most organizations.

DIFFERENT KINDS OF ORGANIZATION

Working organizations can take a variety of forms. This is particularly striking if one looks at different periods of history (Chapter 2), or at different countries today (Appendix B). Part of the difference is due to the nature of the work or the technology (p. 48f.). On the other hand, quite different activities can be embodied in identical organizations – factories, churches and schools can be run with essentially the same structure, for example. If we are to consider what kinds of organization are most satisfactory, we must consider the range of alternatives that have been used; we really ought to consider all possible alternatives, but that is more difficult, since no one knows how untried arrangements would work.

One basis for the classification of organizations is in terms of the type of authority used and the main form of motivation appealed to in the members. Etzioni (1961) suggested the following types:

Coercive. Authority rests in the power of punishment; the members do not enjoy being there at all, and are motivated primarily by fear of punishment. In the past a great deal of work was organized in this way – Roman slaves, and workers in the Industrial Revolution. The latter were motivated both by fear of punishment and by fear of dismissal and consequent starvation.

Utilitarian. Authority rests on the power to reward, and workers will work in exchange for rewards, usually money. This is the main system in modern industry, especially where wage incentives are used.

Moral. In research establishments, hospitals, voluntary and professional organizations, the members work because they believe in the importance of the organization's goals, and are personally committed to them. Authority rests on a leader's ability to appeal to these motivations in the members. The feudal system was partly coercive and utilitarian, but tenants were also committed by sworn obligations, and believed in the right of their landlord to their work and obedience. In more recent times there has been a high degree of commitment among entrepreneurs and senior management, but very much less among their subordinates, some of whom are completely alienated from the goals of their organization.

Pugh and Hickson (1968) carried out a statistical study of 52 British firms and other work organizations. Each was assessed on six dimensions of organization – number of specialized departments, number of specialized jobs within departments, extent of standardization procedures, written definitions of roles, centralization of decision-taking, and number of levels in the hierarchy. A statistical analysis was carried out and four main types of organization were found.

First there are the large manufacturing concerns with highly structured working methods, a lot of job specialization and highly formalized roles, a lot of people not directly engaged in work (researchers, planners, etc.), and decentralization of work procedures. Then there are government and other administrative organizations with highly centralized personnel procedures, elaborate committee structures, but little standardization of working methods. Thirdly, there are the small firms, with between 250 and 750 staff, little specialization or standardization, and a fairly low degree of centralization. These are owned by a small number of people who are also directors, and it is suggested that they are run by implicit customs rather than by explicit regulations. One third of the total had average scores on all the variables, and had no distinctive features in terms of these measures.

A number of studies have shown that the design of working organizations is affected by the nature of the work done. As we saw earlier, Woodward (1965) found that the number of levels in the supervisory hierarchy was typically three in unit or batch production, four in mass production and six in process work; the span of control also varies, being greatest for mass production. She reported that the most successful firms of each type were those that were near the typical structure for each type of work. Burns and Stalker (1961) found that the organizational structure varied with the rate of change of the technology. In large manufacturing firms with a slowly changing market and technology there is a 'mechanistic structure', like the first type above. However, in industries undergoing rapid change, like some of the Scottish electronics firms which they studied, a more 'organic' structure had developed, with a more flexible and less hierarchical structure, and less role specialization. Individuals had more general responsibilities to the whole organization, instead of carrying out a single clearly defined role.

IDEAS ABOUT ORGANIZATION

In the nineteenth century in England there was a slow growth of management practices to deal with the increased size and technological complexity of industrial concerns. At first each firm was dominated by one man, the entrepreneur owner–manager, who did all the different management jobs himself, and exercised a highly personalized control over everyone; there were no regular methods of working or of dealing with personnel. With increased size the span of control became too great for one man to handle and a regular chain of command was established with salaried foremen and managers. Sometimes different partners were responsible for the different finance, etc. With the increased scale and the rise of professional managers came a carefully planned work layout, division of labour, carefully organized mass production methods, definition of duties, and regular personnel practices. The majority of owners and managers regarded the labour force as a hostile group whose culture had to be destroyed and character reformed by means of economic incentives and punitive discipline. A minority of men like Robert Owen took a different view, and were concerned for the welfare of their employees and were successful in winning their cooperation (Pollard, 1965).

There was very little formulation of the principles of management or the theory of organization until about 1900. Then Fayol put forward his fourteen principles, and similar ideas were later formulated by Mary Parker Follett, and introduced in England by Urwick. 'Classical organization theory', as it became called, was not based on research, but on the observation and experience of a number of early industrialists and soldiers. The principles were the methods of management which they had seen used and which seemed to work. They also contained a number of ideas and assumptions about the social psychology of workers. Some of the main ideas of classical organization theory are: (1) *span of control* – executives should have no more than five to seven subordinates reporting to them, first-line supervisors no more than twenty; (2) *chain of command* – there should be a continuous chain of command, each person reporting to his immediate superior, in a pyramidal structure; (3) *written responsibilities* – there should be clear and written responsibilities for every job; (4) *division of labour* – the work should be divided up so that no one has duties which are too varied or unrelated; and (5) *handling procedure* – workers should be motivated by economic incentives, controlled by fair discipline and impersonal rules, and be promoted on the basis of technical competence.

These principles contain a certain amount of sound guidance. The second embodies the idea that each man should have one boss: this is often not followed, and the same person may have to report to two or more supervisors, which can easily create serious conflicts of role for him. The third leads to the development of clear job descriptions, and to thinking out clearly what each person should be doing. If this is not done those concerned will not know what they are supposed to be doing, and may not put their efforts in the most useful direction.

However, the principles of classical organization theory have been extensively criticized in the light of later research and experience. Here are some of the main points.

The first of the main ideas above, the principle of span of control, is not universally true. In particular, the organization can be much flatter at higher levels than was recommended. A vice-president of Sears Roebuck can have 200 store managers reporting to him if he has access to adequate measures of performance. The second, the hierarchical structure, has been found to cause communication difficulties, alienation at lower levels, and general ineffectiveness. The reasons for this, and the possible alternatives are discussed below. Further, no account is taken of the formation of working groups and other lateral and informal relationships (Bass, 1965).

The fourth, division of labour, has resulted in workers doing very boring, repetitive jobs, sometimes repeated every minute or even more frequently. This has caused very low levels of job satisfaction (p. 253 f.). As for the fifth, it is assumed that workers are naturally lazy and uncooperative and need to be controlled by payment and punishment. No reference is made to eliciting their cooperation, to their participation in decisions, or to personal relationships between leaders and those led (Bass, 1965; Massie, 1965).

A further development of this approach was Scientific Management, due to F. W. Taylor and others. Here the emphasis was on time and motion study combined with wage incentives. It is interesting to note that Taylor saw this as a way of bringing about cooperation between employers and workers, and of removing both trade unions and dictatorial managers (Taylor, 1912, reprinted in 1947).

The next set of ideas about management which developed is usually known as the Human Relations movement. It began with the Hawthorne experiments in the early 1930s and was widely approved of by social scientists (though not by managers) in the 1950s. The Hawthorne investigations included a study of informal organization and output restriction in the Bank Wiring Room, a survey of workers' complaints, and the famous experiment in the Relay Assembly Test Room (Roethlisberger and Dickson, 1939). The latter experiment appeared to show that output was more affected by social relations within the group and with the supervisors than by wage incentives and the physical conditions of work. In my opinion, these conclusions were unfounded (see p. 106). These experiments were initiated, and the general human relations outlook propagated by Elton Mayo (1933, 1945).

After the Second World War research in industrial social psychology, mainly in the U.S.A., extended the human relations approach in three related directions. First, research at the University of Michigan and elsewhere showed that democratic styles of supervision led to more output and job satisfaction (e.g. Likert, 1961). Second, laboratory and field studies of small social groups showed that social relationships *within* groups affected productivity. Third, many surveys were made of job satisfaction and it was found that social factors, such as relations with peers and supervisors, were important in satisfaction with work; it was also widely believed that job satisfaction was correlated with, or was a cause of, high productivity.

The human relations outlook had a considerable impact on American and British industry, particularly on supervisory and management training courses, though personnel departments were usually more enthusiastic about it than production departments. The movement helped to reform industry and improve the way in which workers were treated. Other factors in this improvement were the influence of the trade unions and a shortage of labour during part of the period in question.

The human relations movement has been criticized as being too pro-management, a way of manipulating workers; since one of the main goals of the movement was to increase job satisfaction, this objection seems unreasonable. The opposite objection has also been commonly made – that it is too concerned with job satisfaction, and does not pay enough attention to making a profit and staying in business; this is equally untenable, since all of the changes suggested have been shown to increase productivity.

We now turn to more serious objections, based on research, which suggest some revision of the Human Relations ideas – though not their rejection. The direct effects of new styles of supervision and group composition on productivity are modest

– of the order of 10–25 per cent. There are additional indirect effects, however, through reduced absenteeism and labour turnover, better communication and cooperation. Job satisfaction is usually *not* correlated with rate of output – happy workers do not work harder, though they are absent less and their turnover rate is lower (p. 238f.).

Democratic-persuasive styles of supervision are not invariably the most effective, and supervisors need to have a 'concern for productivity' as well as a 'concern for people' (see Blake and Mouton, 1964). The human relations people said nothing about the role of technological factors. The Tavistock Institute, and other researchers, have drawn attention to the importance of looking jointly at social and technological factors. The human relations people said little about changing organizational structure, apart from changing the relationships in existing structures. As described in this chapter it may be very advantageous to change the shape, size, structure, and formal arrangements for participation in decisions.

A number of sociologists have been very critical of bureaucratic organizations. One of the most frequent criticisms is the tendency of people to become too attached to 'red tape', i.e. to pursue administrative procedures at the expense of the real goals of the organization. Merton (1957) has suggested that this is because an effective organization depends on strict devotion to regulations, so that there are strong social pressures to conform, and as a result some people take the rules, regulations and administrative procedures as ends in themselves. Little is known about the conditions under which this takes place; it is probably more common among obsessional personalities, in circumstances in which there are strong sanctions for failing to keep to the regulations.

Parkinson (1957) pointed to a number of related kinds of organizational pathology. 'Parkinson's Law' is that 'work expands so as to fill the time available'. Parkinson also observes how people build empires regardless of the amount of work to be done, and shows how officials in the British Navy expanded far more rapidly than the Navy as a whole, and the Colonial Office expanded while the actual colonies were contracting.

Again, little is known about the precise conditions under which unnecessary officials are able to multiply.

A number of sociologists have criticized excessively hierarchical structures on the grounds that vertical communication is difficult (p. 194 f.), and that those at the lower levels can exert very little influence on what happens and thus become alienated (e.g. Blau and Scott, 1963). We have already considered one solution to this problem – the introduction of democratic-persuasive supervisory skills. Another solution is to have formal arrangements for participation in decisions (see Appendix A, p. 203 f.). A third solution is to change the structure of the organization, by decentralization or by having fewer levels and a larger span of control.

Peter (1969) proposed the 'Peter principle' which is that 'in a hierarchy every employee tends to rise to his own level of incompetence', i.e. people get promoted until they reach a job which they are unable to do. It is certainly quite common for a man to be promoted to a new job which he does less well than his previous job. But this is often because the new job calls for different abilities – as when a skilled workman becomes a foreman, or an engineer a manager. In organizations expanding rapidly there may be meteoric promotion of individuals to positions that are beyond their abilities. On the other hand, prestigious organizations that are not expanding much, and which are able to attract very talented applicants, may be forced to employ many people *below* their true level. In both cases better manpower planning is needed.

ROLES AND ROLE CONFLICT

To understand how organizations function we have to study the patterns of social interaction between the members. Every member of an organization occupies a *position*, e.g. foreman, shop-steward, personnel manager. For every position there is a *role*, i.e. a pattern of behaviour typical of the people in that position. The role may include the work done, ways of behaving towards people in other positions, styles of non-verbal performance, attitudes and beliefs, clothes or uniforms worn, and style of life outside work. The different roles in an organization *interlock*, like the roles of doctor and patient, or teacher and pupil – the two roles fit together, one role elicits the other, and one role cannot be performed unless someone plays the other. Organizations can be regarded as systems of interlocking roles.

Why do all foremen behave in a similar way, that is different from the way personnel managers behave? The interlocking of roles is one factor; the organization has grown or has been built with a particular design, and each role interlocks with the others – if a doctor plays the doctor role the patient has to play the patient role, and the same is true of other pairs of roles. Each person is expected to play his part, not only by his immediate superiors, but also by peers and subordinates who want him to do things for them or collaborate towards group goals. The nature of the job produces role behaviour, since it can only be performed effectively in certain ways. The role is often the best way of doing a job. On the other hand, there may be considerable cultural variations in the roles for similar jobs, for example the role of a first-line leader. There is selection for the job – only certain people can become managers. There is also self-selection – only certain people want to. There are various social learning processes which succeed in making new occupants behave like old ones – imitation and instruction, both on training courses and on the job.

The extent to which an individual's behaviour is pre-programmed varies according to his status. People in less skilled jobs have little scope for variation from their standard role; more senior people have considerable leeway to do their job as they like, though still within the broad limits defined by the role (Cyert and MacCrimmon, 1968). Behaviour also depends on personality, as well as role, and this becomes more important the more a role allows for variation. The extent to which a manager behaves in an authoritarian way, for example, depends both on the role *and* on his personality; personality has rather less effect on the behaviour of a skilled manual worker.

It is sometimes said that behaviour in organizations is, or ought to be, 'impersonal'. This is a rather misleading notion.

It is true that interpersonal behaviour in organizations follows standard patterns that have been worked out in the past, so that when one man is replaced by another things carry on much as before. On the other hand, this does not mean that any of these relationships need be cold, distant or unfriendly. The relation between nurses and patients in hospitals is a role relationship, but it is also marked by warmth and care. In addition, although there is considerable standardization of role behaviour, there is variation between the behaviour of different personalities. Behaviour is affected both by the individual and by the role.

Members of organizations often experience *role conflict* when other people have different expectations and exercise different social pressures from one another about the role they should be performing. Kahn and his colleagues (1964) found that 48 per cent of a sample of American industrial employees experienced such conflict, for example between the demands of management and the unions, between those above and those below, or between company and clients. *Role ambiguity* occurs when people do not agree about what the role should be and people do not know what is expected of them. Kahn and his team, in their industrial survey, found that 35 per cent were disturbed by lack of clarity about the scope and responsibilities of their jobs. This was particularly found in new jobs where there was no established tradition.

When a person experiences role conflict or ambiguity he tends to be tense and unhappy, is dissatisfied with his job, tends to withdraw from social contact with those exerting conflicting pressure, and becomes bad at his work. He may also attempt to resolve the conflict or ambiguity in various ways – by giving one demand priority over another, bargaining with those exerting pressure on him, seeking official clarification or guidance, or trying to make changes in the organizational structure. Organizations can avoid or reduce role conflict by introducing appropriate rules, e.g. preventing husband and wife from working in the same part of the organization, or protecting from sanctions people who might easily incur them, such as lawyers or trade union organizers.

There can also be conflict between an individual's needs or

personality and his role. For example, a professor may be more interested in research than administration, an authoritarian person may find himself in a democratic organization, women workers may be primarily interested in the social life of their firm. This kind of conflict can be avoided by selecting people with the right abilities, needs, interests and personalities for the particular job. Existing selection procedures could be improved by putting more weight on the individual's needs and interests, so as to bring about more alignment of individual and organizational goals. During his training and the early period in his job, a person's goals may change to fit his role better. This applies particularly to doctors, clergymen, marines, and others whose initial training period is long and emotionally arousing and who become very dependent on their trainers. Supervisors may be able to modify personal goals by showing individuals how their needs can be met within the organization. The organization may isolate those with inconsistent goals and avoid giving them jobs such as representing the organization in dealings with outside bodies. If the individual becomes influential in the organization he may be able to modify the organizational goals to be more compatible with his own. If all these processes fail, he will simply leave: indeed most labour turnover can be ascribed to conflicts of this kind (Cyert and MacCrimmon, 1968).

COMMUNICATION IN ORGANIZATIONS

A social organization consists of a number of people occupying positions who have a settled pattern of communication and interaction with one another. These communications go to people above, below and on the same level, to people in the immediate group and to people outside it. We have already described social behaviour in working groups; now we shall deal with interpersonal behaviour in the wider organization. Some communication goes through the formally approved channels; some does nòt. While it is essential to limit communication to definite routes, these are often inadequate, and extra 'informal' channels have to be created, for example between opposite numbers in different sections of an organization whose official channels are through a shared superior. Communication may be about work or about matters apparently irrelevant to the job, but both are probably important; gossip and chat play an essential part in maintaining cooperative relationships between people.

Lateral communication is to other members of the organization of about the same status, often in different sections or departments; such social contacts may be allowed for in the organization chart, but generally they are not. Inside working groups there is, of course, a lot of lateral communication, such as help and information about the job.

It is found in American firms that 41 per cent of messages sent or received by line production managers are with other managers at the same level (Landsberger, 1961–2). These contacts with other departments are needed to get the work done, and may be quicker than using official channels, but they involve conflicts of interest and outlook. The following social techniques are commonly used here: appealing to rules or a common authority; evading the rules, e.g. ignoring requests; relying on friendships, past or future favours, or using political allies; persuasion, or showing the other the nature of the problem; trying to change the work-flow or other aspects of the organizational arrangements in an advantageous way (Sayles and Strauss, 1966).

Lateral relations between managers can take a number of forms. Junior managers may form cliques with the aim of increasing the status or other rewards of members and generally controlling events at work in their favour (Dalton, 1959). The working of organizations is often helped by lateral friendships, which create additional channels for cooperation and the flow of information. Another kind of lateral communication is the spread of information and rumours through the 'grapevine'. Such information travels surprisingly fast, and is sometimes quite accurate. It plays a useful function in satisfying curiosity and providing topics for enjoyable gossip, as well as keeping people informed about what is going on.

193

Downward communications are the main kind envisaged by classical organization theory and shown on organization charts. In fact such communications usually involve two-way interaction – questions lead to answers, and it is important to know whether instructions have been understood. We shall deal here with interactions which are *initiated* from above. First, instructions about the job: how this is done depends on the style of leadership used and the amount of delegation of responsibility practised in the organization, and can vary from orders to advice or guidance. This is discussed in more detail in Chapter 7. Second, information may be given about a subordinate's performance, as in an appraisal interview. Other information may be passed on about organizational matters or impending changes. Third, communications from experts need not be 'downwards' in terms of the organizational hierarchy, since the most expert person on a given matter is not always the most senior. Special lines of communication may be built up, in which people consult 'opinion leaders' on certain matters, who in turn consult even better informed experts. Fourth, two-step and indirect communication: a manager often wants to communicate with people two or more levels below him in the hierarchy; he has two main ways of doing so, neither of them very satisfactory. He can go through the 'usual channels' of speaking first to his subordinates, but at least four separate messages are needed before any feedback is received. There are also likely to be various delays and distortions; for example, the intermediate supervisors may re-interpret or play down the instructions; or when these arrive they may be so mysterious that 'research' has to be done to find out what they are really about. The senior manager can otherwise use letters, notices, or the public address system, which is faster and avoids distortion; however, there is no way of verifying that the information has been received or understood. Such methods can be improved by asking supervisors to reinforce them, or encouraging subordinates to discuss any problems with their immediate superiors.

Upward communication. Seeking help: it might be expected that workers would often seek help from the most knowledgeable and experienced person available – their immediate supervisor. It has been found, however, that it is more common for help to be sought from equals (and for it to be reciprocated), apparently because this avoids loss of reputation (Blau, 1955). Reporting progress: while it is essential for senior staff to have fast and accurate information about how the work is going, difficulties encountered, etc., it is often very difficult for them to find out what is going on. Bad news is likely to be ill received and may reflect on the competence of the person who brings it; consequently such information is delayed and distorted – supervisors and managers are told what they want to hear, and when they are thought to be in a good enough mood to hear it. Upward communications are less accurate when the senders are keen to be promoted (Read, 1962). Suggestions and complaints: although people at lower levels may be reluctant to report difficulties or lack of progress, they like to be consulted, to air their grievances and to have their ideas heard at higher levels. In old-fashioned and authoritarian regimes this does not happen, and managers often create barriers to upward communication by isolating themselves in their offices. In more modern organizations upward communication is achieved by consultative styles of supervision, suggestion schemes, representation on consultative committees and through trade unions and appeals channels. In most organizations there is a means of appealing against the decisions of the immediate superior; this involves by-passing him, and is probably rarely used because it damages relations with him. On the other hand, the existence of an appeals channel may make supervisors more ready to listen to their subordinates.

CONFLICT BETWEEN GROUPS

Line and staff. The classical bureaucracy, with a military hierarchy of authority, is not the usual design for working organizations. Most industrial firms have 'staff' departments, such as personnel, research and development, production planning, work study and accountancy. This is because the skills involved are so diverse that managers cannot be experts in them all. The staff departments are usually in an advisory relationship to line managers; this does not always work easily since the staff managers are typically younger, better educated, and of higher prestige, but of lower occupational potential, than line managers. Line managers see themselves as hard-headed, realistic, practical men, whose job is to get the work done and show a profit. Staff departments may have other interests; for example, personnel departments may be concerned about job satisfaction or career planning, and will know more about their particular field than line managers. While staff are supposed to 'advise', they may want to go further than this and make decisions, with the result that line managers fear that their authority will be undermined. In some firms the staff do in fact become very powerful, and do more than advise. In addition, line managers may be given conflicting advice by a number of different staff experts (Dalton, 1959).

The alternative to having both line and staff managers is to have integrated functional groupings. This design has been used in American military and industrial research organizations. 'Functional teams' are constructed, each team containing all the necessary expertise to tackle its task. The members may be seconded from existing departments when a special project team coexists with a traditional structure, and the membership may change as the task moves to different stages (Bass, 1965). It is, however, necessary for staff to keep in touch with their fellow experts as well.

Management and unions. As the result of historical developments during the last hundred years, the interests of workers are now represented primarily through their trade unions. The balance between conflict and collaboration may take various forms – armed truce, working harmony and collaborative effort (Stagner, 1956), depending on numerous factors, economic, political and personal. This situation has a number of interesting social psychological features. The conflict is partly due to different ways of seeing and interpreting the working situation: in one study it was found that 14 per cent of union members and 54 per cent of managers thought that labour trouble was mainly caused by outside union organizers (Bass, 1965, p. 347). The two sides also differ in the extent to which they see managers and union officials as honest, fair, trustworthy, cooperative, etc. (Haire, 1955). While there may be genuine grounds for grievance, workers are often discontented for a variety of reasons which are not understood, and tend to respond in a standard, ritualized way by demanding higher wages.

The main strategy used by unions is the exercise of collective bargaining – management can afford to lose one discontented worker, but cannot replace all of them. The grievances of individuals are taken up by union officials; stronger strategies are go-slows and strikes; it is very rare for managers or machines to be attacked. Management can replace workers by automation, promote union leaders into management, or run organizations in a way that produces greater satisfaction. Negotiation between management and unions has become smoother and more professional. In one British study it was found that 98 per cent of managements exchanged statistical information with unions (National Institute of Industrial Psychology [N.I.I.P.], 1952); more use is made of professional mediators and arbitrators; disputes are often resolved constructively, as in productivity bargaining.

Despite such improvements, however, there is still a very large number of strikes, and there is often considerable suspicion, misunderstanding or hostility between 'management' and 'labour'. The system of trade union representation and bargaining itself perpetuates the idea that there are 'two sides' in industry – despite the fact that managers are usually salaried employees themselves, and the fact that a large proportion of employees occupy intermediate positions. The system also emphasizes the conflict of interests between management and labour, rather than the area of common interests – both sides want to keep the firm in business, and therefore to compete successfully with other firms, both sides want to keep efficient workers with the firm. For these reasons some social scientists think that it would be better if workers could participate more directly in decisions in the firm, in some form of 'industrial democracy'; this will be discussed below. The unions can play a very active role in industrial democracy (as in Western Germany), or a rather minor one (as in Yugoslavia).

In any case the position of the unions is far from satisfactory. A very small proportion of members are actively interested and few attend meetings; they and the officials carry a great deal of power; votes are usually quite unrepresentative; since membership is voluntary, to keep their members the leaders must keep satisfying their needs, which leads to constant warfare with management; the higher leaders are often quite out of touch with the ordinary members (Allen, 1954); and it has proved impossible to control small numbers of fanatical individuals, often communists, responsible for unofficial strikes.

THE OPTIMUM DESIGN OF WORKING ORGANIZATIONS

From research discussed above we can outline the kind of working organization that will be most effective and produce most satisfaction among its members.

Size. Since the Industrial Revolution there has been a continuous increase in the size of working organizations – for technological reasons, and to take advantage of other economies of scale. By size one usually means the number of people working at a particular location, though it may be necessary to take account of several plants together if there is centralized administration. It has repeatedly been found that in smaller units job satisfaction is greater, absenteeism, labour turnover, accidents, and labour disputes are less, in many cases by a large amount (Revans, 1958). For example, the Acton Society Trust (1953) found that the rate of absenteeism correlated ·67 with size of coal mine and ·60 with supervisory span of control; rather smaller correlations were found for shops and factories. The accident rate in coal mines was nearly twice as high in the larger mines as in the smaller ones (Figure 14).

However, no consistent relationship has been found with productivity; in some studies a curvilinear relationship has been found, with units of 1,500–2,000 doing best. Size can be

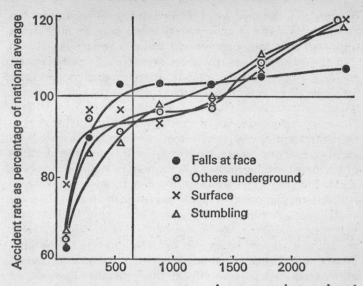

Figure 14. Accidents and size of mine (from Acton Society Trust, 1953).

kept down by decentralization; this is easier when sub-units are independent (e.g. shops), or can be given specific programmes of work to do. Decentralization reduces communication problems, makes participation in decisions easier, and increases job satisfaction. Weiss (1957) compared centralized and decentralized organizations and found that there was a trend towards less absenteeism, turnover, etc. in the decentralized concern. On the other hand, there are limits to decentralization – depending on the scale of technology, and the degree of interdependence of the separate units. Retail stores are a good example of an industry where decentralization works well.

Shape. Organizations can be 'tall', with a small span of control and a lot of levels in the hierarchy, or 'flat'. This is of interest both because different theories have favoured each variety, and because there have been a number of careful studies comparing organizations in this respect. In a number of American studies of managers and research workers it has been found that for organizations under 5,000 *only*, there was greater satisfaction in flatter organizations. In larger organizations there is some evidence that taller ones are both more productive and more satisfying (Porter and Lawler, 1965).

Democratic–Authoritarian. One of the most important dimensions of organizations is the extent to which authority is delegated and subordinates consulted. Most working organizations in the past have been highly authoritarian – power has been wielded by leaders without consultation, orders given without explanation, and coercive methods used without regard for the welfare of subordinates. In some cases these leaders were benevolent despots, wielding power autonomously, but with regard for what were believed to be the interests of the workers. We showed in Chapter 7 that democratic and persuasive supervisory skills have been found extremely effective in a number of different cultures. Several writers have advocated 'organic' structures in which communication is more open, members contribute on the basis of their knowledge rather than their rank, and status differences are minimized. Burns and Stalker (1961) suggest that this kind of structure is needed in times of rapid technological change. More use is made of informal links in organic structures, but there has to be a clear formal structure as well if anarchy is not to develop.

Formal participation in decisions. It is fairly common to use committees to improve decision-taking, and also to involve more junior personnel in management decisions. In most organizations such participation goes down as far as junior management, but no further. Job satisfaction and commitment to an organization are much greater in the more senior ranks; discontent and alienation are found more at the bottom. This is partly due to the greater rewards and autonomy at the top, but also partly because of greater participation in decisions. We shall see that experiments with 'industrial democracy' in a number of different countries appear to have been successful.

When all members of an organization can participate in management via their elected representatives, it appears to generate a spirit of cooperation, produce more suggestions, and an increase in output; at the same time workers feel less alienated, and strikes are reduced (see p. 203 f.).

The detailed design of working organizations. The detailed organization has still to be constructed for dealing with problems of coordination between different departments, information flow, control of cycles of operation, and introducing innovation. In practice the chart is designed by managers in the light of their experience, and modifications are made if things do not work smoothly. Industrial consultants give advice on the basis of *their* experience – we described an example of this earlier (p. 49). Consultants may also formulate general principles, or models, about how organizations work. Miller and Rice (1967) offer a model of organizations based on a flow diagram and general systems theory. While suggestions for organization charts follow from the model, no data is presented to show that they work any better than other designs. A number of American organization experts have proposed a logical approach to organization design, based on planning the flow of information and providing corrective feedback where necessary. It is possible to build computer models to design complex organizations in this way (Haberstroh, 1965). Again no data is presented to show that the designs work. These models have been criticized as being too rational and paying too little regard to the motivation of workers (Burns, 1966).

PRODUCING ORGANIZATIONAL CHANGE

Deciding on the best design for an organization is only the first step. There is still the problem of introducing the necessary changes. Changes in organizations cannot be brought about simply by telling people about the new arrangements. There is great resistance to change – people fear loss of income or status, or changed relationships with other people; some may choose the even greater upheaval of leaving the organization entirely – in fact labour turnover is a common result of changes. Members need to be taught and persuaded to accept the new arrangements; there are several ways of doing this.

Persuasion is usually necessary and can take place at public meetings or via public address, notices, leaflets, etc. It should be carried out by the most senior officials – who have the most power. Persuasion is easier if it can be shown that the change will bring some real advantage to the individuals concerned, such as increased pay or status. The techniques of presentation have been described earlier.

Training is usually a necessary part, especially if new social skills are needed by managers or supervisors. It is important for senior members of the organization to support the training, and it is useful if they can act as trainers. (The different methods of training were described earlier.)

Group methods. Changes can be introduced to a group by discussing them with the group, persuading the group of the advantages of the new scheme, working out with it acceptable ways of implementing them, and bringing the group to make a decision to accept the changes (p. 149f.).

Blake's strategy. Blake and Mouton (1965) have reported a scheme for changing the pattern of relationships (not the organizational chart) within an organization. There are six stages: group laboratory sessions are used to demonstrate interpersonal phenomena and skills, such as the use of power in supervision and ways of dealing with conflicting ideas about how work should be done; trainees are helped to analyse the working of their own work teams; lateral links between colleagues are strengthened; diagonal slice groups discuss new organizational goals; help is given with the detailed implementation of the changes; and there is consideration of further areas where changes are needed. This approach in a firm of 4,000 employees, including 800 managerial and technical staff, over a five-month period, produced increases in productivity and profits, together with better ratings by subordinates of managers' performance. There also appeared to be improvements in supervisory skills and managers' relations with subordinates.

Mann's strategy. Mann (1957) has developed a combination of group discussion and feedback from social surveys of an organization. Often when consultants present such survey material, the data are quietly filed and no action is taken. According to Mann's system, feedback sessions are arranged in which the managers of each section discuss the results, with a view to doing something about them. Each group discusses the problem at its own level and receives reports of the discussion of more detailed problems at the next level below. Mann has found that this method leads to changes in employee attitudes and in supervisory behaviour.

The follow-up studies of these more complex ways of producing change have not been sufficiently rigorous to provide conclusive evidence, but certain conclusions can be suggested: simply announcing changes, or giving lectures, is not enough; persuasion and active involvement of the groups concerned in the change is more effective; training may be needed in specific social skills, together with changes in the selection procedure.

APPENDIX A: INDUSTRIAL DEMOCRACY

One of the main sources of discontent in traditional industry is the feeling, on the part of the majority of those at lower levels, that they are not consulted, and have no say in what happens. As we have seen, upward communication is often very difficult. This leads to a feeling of alienation in which many workers feel that they do not belong properly, and are not interested in productivity or other organizational goals. We have seen that styles of supervision that encourage participation in decisions lead both to higher output and to greater job satisfaction (p. 148f.). We have also seen from studies of decision-making groups that groups make better decisions than individuals (p. 130f.), *and* produce greater commitment to the decision taken.

Industrial democracy consists of the creation of formal channels for participation or consultation by a system of committees and elected representatives. This can be a supplement to normal trade union negotiation, can be integrated with it, or can be a substitute for it. There are different degrees of participation in decision-making by workers, from being able to make suggestions, to being consulted (but their decisions not being binding on management), to the right of veto, the right of joint decision, to overall control (Blumberg, 1968). Employees may participate in decisions on very trivial issues, or in more important matters to do with the speed and method of working, pay and promotion, or wider matters. There are also several different ways of representing employees. One, direct representation on the board of directors, as in Yugoslav factories, or on an equivalent high-level committee, as in West German industry. Two, joint committees representing different levels of employees, as in British joint consultation, and the American Scanlon plan.

We shall discuss the Yugoslav and kibbutz versions of industrial democracy in Appendix B. Here we shall look at three examples–from Britain, Western Germany and the U.S.A.

The British system of joint consultation involves setting up joint committees of representatives of management and of other groups in the organization to discuss a wide range of problems connected with running the enterprise. There may be a number of such committees at different levels of the organization – one dealing with the affairs of the whole concern, others dealing with divisions within it. These committees may have decision-making powers, but they are more often advisory. The members are elected and are expected to represent the interests of their group rather than act with delegated powers (N.I.I.P., 1952).

Joint consultation was set up in many industries in Britain

during the Second World War, especially in armaments factories, to obtain greater cooperation from workers. After the war many firms abandoned it, but it was built into the organizational structure of the nationalized industries, on the theory that joint consultation would produce a cooperative industrial society, while collective bargaining was appropriate to areas of conflict, e.g. wages. Since the war there has been a gradual decline in the use of joint consultation by private industry, and it has come to be seen as a minor tool of management.

There have been a number of studies of the success of joint consultation, in particular a survey by the National Institute of Industrial Psychology (1952) of 545 firms which used it. This survey found that most firms had certain 'problems', e.g. absenteeism, promotion prospects, canteen, safety and accidents; nearly all the firms surveyed discussed these matters during joint consultations; an index of the extent to which joint consultation had contributed to the solution of these problems was worked out – averaging about 50 per cent. Attitudes to joint consultation were also studied: the most senior people in firms supported it most, workers and foremen least, while 10 per cent of foremen resented it – their power was weakened since their subordinates had access to the joint committee. Jaques (1951) describes the reorganization of a joint consultation scheme that was not working very well. The main points of the revised scheme were: (1) all five levels in the hierarchy were represented, not just the top and the bottom; (2) the joint committees were given power to take real decisions, instead of just being advisory; and (3) the shop-stewards were integrated into the scheme by a number of them becoming representatives.

While it is clear that joint consultation is not wholly successful and not wholly accepted, it is hard to agree with Clegg's conclusion that 'joint consultation can be written off as an effective instrument of industrial democracy' (1960). The N.I.I.P. study shows that joint consultation is effective when the conditions are right, and the Jaques study underlines some of those conditions.

Codetermination (Western Germany). The main feature of this system is the establishment of supervisory boards, which are rather like boards of directors and meet monthly; five of the eleven members are elected representatives of the workers in the coal and steel industries, one third in the case of all other industries. Three of the labour representatives are nominated by the unions. These boards are different from the British joint consultative committees in that they take final decisions on all matters. There is also a labour director who is nominated by the union, though paid by the firm, who is one of the three members of the management board. This board consists of three directors who run the firm – the technical, commercial and labour directors. They meet weekly, and they carry out the policy decided by the supervisory board (Schuchman, 1957).

There is a long history of this kind of management–worker cooperation in Germany; the present system dates from 1947 when the system for the coal and steel industry was established by law under the Allied Control Commission; in 1952 a slightly different law was passed for the other industries. This system has been in operation throughout West German industry ever since.

It might be expected that this system would undermine the unions. However the unions have been strongly in favour of codetermination and believe that it is important for them to penetrate into and participate in management. It was found that 63 out of 252 labour representatives on supervisory boards were union officials, that unions were mainly responsible for choosing labour directors, and that union independence has not been weakened (Blumberg, 1968).

It is difficult to assess the success of codetermination in Germany since it has been adopted by entire industries at the same time, and other changes have taken place during the same period. In the first place it seems to have worked smoothly: the labour members have acted responsibly, with due regard for organizational goals; the work of the supervisory boards has been different from management–trade union negotiations in that a wider range of issues has been discussed. Nevertheless there have been conflicts of interests on some matters, which have had to be negotiated in the usual way. The labour directors have been able to improve personnel management and to break down some of the previous authoritarian relationships with workers (Clegg, 1960). Surveys have found that most workers are in favour of codetermination, though many of them know little about it. The number of days lost through strikes has been less than before the war, particularly in the coal and steel industries, where codetermination was applied first. It is generally believed that the long period of industrial peace during a period of rapid technological change, and the great increases in productivity, are partly due to codetermination.

There have been some difficulties. The labour director and other labour representatives, although partly or wholly appointed by the unions, have sometimes been regarded with suspicion by workers and unions: they draw large salaries, they have managerial responsibilities, and are suspected of having gone over to the other side. Some employers have also managed to outwit the labour representatives by forming sub-committees, on which labour is not properly represented. However, the general experience has been that the power of management, unions and shareholders has not been much encroached upon, and decisions have been arrived at which are acceptable to all parties.

The Scanlon plan (*U.S.A.*). This scheme has two main components. First, departmental production committees are set up consisting of elected worker representatives and a member appointed by management, usually the supervisor. There is also a company-wide committee with representatives from both sides. The committees meet at least once a month and discuss suggestions for improving working methods and increasing efficiency. They are given considerable power of decision-taking, though a limit is placed on their expenditure. Second, the committees work out a 'formula' according to which a proportion of the savings made in labour costs is paid to workers as a bonus, over and above the rates set by collective bargaining. Usually 75 per cent of savings is paid as bonus. The firm makes a small profit on labour costs and better use is made of the capital assets.

The Scanlon plan was put forward shortly after the war (Scanlon, 1948), and has been applied in a number of American companies since then. However, it has not been as widely used as the British and German schemes discussed, and it has often been used in firms that were in difficulties.

Again it is difficult to assess how successful this system has been. It is found that workers are given much more information about production costs, competition, etc. They also have more suggestions to make. It seems likely that workers become more concerned with efficiency, and internalize the goals of the firm. Katz and Kahn (1966) conclude that

the Scanlon plan appears as a creative solution to many of the typical problems of large organizations. It adds strong positive factors to the usual army of 'motivators', and it adds no penalties. There is a formal enlistment of the peer group via the representative committee structure, and such groups are strengthened through the close linkage of reward to group and super-group contributions to system efficiency. The job of the individual worker is enlarged and enhanced by the recognition and encouragement of innovative contributions, and the model of leadership which is called for comes much closer to the values of democratic practice as they exist in our culture and institutions outside industry.

Most of the case studies reported, though not all, show increases in productivity per unit of labour of the order of 25 per cent with corresponding bonus payments (Lesieur, 1958). The plan appears to have worked best in rather small firms, of a few hundred workers.

Supervisors, who are no longer in complete control of their departments, have put up some resistance. It needs the enthusiastic support of management, and action must be taken on suggestions that are made at the committees. Local unions have been happy with the scheme, but the central offices of unions have felt that the local unions become too identified with management. The scheme does not, of course, replace collective bargaining, but is supplementary to it.

Experiments in participation. There have been a number of American experiments in which participation in decision-making has been introduced (for reviews of the literature see Blumberg, 1968; Lowin, 1968). We will describe some of the most interesting studies briefly.

In a pyjama factory there was an increase of 14 per cent in output when participation was introduced in connection with production changes – compared with a drop of 17 per cent in control groups. There was also an increase of 18 per cent in a later replication. No workers left from the experimental groups during the experiment compared with 17 per cent from the control groups. Even better results were obtained with groups of workers who participated fully in decisions rather than through their representatives (Coch and French, 1948). Fleishman (1965) carried out a similar study, comparing workers who participated directly in decisions and others who did so via elected representatives. In this experiment, however, equally favourable results were obtained in both cases, in that the usual drop in productivity following change of product did not take place.

A field experiment was carried out in which the level of decision-making in a large insurance company was changed: in two sections worker participation was increased, in two sections it was reduced. Productivity increased in all sections – probably a Hawthorne effect; satisfaction increased under participation and decreased in the no-delegation sections (Morse and Ricmer, 1956). A number of technical difficulties arise with these and other field experiments, e.g. the possibility of Hawthorne effects; these experiments are extremely difficult to do, and it is not possible to control all the variables. However, there are a considerable number of such studies, some with larger increases of productivity, or drops in labour turnover (250 to 5 per cent in one case), and the overall body of data is impressive.

The success of industrial democracy. We can consider the three schemes just discussed, the Yugoslav and Israeli experience to be described in Appendix B and the results of the American field experiments. Increases in production were found in the field experiments; they were also found in Germany, Yugoslavia, Israel and in some applications of the Scanlon plan, but there were other changes as well in these cases.

A fall in strikes was found in Germany, very low absenteeism in the kibbutz, and decreases of turnover in the field experiments. Changes in worker attitudes and job satisfaction were found in the field experiments; no survey data is available from the national schemes, but it is widely reported that there has been an increased spirit of cooperation, more team-work, less hostility between groups and more suggestions.

Some research has been carried out into how representatives and committees have actually functioned. Members of committees experience conflict – between being representatives of workers and running the affairs of the firm. There can be a real conflict of interest between workers' representatives and management over wages, for example. However, wider issues are discussed than those involved in usual trade union bargaining, especially in the personnel field. There is little discussion of production, finance and sales, though here there may be no conflict of interest and representatives may take a company point of view. The managers, who know most about these things, still manage. Management do not feel that their power has been much diminished, and representatives do not discuss committee decisions with their often apathetic colleagues, who regard the committees as places for airing minor grievances. The actual spread of power in many schemes has therefore been rather small (Emery and Thorsrud, 1969).

Studies of these schemes (N.I.I.P., 1952; Emery and Thorsrud, op. cit.) suggest some of the conditions under which participation is successful.

Management should be in favour of the scheme, take it seriously, see that issues are properly discussed on the committees, and should not just rush through their carefully prepared plans. The committees are taken more seriously by management and workers if they have real power and are more than advisory bodies – as they have been in most of the British schemes. It is interesting that in two of the most successful schemes – the Yugoslav one and the Scanlon plan – the committees decide the level of bonus payment. All levels in the hierarchy should be represented, not just the top and the bottom. Supervisors need to be of a higher calibre – since they are likely to be short-circuited by complaints to committees. Their formal power is slightly reduced, and they need additional skills of persuasion and consideration. Representatives should sit on committees which deal with matters that they are able and willing to discuss. A number of studies have found that employees are keener to participate in decisions about their own departments than about company affairs (Hespe and Little, 1971). Where there is a strong trade union it should be closely involved, for example by shop-stewards serving as representatives. Otherwise the new committee structure can act as a substitute for the unions, as in Yugoslavia.

APPENDIX B: WORK IN ISRAEL, YUGOSLAVIA AND JAPAN

WE traced earlier the history of work as it has developed in the West, and in most of the book we have been dealing with research on work as it is known today in Britain, the U.S.A. and western Europe. We are now going to make a short digression to consider three quite different, and apparently very successful, ways of arranging work. It is possible that valuable lessons can be learned from these examples, but we must remember that they are each placed in a distinctive cultural and ideological setting.

ISRAEL

There are several kinds of working organization in Israel, but the one of greatest interest for our purposes is the kibbutz. The first kibbutz was founded in 1909 and many more have grown up since. Kibbutzim vary in size from 100 to 1,000, being typically about 350; 3 per cent of the population now belong to them, though a larger number belong to the Moshavim – farmers' cooperatives – which are somewhat similar.

The kibbutz is based on common ownership of property, so that the residential community is also a working unit with no differences of wealth or status. Originally they were collective farming communities, and they farmed virgin soil with inexperienced workers, little capital, and problems of military security. The early kibbutzniks were very poor, lived in tents, and worked very long hours. Now they are much more prosperous and live in comfortable apartments in well built villages, and have the latest agricultural machinery. For some time they have had small workshops to serve the farms, but during the last fifteen years they have, for economic reasons, established a large number of small factories, partly to provide employment for older members and new immigrants. Most of the factories now have 50–100 workers. In addition to kibbutz members there are paid workers – taken on partly because of the need for particular skills and partly because of government pressure to employ new immigrants.

There are no incentives in the usual sense. Hired workers are paid, but kibbutz members, who work longer hours and have shorter holidays, are not. They work for the community as a whole, and in turn their needs are met on equal terms with everyone else's, depending on the prosperity of the kibbutz. The productivity per work day of each section is calculated in order to check the efficiency of different work groups. There is no desire for promotion, and little advantage in becoming an official, which is only temporary in any case. According to reports of observers, the majority of members appear to be prepared to work hard on this basis, and many will volunteer for extra work after nine or more hours of work. This motivation is partly sustained by group pressures and the influence of informal leaders. How is such commitment to organizational goals achieved? It has been shown that successful American utopian communities differed from unsuccessful ones in their use of a number of 'commitment mechanisms' such as sacrifice, investments (so that it would be costly to leave), mortification (i.e. reduction of individual identity), and surrender of decision-making to the social system (Kanter, 1968). Clearly the kibbutz differs from orthodox industry in possessing several of these commitment mechanisms.

The most important group is the kibbutz as a whole. This is rather a large group and there are various sub-groups – based on the different nationalities present, and the different work done. However, all members feel that they are members of the kibbutz as a whole and that they own it. All goods are shared equally between members, and they know that their prosperity depends on that of the group. There are strong social pressures to behave in the accepted manner, and anyone who does not work hard enough, for example, is the object of intense disapproval, and is ultimately forced to leave the community.

The only official supervisors are the work coordinators, who allocate jobs, and the production manager. However, they have no official powers of reward and punishment, and have to rely on persuasion and social skill. In addition to formal leaders, informal leaders emerge, and play an important role. Other supervision, for example of the hired hands, is performed by working kibbutzniks. No special importance is attached to supervision, and it is not carried out very vigorously. It is assumed that people will work without supervision.

A kibbutz is governed by the weekly meeting of all the members, although in practice only 25–75 per cent of them attend. The democratic process has been weakened with increasing size, and the increasing power of the committees and secretariat. There are elected committees to deal with the coordination of work, production, education, leisure and culture, etc., each with one of the elected secretariat as chairman. As many as 50 per cent of kibbutzniks may serve on one committee or other. Final authority resides in the assembly of all the members of each kibbutz or factory.

A number of officials are elected by the weekly meeting for one-year periods. In addition to the work coordinators and the production manager, there are various secretaries, each helped by a committee. A factory is run by a team of three or four managers, appointed by the weekly meeting, who are in charge of production, sales, accounts, etc.; they must consult the assembly of workers and for important decisions must consult the weekly meeting as well. There is no great enthusiasm to become an official since this involves extra work, being away from home and the difficulties of organizing others, while there is no pay and little status attached to the job. In practice, the officials have to see a lot of each other and of officials elsewhere, so that a slightly superior group is formed of those who are concerned with administrative matters. In one kibbutz the offices rotated between 12 of the 140 members (Zweig, 1959). No permanent status is given to people with special qualifications, and it is believed that skilled manual work is the highest form of work.

Economically the kibbutzim have been very successful; as we have seen, they have become very prosperous compared with the early days of extreme poverty. They have installed the latest agricultural machinery and set up small modern factories. Factory work is not very popular, and intrinsic satisfaction here and on the farms is sometimes low. On the other hand, there is little absenteeism and few leave the kibbutz – about 5–6 per cent per year, mostly to get more skilled jobs elsewhere. Work is satisfying in other ways, it has emotional overtones devised from its direct contribution to the community, and the sense of working as part of a cohesive group (Zweig, 1959; Weingarten, 1962; Friedmann, 1965).

YUGOSLAVIA

Most industrial development in Yugoslavia has taken place since 1945, when a quite distinctive form of social organization was devised by the new communist government.

Yugoslav factories are owned by the state and controlled by their workers – following the ideas of Robert Owen, guild socialism, G. D. H. Cole and others. Although the state is not democratic, the factories are – the reverse of the situation in other advanced countries. Despite a difficult political climate, powerful unions and illiterate workers, the Yugoslav system has worked well during a period of rapid technological change, and has gradually changed in the direction of becoming more democratic and independent of control by the government or the unions.

Payment does not depend on individual efforts, but on the productivity of departments and of the whole factory. There are, however, differences in the rates paid to individuals according to their level of skill and responsibility. There is thus a double incentive – group piecework based on a fairly large group, and an incentive to qualify for a higher level of skill. The distribution of payment is in the hands of the workers' council: they can pay out as much bonus over the basic rate as they like after costs and taxes have been met – this was the equivalent of two and a half months' pay in 1957.

The working group for many purposes is the factory as a whole. Considerable loyalty is generated, workers feel that the factory belongs to them, their wages depend on the productivity of the whole concern, they have a say in how it is run and individual energies appear to be directed towards organizational goals. Departments also function as working groups, especially when there is a departmental workers' council and separate accounting, so that wages depend on the productivity of the department.

The position of supervisors is weakened by the ease with which workers can complain to one of the committees about a wide range of matters, including holiday dates, jobs allocated, etc. A very large number of such appeals is made. Supervision has to be of a more persuasive kind and a lot of attention has to be paid to the wishes and welfare of workers. Supervisors are given training courses, in addition to experience of serving on committees.

The administrative structure consists of a regular administrative hierarchy, with technical staff, closely linked to a system of workers' committees. Each factory has a director who is in charge, though his power is somewhat limited by the workers' committees, and he is answerable to the government as well. He is appointed for a period of four years by a committee of representatives of the workers' council and other local organizations. He is paid about five times as much as unskilled workers. Each department of 150 men has a manager and smaller units a supervisor; they are appointed by the workers' council, their jobs are openly competed for, and they are paid according to their position in the hierarchy. There are technical staff with degrees or other qualifications such as engineers, chemists, research workers, accountants, sales and financial experts. Workers are graded according to skill, decided by vocational examinations. Although the hierarchy of authority is a conventional one, with differentials of power and pay, it differs from the British and American system: managers and workers are not divided into different castes; status differences between them are reduced; through their experience on committees workers get experience of management problems, and become well informed about the issues facing the firm; there is little hostility to management; workers can be promoted if they pass the relevant exams and are approved by the appropriate committee.

Every factory has an elaborate system of committees so that workers are represented in several ways. The workers' council has 15–120 members, according to the size of the factory, typically 20–22, representing different sections and levels of the organization; it meets about once a month to take decisions on all aspects of policy. Although members of the council are elected, the nominations until recently were made by the union; since 1964, however, the nominating procedure has been liberalized and the power of the unions reduced. The director and his staff are active and influential members of the council, and can usually get their ideas accepted, especially on technical matters. The management board consists of between five and eleven members who are appointed by the workers' council and are usually members of it, and the director. It carries out the policy made by the council, and usually meets weekly. Workers' councils are formed at departmental level, especially in large or geographically dispersed firms. Where possible accounts are decentralized, so that departments are financially autonomous. There are more specialized committees dealing with finance, sales, and other such areas. The members of these committees receive no extra pay, often meet after hours, and have no individual power, status or privileges. Turnover of membership is rapid, and members are often removed on the initiative of one group or another, for laxity or other minor offences. However, during the 1950s half to one third of all workers served on committees, 75 per cent being manual workers. Those most in evidence were male skilled workers and members of the communist party (Blumberg, 1968). Experience of committee work is regarded as a form of training and as a vehicle for promotion. The committees are also regarded as a channel of information for management to find out the views of workers, and in addition for workers to learn about the problems facing management. The committees work closely together with management and exercise considerable influence over matters of wages and working conditions, though less on more technical aspects of production (Kolaja, 1965).

The unions are less powerful than before but still exert a certain amount of power, for example influencing the selection of committee members. Their role now is more one of helping individuals with grievances or problems. The union is also dependent on the workers' council for funds. The internal representation system has made the unions largely superfluous, and strikes have vanished.

Productivity has been rising at about 7 per cent per year, wages at 10 per cent per year during recent years (Blumberg, op. cit.). There has been very little resistance to change during this period of rapid technological change. Communications within firms have been greatly improved, barriers and hostilities between groups have largely disappeared, and there is evidence of increased loyalty and commitment to firms. The workers' committees have worked well, and members have acted responsibly on them.

JAPAN

The Japanese industrial revolution started between 1929 and 1937 (when the war with China started), and began again after 1950. Japan has few raw materials, and her economic growth has been achieved by the manufacturing and processing of raw materials, as in the steel industry. The first phase of economic growth was mainly associated with a small number of large family firms, or *zaibatsu*. These firms were each owned by a family, or group of families, which demanded absolute loyalty, and which were feudal; each had a monopoly position through controlling a whole group of firms. A number of observers have said that industrialization was made easier through the adoption of traditional forms of social organization, such as the feudal hierarchy (Abegglen, 1958); others have argued that traditional structures have been harmful through delaying the introduction of democratic management techniques and other innovations (Odaka, 1963).

There was little economic growth from 1945 to 1950: much of industry was in ruins, there were large reparations to be made, and the Allied occupation suppressed the *zaibatsu* as being illiberal and monopolistic. After 1950 the situation changed: it was accepted that further reparations were impossible, the Americans paid large sums on account of bases connected with the Korean war, and there was a high rate of savings and investment in imported technology. Pressure on the *zaibatsu* was eased, and to a large extent these monopolistic family groupings of firms were re-formed (Allen, 1965). Between 1953 and 1961 there was an increase in the G.N.P. of 217 per cent.

Japanese success in the export market, mainly to the U.S.A., has been largely due to low wages keeping prices down. The large increase in output was partly due to the very undeveloped state of Japanese industry at the end of the war (*Economist*, 1963). Until about 1955 there was a relatively low rate of mechanization, the aim of management being to make use of the large labour force already on the payroll. It was estimated in 1958 that Japanese factories were running at about 20 per cent of the output per man of equivalent American firms (Abegglen, op. cit.). Since 1955 there has been a great deal of capital investment in new equipment in order to increase the productivity for the export market of the labour force; it is now reported that there is actually a labour shortage, which is an additional reason for mechanization (*The Times*, 1969).

The large firms offer larger salaries, excellent welfare facilities, and social prestige, so that employment is keenly sought. The educational system has been changed since the war and it now provides the normal means of job selection. Depending on their final examination results, people enter more or less desirable firms and at different levels. A person with middle school education will enter a firm as a manual worker, and cannot rise above charge-hand; a graduate enters as an assistant manager and is slowly promoted up the hierarchy. A social survey, however, found that 91 per cent of respondents did *not* think that education should determine seniority in this way (Whitehill and Takezawa, 1961). Once a person has joined a firm he enters into a long-term commitment. The extent of this commitment has probably been exaggerated by some writers; in fact there is a certain amount of labour turnover, and the majority of workers accept that it may be necessary to discharge unsuitable workers after a definite period has been given for improvement, or that they should be kept on until they can find another job (Whitehill and Takezawa, op. cit.).

Wages depend primarily on age, length of service, education and rank in the hierarchy. Managers are paid only about 50 per cent more than manual workers. In addition to their pay, employees get free meals, low rent housing, cheap medical services, schools for children, a pension and other welfare facilities. Very little use is made of wage incentives. A monthly productivity allowance is paid, and also a twice-yearly bonus, based on the firm's efficiency, but these are fairly stable parts of the total wage, and it is doubtful whether they have any incentive effect. There is also some variation in wages based on estimates of individual efficiency, but this forms a very small part of wages (Abegglen, op. cit.).

Promotion in the management hierarchy depends mainly on initial education, the point of entry into the firm, and length of service. Rank is closely tied to age, and a manager should not supervise an older person (apart from manual workers). However, recognition can be given to effective managers by promoting them to a deputy or supernumerary post: these do not carry much more salary, but do give more status. Incompetent managers may find that an additional person has been appointed to the same position, or that there are other managers with overlapping authority doing his job.

The traditional form of social organization in Japan is one of close interdependence in family groups. This structure is transferred to the work situation, so that work groups are very close-knit. Groups usually have about ten members, under the equivalent of a charge-hand, who is really one of the group and has little supervisory authority. The social atmosphere has been compared to that of a hearty public school (*Economist*, 1963). There is no feeling of inferiority among manual workers despite the hierarchy of which they form the lowest rank. Instead, they have a feeling of sharing in the collective success of the firm. A very strong feeling of identification is created, since many employees spend their whole careers with the firm and live in company houses. In some firms the day is started by singing the company hymn. Whitehill and Takezawa (op. cit.) found that 32 per cent of their sample thought of their company as 'very much like a big family to which he may belong until retirement' and a further 32 per cent as 'a part of his life at least equal in importance to his personal life'. The majority welcomed company involvement in their private lives in respect of providing housing and other benefits, and in arranging outings, but did not like company involvement in religion or marriage – apart from offering advice.

There are several traditional forms of relationship with older persons in Japan. The *uyabum-koyun* relationship is a formal relation with a kind of foster parent in which the older person shows both love and protection, but also harsh authoritarian rule; the junior person shows unquestioning obedience, dependence and loyalty (Bennett and Ishino, 1963). This relationship plays a central role in Japanese society and is found to carry over to relationships with supervisors in small firms. In larger firms the rather less formal, though still paternal, relationships of the *batsu* or clique are found, in apprenticeships, between workers and foremen, and in groups of managers from the same university (Abegglen, op. cit.). In addition to the charge-hands referred to above, there are foremen who work in offices and look after about three charge-hands and their sections. They have little responsibility and do not participate in managerial decision-taking. They are much concerned with the welfare of their men, including their family affairs. No formal training is given to supervisors, who pick up their skills on the job.

The management structure is very hierarchical – there are typically six levels with a span of control of three at each level and great differences of status between levels. Above the foremen come section heads, divisional managers and the board of directors. The highest level consists of members of the family who own and control the firm, and the next level consists of senior managers who may be literally adopted by that family and are expected to show a high degree of loyalty to it (Harbison, 1959). There are also many assistant managers at each level, with considerable overlapping of authority so that there is little individual responsibility. The large number of managers is partly the result of the policy of promotion by seniority and the practice of not discharging anyone.

Paternalistic relationships extend up the management hierarchy. The pattern varies from primarily benevolent, patriarchal and familial relationships to more despotic, authoritarian and exploiting ones. There has been little delegation, decentralization or industrial democracy, though this is now changing. Trade unions have grown in power recently; they negotiate with those managers in a firm who specialize in industrial relations. This has led to a new dependent relationship with these managers, who are given loyalty in exchange for protection (Levine, 1958). There is some interest in participation in decisions; consultative supervision is disliked, but workers like their views to be represented by third parties – foremen or union representatives (Whitehill and Takezawa op. cit.). There is probably a general change of attitude to authority among the young in Japan, as is shown by recent student disturbances.

In a recent study Frager (1970) found that Japanese students conformed less than American students in experimental group situations, and showed a large amount of anti-conformity (actual moving away from the norm); anti-conformity was most common among male students with high scores on a test for alienation.

Economically these Japanese firms have been very successful – in spite of a greater concern with the welfare of employees than with production, in spite of a system of promotion by seniority rather than competence, and in spite of very little competition between firms. As far as can be judged, the workers are very happy in their work. There are some points of strain in the system – the excessive competition to enter these firms, the increasing power of the trade unions, and increasing demands for participation and a less rigid social structure, but the authoritarian structure has worked remarkably well so far, probably because it has fitted traditional culture and socialization, and provided such a high level of security and other rewards. Japanese managers are well aware of the management practices used in Western countries, but have been very slow in introducing these techniques.

Although these three kinds of industrial organizations are set in different cultures to ours, I believe that we can learn important lessons from each of them. From the kibbutz industries we see that when people are deeply committed to the community work takes on a new meaning, and they will work hard for low wages, including unpaid overtime. Under these conditions it is not necessary to pay the managers any more than the workers.

From the Yugoslavian experience we see how industrial democracy is possible and apparently successful, even in a non-democratic country, and with a relatively uneducated and unskilled labour force.

From Japan we learn that industry can be extremely profitable when one of the main goals is the welfare and security of the employees, even though money appears to be wasted on redundant personnel.

CHAPTER 9

JOB SATISFACTION

The measurement of job attitudes – the causes of job satis-faction – the relation between job satisfaction, productivity, absenteeism and labour turnover – Appendix A: Herz-berg's two-factor theory – Appendix B: mental health and work.

THE MEASUREMENT OF JOB ATTITUDES

THE primary goal of work is presumably production. How-ever, since people spend eight or more hours a day working, it is also important that they should enjoy their work. Further-more, if workers are discontented there is an overall decline in their effectiveness as workers.

The easiest way to find out how much a person enjoys his work is to ask him. A number of the early surveys were carried out by Hoppock (1935) who used questions like 'choose one of the following statements which best tells how well you like your job' (seven alternative answers from 'I love it' to 'I hate it'). Later studies used a larger number of questions, as many as 150 in one case, inquiring about many different aspects of the job. A number of statistical analyses have been carried out, and the following are the areas of satisfaction which have appeared most commonly:

Satisfaction with company and management.
Satisfaction with supervision.
Satisfaction with co-workers.
Satisfaction with financial rewards.
Satisfaction with working conditions.
Satisfaction with job content.
Satisfaction with promotional opportunities and status.

In most recent studies Likert-type scales have been used. These consist of a series of questions, with five alternative

responses. For example, to measure satisfaction with co-workers, there might be eight items, of which one was:
'In your department is there . . .?
a. A very great deal of friction
b. Quite a bit of friction
c. Some friction
d. Little friction
e. Almost no friction.'

When it is said that there is a factor of satisfaction with co-workers this means that a number of questions about co-workers are found to correlate highly together. An average of the replies to these questions gives an individual's degree of satisfaction with his co-workers; a profile can then be plotted for his satisfaction in different areas.

For administrative purposes it is very useful to know which sections of an organization are unhappy about what. To find this out a fairly lengthy questionnaire can be given, covering many detailed aspects of work and organization. Another method is to use a free response method. General Motors ran the 'My Job Contest' in which contestants wrote essays about 'Why I like my job'. Content analyses were made of the replies, and it was found that certain topics were mentioned very frequently (e.g. cafeteria, steady work), while others were mentioned more rarely, and that the topics mentioned varied greatly from one department to another (Evans and Laseau, 1950).

Despite this evidence that job satisfaction consists of a number of smaller components, several recent studies have shown that the components all correlate together, and that there is a general factor of job satisfaction, rather analogous to the general factor of intelligence. In one investigation a 76-item questionnaire with 14 sub-scales was given to 472 workers of different sorts, and a strong general factor was found which correlated 0·78 with confidence in management, 0·71 with satisfaction with personal development, 0·67 with satisfaction with supervision, etc. (Wherry, 1958). In other words, people who are satisfied with one aspect of their work tend to be similarly satisfied with other aspects.

Rather lower correlations than these have been found in other studies, for example the correlations of 0·20–0·68 found by Hulin and Smith (1967), shown in Table 7 on page 243. There is no doubt that there is a fairly strong general factor of job satisfaction, though some groups of workers are satisfied in some respects but not in others, such as workers on assembly lines who are satisfied with their pay but dislike the work itself.

Are these various measures of job satisfaction valid? Do they really measure job satisfaction? They have *internal* validity, in that the items correlate together, they have *face* validity, in that the items are all obviously about job satisfaction. There is evidence of *construct* validity, in that there is some correlation between these measures of job satisfaction, labour turnover, and absenteeism though the correlation is rarely more than 0·30 (p. 240 f.). There is usually no correlation at all between job satisfaction and output, though most organization experts believed that there would be (p. 238 f.). Workers could be biased in the way they reply to the questions. No matter how anonymous a questionnaire is said to be, they may not wholly believe this, so that replies about discontent with supervision, or satisfaction with pay, might be modified. Usually these surveys are conducted by the organization itself, so that replies are made on the assumption that the administration will read them. Perhaps the most honest replies are given at 'exit interviews' with those who are leaving, but this is of course a discontented sub-group.

Sociologists have approached the problem of satisfaction in terms of the concept of 'alienation'. Marx maintained that workers in the Industrial Revolution became alienated or estranged from their work, and from the product of their work, as a result of the division of labour and their exploitation by employers. Later sociologists have expanded the concept of alienation and four kinds are now recognized:

Powerlessness – lack of control over management policy, the conditions of employment or the immediate work process.

225

Meaninglessness – inability to see the purpose of the work done or how it fits in to the whole production process.

Isolation – not belonging to working groups or guided by their norms of work behaviour.

Self-estrangement – failure to regard the work as a central life interest or means of self-expression, experiencing a depersonalized detachment while at work (Seeman, 1959; Blauner, 1964).

The first three factors correspond to traditional aspects of job satisfaction. Powerlessness is closely related to lack of autonomy in work, and also to lack of satisfaction with supervision, and inability to participate in decisions. Meaninglessness is primarily related to the nature of the task, and to the extent to which the work of individual workers and members of groups adds up to a meaningful whole. Isolation is identical with lack of satisfaction with the group, or co-workers. Self-estrangement is a new concept. Workers may be alienated in all these ways but still be satisfied with their pay. On the other hand, there is a strong general factor of job satisfaction, and the various aspects of alienation will correlate fairly highly with this, so that it may be unnecessary to treat it as a separate feature of work attitudes.

Sociologists have found workers who are alienated but satisfied – they may suffer from a sense of meaninglessness or powerlessness, but they are contented with their pay (Goldthorpe, 1968). Such workers have not developed any intrinsic motivation for work.

THE CAUSES OF JOB SATISFACTION

It is difficult to say how many people are satisfied with their jobs. When asked Hoppock's single question, only about 13–21 per cent of people in over 1,000 separate surveys in the U.S.A. said they were dissatisfied. However this may be an underestimate of discontent, since larger numbers say that they would prefer a different job or would do something different if they could start again (Table 3). It could be argued that even if the great majority *say* they are satisfied they ought not to be, in view of the boring nature of their work, or their unpleasant working conditions. On the other hand, observers may fail to appreciate the meaning that can be injected into simple jobs, and the satisfaction that can be obtained.

There are, however, large differences between the satisfaction of people in different jobs. Table 3 shows some of the results of an American national survey of 2,460 people (Gurin, Veroff and Field, 1960).

Table 3

	Very Satisfied (%)	Satisfied (%)
Professional, technicians	42	41
Managers, proprietors	38	42
Clerical	22	39
Sales	24	44
Skilled	22	54
Semi-skilled	27	48
Unskilled	13	52
Farmers	22	58

Another survey asked people in different occupations if they would choose the same kind of work if they were beginning their career again (Table 4).

However, these results do not tell us what it is about the work of mathematicians and managers which makes it more satisfying than the work of unskilled workers of various kinds; it could be pay, status, the interest of the work, or other factors.

Investigators have tried to discover the basic causes of job satisfaction in several ways. One way is to ask people to place different factors in order of importance to them. The results of such a survey (of 3,345 male applicants to a firm) are shown in Table 5. Another approach is to find how large a correlation there is between satisfaction and a particular factor, and overall job satisfaction, which gives rather similar results.

Table 4

	(%)
Mathematicians	91
Lawyers	83
Journalists	82
Skilled printers	52
Skilled car workers	41
Skilled steel workers	41
Textile workers	31
Unskilled car workers	21
Unskilled steel workers	16

Percentage of workers who would choose the same work again (Blauner, 1960).

The precise order of these factors varies somewhat between surveys, depending on the social and economic conditions, and on how the question is asked. For example, the survey above places security higher than it appears under better economic conditions (Viteles, 1954; Tiffin and McCormick, 1966).

We shall consider the effects on job satisfaction of those aspects of work which have been found to affect it most.

Table 5

Factors	Average rank of each factor
Security	1
Promotion prospects	2
Interesting work	3
Company	4
Pay	$5\frac{1}{2}$
Co-workers	$5\frac{1}{2}$
Supervisors	7
Hours of Work	8
Working conditions	9

Rankings of the importance of different sources of job satisfaction (Jurgensen, 1948).

Intrinsic nature of the work. The interest and other features of the actual job often rank second or third in surveys like the one above. It is particularly important to men, to more educated people, and at higher levels of skill and status (Herzberg, *et al.*, 1957). Table 4 showed that 91 per cent of mathematicians but only 16 per cent of unskilled steel workers would choose the same kind of work again. The question is, which of the many differences between the work of mathematicians and unskilled steel workers is most important? Differences of pay and status will be discussed separately below; in some studies their effects have been eliminated statistically, and the effects of the work itself can be seen.

(*a*) *Variety.* There is a low level of satisfaction with very repetitive jobs. This is true of the length of the work cycle, i.e. the number of operations or the time to complete it; job enlargement results in greater satisfaction. However, the enlarged job should result in a meaningful whole being accomplished. It is also true of job variety, i.e. the variety of alternative complete jobs that are performed over a period of time; satisfaction is also increased by job rotation.

Not everyone prefers varied work; it is found that people of low intelligence prefer repetitive work – there is an optimum level of I.Q. for every kind of work.

(*b*) *Autonomy.* Control over working methods has been reduced by the introduction of standardized methods, following the application of method study. While this has often resulted in greater output, it has also reduced job satisfaction. This is partly because the standard methods do not suit everyone, partly because people like to be free to choose how they will work. Studies of assembly-line and other mechanically paced work show that control over speed of work is also an important source of satisfaction. It has been found that 92 per cent of assembly-line workers would prefer to be off the line, and their rate of labour turnover was twice as great (Walker and Guest, 1952).

Studies of manual workers who are free to choose their own

methods and pace of work, such as railway workers, lorry drivers and salesmen show that they are very satisfied. Many workers in the lower ranks of organizations have hopes of starting their own businesses, and a few try to do this. In Goldthorpe's study (1968) 56 per cent had thought of this, and 19 per cent had either tried it or made plans. This is surely evidence of a desire for autonomy.

(c) *Use of skills and abilities.* Several surveys have found that satisfied workers say that they are able to use their skills or abilities. As we pointed out earlier (p. 96f.), concern with accomplishment and self-expression appear more at higher levels of job status. Self-expression leads to satisfaction only for those who are involved with their work (Vroom, 1962).

How important is the intrinsic nature of the work as a source of job satisfaction? This factor was largely overlooked by human relations writers; on the other hand, the surveys that asked about its importance have all found it very high on the list (e.g. Herzberg *et al.*, 1959). However, a very interesting study by Turner and Lawrence (1966) has shown that there are some workers who are not made happier by having interesting work. Protestant workers from small (American) towns were more satisfied and less often absent if they had jobs which were more complex and required greater knowledge and skill. However, workers from large towns, mainly Catholics and from ethnic minority groups, preferred the simpler, more repetitive jobs. Blood and Hulin (1967) obtained very similar results – satisfaction did not correlate at all with variety and interest of work, or correlated inversely with this in large urban communities with slums, a low standard of living, and a high population density.

Hours of work. Shift work is generally disliked; in view of the increased amount being brought about by automation this is unfortunate. Some people dislike shift work much more than others; Vroom (1964) suggests that this depends on how much their leisure and family activities are disrupted by the particular hours of work, and on how much the disrupted activities are valued. It has been found that absenteeism goes up when more hours are worked per week – but this is probably in order to do shopping, etc., and partly because of the increased wages. Managers, professional people and the self-employed work extremely long hours, and we have seen that these are the people who are most satisfied with their work.

Incentive conditions. (*a*) *Pay.* Better-paid workers are more satisfied, but they also do different work, and have higher status. In several studies all other variables were held constant, and pay was found to correlate about 0·25 with satisfaction (e.g. Remitz, 1960). There is little doubt that pay that is too low, either relatively or absolutely, is a source of dissatisfaction (see Herzberg *et al.*, 1959).

Relative pay is a better predictor of job satisfaction than the absolute amount paid: in one study supervisors earning over $12,000 were more satisfied than company presidents earning under $49,000. People at work have a clear idea of what they ought to be paid, in comparison with others, and in relation to their skill, experience, etc. (Lawler and Porter, 1963). Although there is little evidence that over- or under-payment affects productivity (p. 89), it clearly affects satisfaction.

Human relations writers thought that pay was rather unimportant, despite the fact that nearly all industrial disputes are ostensibly about pay, and the enormous effect pay has on labour turnover (p. 85). Surveys show that pay is rated third to seventh (Tiffin and McCormick, 1966). Goldthorpe (1968) reports that some of his group of affluent workers were *only* concerned with pay, rather than with other aspects of the work; however, this appears from the reported results to be true of only a minority of the sample – e.g. the 18 per cent who gave the level of pay as the only reason for staying, though 67 per cent gave pay as one reason among others.

(*b*) *Occupational status.* The level of satisfaction with different jobs corresponds very closely with the social status commonly associated with those jobs (Table 3). This is true even though many white-collar workers, such as teachers, are paid less than many manual workers, and when the work is objectively dirty or unpleasant (doctors, geologists), or repetitive (royalty, diplomats), or the hours long and inconvenient (politicians, many research workers). Nevertheless many manual workers at low levels of skill, are also very satisfied – depending on other aspects of the job to be discussed later. The more senior members of working organizations have many advantages – higher status and pay, more autonomy, more interesting work, better conditions, etc. Some sociologists have expressed surprise that the lower status members are not *more* discontented, and that higher status members are not *more* contented, than they are. It has been suggested that feelings of 'relative deprivation' in the lower ranks are diminished by people choosing modest reference groups for comparison. Fox (1971) suggests that if lower participants were to compare their lot with the financial rewards, status, autonomy and intrinsic job interest of higher management, 'industrial society in its present form could not exist'.

(c) *Promotion prospects*. American surveys show that opportunity for advancement is usually ranked first or second in importance. Herzberg (1959) found that achievement recognition and advancement were the main causes of *positive* satisfaction. Several studies found correlations between job satisfaction and estimates of the likelihood of promotion. On the other hand, if people expecting promotion do not get it, they will be discontented. For manual workers the actual chances of promotion are often quite small – the ratio of subordinates to foremen may be 100:1. In Goldthorpe's survey of affluent manual workers none thought their chances of promotion were 'very good', though 45 per cent thought they were 'fairly good'. In the same study the corresponding percentages for white-collar workers were 13 per cent and 53 per cent. The importance of promotion is quite different for people in different social classes and at different skill levels. For managerial and professional people work is part of a career, and promotion is of the highest importance. For unskilled and semi-skilled workers promotion is less likely, and is less sought after.

(*d*) *Security*. Findings on the importance of security are contradictory. The results depend on the country and historical period in which studies have been carried out. Those done in Britain or the U.S.A. during the 1930s usually found that security was thought the most important feature of a job (Viteles, 1954). Though it has dropped from first place in more recent surveys, it still comes very high on the list. When people are worried about losing their jobs this is found to spread to discontent with all other aspects of their work (Grove and Kerr, 1951). The people who are most concerned about security are those in the lower income group, and whose fathers were in unskilled or semi-skilled jobs – presumably because there is less security for less skilled workers. On the other hand, it is also found that more intelligent people are also very interested in long-term security (Wilkins, 1950–51). In Britain some of the elements of security are provided by the state – health and unemployment insurance, and pensions. What workers would really like is guaranteed employment; despite a greatly improved employment situation, memories of the depression of the 1930s linger on. So far no solution to the problem of providing guaranteed employment has been found within western capitalism, though the problem has been solved in other countries, such as Japan and Israel.

The work group. Many studies have shown that job satisfaction is affected by relationships in the work group. For example, it was found that 65 per cent of regular group members were satisfied, compared with 28 per cent of isolates (Zaleznik *et al.*, 1958). Job satisfaction is greatest when it is possible to have the desired kind of interaction with desirable people; the research problem is to specify what is desired.

(*a*) *Cohesiveness*. Satisfaction is greatest in cohesive groups. The conditions for cohesiveness are discussed elsewhere –

frequent interaction, group members of similar background and values, democratic leadership skills, members brought together by the work-flow in a cooperative manner (p. 117f.). A number of studies have shown that labour turnover is much less in cohesive groups (e.g. Van Zelst, 1952).

(b) *Popularity.* There is a close correlation between popularity and satisfaction – as high as 0·82 in one study (Van Zelst, 1951) – and unpopular members usually leave.

(c) *Group size.* Smaller groups have higher satisfaction than larger ones; the reason is probably that in smaller groups each member can exert a lot of influence and talk as much as he likes, while in large groups the majority will be at the lower end of the dominance hierarchy.

(d) *Opportunities for interaction.* Satisfaction is high when there are opportunities for interaction, and reduced when noise or physical separation makes this difficult.

Human relations writers believed that the work group was the *main* source of satisfaction: surveys show that workers place it between third and eighth in importance (Tiffin and McCormick, 1966). The work group is apparently more important in some kinds of work than others. Sometimes the work is normally carried out by teams, where the members are dependent on each other, are exposed to common stresses, and are isolated from other groups. Some of these conditions apply to trawlermen, railway men, steelworkers, printers, firemen and textile workers. In all these cases the group is of great importance and a major source of satisfaction. In much factory work, and particularly on assembly lines, however, such team-work does not occur, and the working group is not an important source of satisfaction. In his study of assembly-line and other factory workers Goldthorpe (1968) found that only about half of them talked much to other workers, that 68 per cent would not be much bothered about being moved to another group, and that 45 per cent had no close friends at work.

The nature of the occupational community is a related source of job satisfaction. Some occupations produce communities in which workers meet each other after hours, talk shop, have their own little cultural world, and their own status system. This happens when the community is residentially set apart, as with mining and universities, or works special hours, as in printing. It has been said that 'railroading, like music and thieving ... is a world by itself' (Caplow, 1954). Members of such communities are happier with their work than, for example, urban factory workers, who rarely meet one another after hours to talk shop, probably because of the closer social integration, and the linking of work and leisure activities (Blauner, 1960).

Supervision. A number of studies have shown a strong correlation between job satisfaction and various aspects of supervision. There is some doubt about some of these findings, since they could be due to satisfied subordinates describing the leadership styles of their supervisors in more favourable terms. This has been met by a number of field experiments in which supervisory style was manipulated experimentally. Supervision is more important to women than men.

(a) *Consideration* is the degree to which a leader shows warmth in personal relationships, trust, readiness to explain actions and listen to subordinates. It is closely correlated with the satisfaction of subordinates: this correlation can be as high as 0·70 (Halpin and Winer, 1952); in another study 97 per cent of satisfied employees said that their 'supervisor thinks of employees as human beings rather than as persons to get the work done' against 33 per cent of the unsatisfied; 81 per cent of the satisfied thought their 'supervisor has an interest in me and understands my problems' against 29 per cent of the dissatisfied (Likert, 1961).

(b) *Participation in decision-taking.* A number of studies have found that a democratic style of leadership, allowing influence in decisions, also increases job satisfaction (p. 151). Other studies, however, have found that subordinates are most contented if they are left alone by the supervisor – this increases control of their own activities, but does not necessarily give them much influence over the affairs of the group.

How important is supervision as a source of job satisfaction? This is another factor whose importance was stressed by human relations writers; but surveys show that workers rank it between third and seventh (Tiffin and McCormick, 1966). As with the work group, the importance of supervision probably varies according to different working situations. Goldthorpe (1968) found that most of his manual workers thought they got on well with their supervisors, often because he left them alone. However, the craftsmen and white-collar workers were more concerned with their supervisors, and their styles of interpersonal behaviour.

The company.
(*a*) *Size and shape.* We have seen that absenteeism is much lower, and job satisfaction higher, in small organizations. Here job satisfaction is higher when the organization is flatter and there are fewer levels in it (p. 198f.).

(*b*) *Participation in management.* We have seen also that workers feel that they belong more, are more cooperative and more satisfied if there are formal arrangements for them to participate in decision-making by means of committees with elected representatives.

(*c*) *Other aspects of the company* mentioned in surveys are managers – their training and skill, the nature of contacts with them; personnel policies – appraisal schemes; relations with trade unions – liberal or conservative attitudes; pride of company and product – based on public reputation, social importance, etc. (Evans and Laseau, 1950).

Individual differences. If all the variables considered so far are constant, there are still individual differences in job satisfaction.

(a) *Sex*. Women are more satisfied than men, at both manual and white-collar work. In a study of white collar-workers 55 per cent of men and 35 per cent of women were discontented with their work (Morse, 1953). Women are also more interested in the social aspects of work. It is not known why women are more satisfied; it may be because work is more a voluntary matter for them, because they are able to daydream more when doing boring work, or because of their greater appreciation of social factors.

(b) *Age*. A U-shaped relationship is often found, in which young employees become rapidly disillusioned, are least satisfied in their twenties, but become increasingly contented as they get older.

(c) *Intelligence*. It is difficult to say whether intelligence as such is a source of job satisfaction. Satisfaction is greater if a person's I.Q. is appropriate to the level of skill of his job, so that intelligent people are *less* satisfied doing repetitive work. Intelligent people are more likely to obtain professional and managerial jobs, which are very satisfying for a variety of reasons.

(d) *Personality*. It is commonly found that more neurotic people are less satisfied with their work, as well as with other aspects of their lives. Satisfaction also depends on how far a person can satisfy his particular set of needs in his job. The correlation between satisfaction and extent of participation in decisions has been found to be 0·55 for those setting great store by independence, 0·13 for those to whom it was unimportant (Vroom, 1960).

(e) *Orientation to work*. Goldthorpe (1968) identified a group of British workers whose orientation to work was 'instrumental', i.e. they were interested primarily in the pay, rather than in the work itself or social satisfaction. These were married men with dependent children, many of whom had moved house in pursuit of higher pay, or had gone down the social scale in search of more money. Other groups are those who have 'careers' rather than 'jobs', those who see their work as a vocation or as serving the community, and those who do it mainly because they enjoy the social life.

THE RELATION BETWEEN JOB SATISFACTION, PRODUCTIVITY, ABSENTEEISM AND LABOUR TURNOVER

Productivity. Do happy workers work harder? Many managers still believe that this is the case, and they have often tried to increase job satisfaction in the belief that this would lead to increased productivity. Social scientists also expected that there would be a positive relation between satisfaction and productivity. If people work hard to receive more pay or other rewards, they should be more satisfied; if people are not satisfied with their pay, or other aspects of the rewards, they would be expected to reduce output, to restore equity, or out of sheer frustration. There have been a number of carefully designed studies in which scores on job satisfaction scales have been correlated with measures or indices of productivity. The productivity measures were the actual rate of work of manual workers, the quantity of sales by salesmen or insurance agents, or ratings of efficiency. The numbers involved were typically 100–400 workers performing very similar work, though one study was made of 9,353 insurance agents, and another of 890 workers in an aircraft factory. The correlations found were nearly all positive, but they were also very small, averaging about $+0.15$ (Brayfield and Crockett, 1955; Vroom, 1964).

Another series of studies compared the average satisfaction of work groups with the productivity of these groups. The best known of these was the study on the Chesapeake and Ohio Railroad gangs by Katz and others (1951), who found that the most productive gangs were somewhat *less* satisfied with their work. Other studies have found a range of correlations, some positive others negative.

Are there any special conditions under which satisfaction and productivity go together? Likert (1961) suggested that these two are correlated among workers at higher levels of skill, but not for those on monotonous jobs. There have been a number of studies of workers at intermediate levels of skill – insurance agents, supervisors, IBM operators and air force control tower operators. The average correlation between productivity and satisfaction in these studies was 0·17, i.e. much the same as for unskilled and semi-skilled workers (Vroom, op. cit.). In a study of 563 managers it was found that those rated as more effective were somewhat higher in job satisfaction, especially satisfaction of the need for autonomy and self-actualization, but not for pay (Porter and Lawler, 1968). It is quite possible that productivity and satisfaction are related for highly skilled workers or for workers who are highly involved with their work.

There are probably individual differences which confuse the picture. There may well be workers who work hard when contented; there may be others who are happiest when they can take things easy, and others who work hard to forget their troubles. This is shown in Figure 15. In the central part of the figure are the 'normal' workers who work harder when satisfied. If all workers were like this there would be a strong positive correlation between job satisfaction and productivity. The other two 'deviant' groups appear in the bottom right and top left corners, and greatly reduce this correlation.

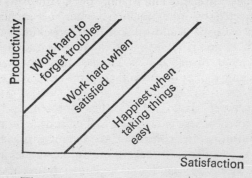

Figure 15. The relation between productivity and satisfaction.

Absenteeism. It might be expected that happy workers would be absent less – surely, if the work is satisfying people will want to turn up to enjoy the satisfaction? This has been found to be so in a number of studies of the satisfaction and absence of individuals and groups, with a typical correlation between satisfaction and absenteeism of about −0·30 (Vroom, 1964). There is a particularly clear negative correlation between satisfaction and *voluntary* or *unexcused* absenteeism rates. Total or overall absence rates are largely due to genuine illness, while voluntary absenteeism occurs simply because workers would rather do something else than come to work. The proportion of total absenteeism which is voluntary can be found by comparing the rate of absence on Mondays and Fridays; Behrend (1951) devised the 'Blue Monday Index' – the difference between Friday and Monday absences per 100 workers. She found that voluntary absenteeism accounts for about 33 per cent of total absenteeism. Neurotic or stress factors account for a further 20–25 per cent of absences (Fraser, 1947). Work anxiety is correlated with low job satisfaction, so this form of absence means low satisfaction.

The link between satisfaction and absenteeism varies for different kinds of worker. A strong relationship has been found between the two among male manual workers and males in the less skilled white-collar jobs, but almost no relationship was found for more skilled males and no relationship at all for white-collar females (Metzner and Mann, 1953). However, absenteeism is affected by other factors besides job satisfaction. If people are badly paid, and will lose pay if absent, they are more likely to turn up. It follows that workers who are dissatisfied with the pay may be absent less – unless they have some better way of making money on days off.

Labour turnover. It might also be expected that satisfied workers would be less likely to leave their jobs. This has in fact been found in studies comparing the labour turnover rates in different departments, or asking individuals about their own past stability and satisfaction. It is estimated that about 60 per cent of labour turnover is voluntary (Herzberg *et al.*, 1957). It is also produced by the same set of conditions that cause absenteeism and low satisfaction – monotonous work, low status, poor relations with groups, unsatisfactory supervision and lack of participation. However, the actual correlation (taking departments as units) is not large – of the order of —0·2 to —0·3 (Vroom, op. cit.; Brayfield and Crockett, op. cit.). Labour turnover depends on other factors besides job satisfaction. In particular, it depends on the availability of other jobs, and it is found to be less in times of high unemployment, and in small towns where there are no other firms offering similar work.

Job satisfaction is an important end in itself. There is not much evidence that 'happy workers work harder', in the sense of working faster. On the other hand, when job satisfaction is high there is a lower level of voluntary absenteeism and labour turnover.

APPENDIX: HERZBERG'S TWO-FACTOR THEORY

Herzberg, Mausner and Snyderman (1959) suggested that there are two factors, corresponding to satisfaction and dissatisfaction. They carried out a number of 'critical incident' surveys in which engineers and accountants were asked to describe occasions when they had felt 'exceptionally good' or 'exceptionally bad' about their jobs. The investigators then coded the extent to which they considered that each critical incident was due to each of a number of possible sources of satisfaction. It was found that the good experiences seemed to be brought about by achievement, recognition, the work itself, responsibility and advancement. Bad experiences appeared to be due to supervisors, fellow workers, company policy, working conditions and personal life. Salary was a cause of both good and bad experiences. Herzberg and his colleagues concluded that 'motivators' (achievement, etc.) mainly affect satisfaction, while 'hygiene' factors (supervision, etc.) mainly affect dissatisfaction, and that satisfaction is mainly due to the motivators, dissatisfaction to the hygiene factors.

A large number of investigations have been carried out to test this theory, and the results may be summarized as follows. First, there is some sense in which satisfaction is not the 'opposite' of dissatisfaction, in that overall measures of these two variables do correlate rather differently with the various source factors, as shown in Table 6. On the other hand, it is perfectly clear that there are not two independent statistical groupings of hygiene and motivator factors contributing to

Table 6

	Satisfaction	Dissatisfaction
Hygiene factors		
Co-workers	6·82	3·82
Supervisor's help	6·12	5·59
Working conditions	6·53	3·24
Managerial policies	5·12	6·73
Motivators		
Recognition	6·32	5·00
Work itself	6·73	5·18
Achievement	7·03	4·82
Promotion	4·59	6·18

Subject ratings of the contributions of different factors to their satisfaction and dissatisfaction (from Lahiri and Srivasta, 1967).

two postulated factors of satisfaction – all factors, hygienes and motivators, contribute *both* to satisfaction and dissatisfaction (Cummings and El Salmi, 1968).

Secondly, replications of the original Herzberg study with different kinds of workers, or by different investigators, have confirmed the original findings. However, if the subjects are asked to report good and bad experiences and rate the contribution of the different sources of satisfaction to the experiences *themselves*, rather different results are obtained. One of these studies was carried out on 93 Indian managers: some of the results are given in the table above. Subjects rated the contribution of each factor to the good and bad episodes on ten-point scales.

It is clear that there is no consistent tendency for motivators to contribute to satisfaction and for hygiene factors to contribute to dissatisfaction. The rather different results obtained in the original Herzberg study and its replications were probably due to the fact that the investigators introduced systematic biases in coding the causes of the good and bad incidents, i.e. ascribing causes of good and bad incidents that fitted the theory.

Thirdly, another group of studies found correlations between overall satisfaction and satisfaction in particular areas, and similarly for dissatisfaction. The results of one study are given in Table 7.

Table 7

| | Males | | Females | |
	Satis-faction	Dissatis-faction	Satis-faction	Dissatis-faction
Hygiene factors				
Pay	0·39	0·24	0·12	0·18
Supervision	0·53	0·25	0·31	0·03
Co-workers	0·48	0·13	0·20	0·08
Motivators				
Work itself	0·68	0·44	0·45	0·43
Promotion	0·40	0·38	0·46	0·14

Correlations between satisfaction and dissatisfaction and five sources of satisfaction (from Hulin and Smith, 1967).

It can be seen that satisfaction is more strongly correlated *both* with motivation and with hygiene factors and not just with the motivators, as the theory maintains.

Fourthly, it has been argued by King (1970) that a re-analysis of the data of Lahiri and Srivasta's study provides support for a weaker version of the Herzberg hypothesis – 'All motivators combined contribute more to satisfaction than do all hygiene factors combined, and all hygiene factors combined contribute more to dissatisfaction than do all motivators combined.' I think that this is very dubious. However, it is interesting that the correlational studies provide clearer disconfirmation of the Herzberg theory than do the critical incident studies. This is probably due to a peculiarity of the critical incident method: probably the recall of incidents is 'selective so that those good incidents which happen to be recalled tend to be biased towards those incidents which were due to one's own efforts (motivators) as opposed to those incidents which were due to the efforts of others (hygienes)' (King, op. cit. p. 28).

The Herzberg theory probably came about because a study using the critical incident method produced certain findings which were mainly a result of using this method. However, numerous studies have now shown that if any other method is used these results are not obtained, so it seems that the theory is simply wrong. The suggestion that dissatisfaction is not the opposite of satisfaction is an intriguing one, and has received some support, though it is not yet clear what the significance of this is.

A number of investigations have been carried out using Herzberg's division of two sources of satisfaction. It has been found that intrinsic factors are more strongly related to overall job satisfaction than extrinsic factors and that individuals at higher occupational levels regard intrinsic factors as more important (Centers and Bugenthal, 1966). The theory has been extremely influential, particularly in directing attention to the importance of the motivators – which it is also assumed will affect the amount of work done, though this was not shown by Herzberg. The theory may also have resulted in managers paying less attention to social factors, which all fall into the hygiene group. Perhaps the most important contribution of Herzberg's writings, like those of Maslow (p. 96 f.), is in pointing to some of the ideal conditions of work; very little attention had been paid to intrinsic features of the work, or to achievement and recognition by the previous generation of industrial social psychologists.

APPENDIX B: MENTAL HEALTH AND WORK

Work is one of the central activities of life, a source of satisfaction and dissatisfaction, the basis of identity and a main object of motivation; it can be the cause of mental health or mental ill health. There is a definite relationship between mental health and job satisfaction − satisfied workers have better mental health (Kornhauser, 1965). However, this is not a one-to-one relationship, and the pattern of causation for the two dimensions is somewhat different. We shall show, for example, that people with wide supervisory responsibilities are very satisfied, but also tend to suffer from psychosomatic complaints.

Many workers suffer from mental ill health in one form or another. In a study of 3,000 engineering workers in Birmingham it was found that about 10 per cent were suffering from 'disabling neuroses', and another 20 per cent from minor neurotic complaints (Fraser, 1947). In a national sample survey of 2,460 Americans 31 per cent said they had problems on the job and 26 per cent both had problems and did not really feel adequate at their jobs (Gurin *et al.*, 1960). Neuroticism is a matter of degree − everyone is a little neurotic − and the percentage said to be neurotic depends on the cut-off point used. 'Disabling neurosis' may affect 10 per cent of workers, but any larger percentage goes into very mild degrees of 'neurosis'.

Several different criteria of mental health have been used. Certain psychiatric complaints are found to be related to working conditions, notably psychosomatic complaints such as high blood pressure, ulcers and heart disease (Doll and Jones, 1951). In several studies people were interviewed about worries, problems, anxiety or tension experienced while on the job or directly related to the job (e.g. Gurin *et al.*, 1960). Other studies have used interviews which have covered a wide range of signs of mental ill health, without making specific reference to the work situation (e.g. Kornhauser, 1965). It is not clear how far work-related problems are correlated with general mental ill health. It is possible that some people are only maladjusted at work or vice versa. On the other hand, several studies have found that the same people seem to have symptoms of different kinds, and the patterns of causation for work-related and general symptoms are very similar.

People not working often feel very depressed. We referred earlier to the distressed state of the unemployed; some people become disturbed when away from work, because they have too much time to think about their personal problems. Mental hospitals often have protected workshops where patients can become accustomed to work, and this is regarded as an essential part of the treatment. Of course, these observations have been made in cultural settings where work is regarded as an important part of life. If leisure becomes a more important alternative to work, not working may become more socially acceptable.

I shall now consider the working conditions which have been found to affect mental health.

Nature of the work. Mental health has been found to be very low among semi-skilled factory workers on production lines, doing repetitive, monotonous work. Further investigations showed that this was not due to fatigue produced by the speed and intensity of work; the jobs were reasonably free from physical and mental strain. On the other hand, mental health was low among those workers who felt that they had no chance to use their abilities. It was suggested that low-grade work caused 'lowered self-esteem, discouragement, futility, and feelings of failure and inferiority in contrast to a sense of personal growth and self-fulfilment resulting from more varied, responsible, challenging undertakings that afford opportunity to develop and use one's ideas and skills' (Kornhauser, 1965).

Jobs may be stressful in others ways. Under battle conditions everyone collapses with a 'war neurosis' if left in action for too long. It has been found that psychosomatic illnesses are common among men who work the switchgear on electric railways – where there is a constant danger of electrocuting their mates. A high rate of breakdown has also been reported for people working in television, perhaps due to the constant crises and tension. The introduction of electronic data processing in one firm led to an increase in neurotic symptoms;

the employees thought that standards were higher and deadlines more important (Mann and Williams, 1962).

Job status. Mental health at work, like job satisfaction, also
varies according to status. Some 407 workers in car factories
were interviewed together with other groups. The percentages
with 'high' general mental health were as follows (Kornhauser,
op. cit.):

white-collar	65
skilled and high semi-skilled	57
ordinary semi-skilled	37
repetitive semi-skilled	18

Gurin and his colleagues (1960) found the same trend continued to higher levels of job status, professional workers
having the greatest feelings of adequacy, though unskilled
workers reported the fewest work problems. People in the jobs
of highest status were most involved in their jobs, and expected
to be rewarded by having responsibility, and pleasant social
relations; these expectations were gratified, resulting in greater
job satisfaction; on the other hand, they ran into more problems at work – senior people are there to deal with difficult
problems. It has been shown that there are great differences
between workers at different levels of skill in their frequency of
going to the dispensary at work: low skill workers go to the
dispensary about four times as often as high skill workers. It
is suggested that low job status leads to low self-esteem which,
in turn, produces low mental health (Kasl and French, 1962).

However, jobs involve a number of other factors that
might affect mental health – autonomy, pay and nature of work.
It was found that supervisors reported sick *more* often than
those in non-supervisory jobs of the same status; the number
of supervisory visits by supervisors to the dispensary was 63
per cent greater in one factory, 9 per cent in another (Kasl and
French, op. cit.). In a different study it was found that 42 per
cent of executives reported two or more psychosomatic ailments, compared with only 25 per cent of professional men

(Rennie and Srole, 1956). It looks as if certain dimensions of job status can lead to worse mental health. A number of studies have found that foremen, managers and doctors have high rates of heart disease and ulcers, and higher cholesterol level. Doll and Jones (1951) found that ulcers were associated with job status in the ways described, but had no correlation with home worries.

Competition. Studies of high blood pressure, ulcers, heart disease, and other psychosomatic conditions have found that these occur most commonly in men in their forties and fifties, in supervisory or management positions, who are under the pressure of deadlines, intense competition, long hours or doing additional jobs. There is also evidence that these diseases occur in men who have fairly low job status, but who are very ambitious, conscientious and hard-working (Kasl and French, op. cit.).

The working group. Job satisfaction is greater among workers who belong to a cohesive group and are accepted by it. It seems likely that belonging to such groups can also provide emotional support, and reduce anxiety created by pressures from managers, or others outside the group (Seashore, 1954). Therapy groups are, of course, used to treat neurotic patients, and it is probable that groups can be therapeutic in other settings too. On the other hand, if a person is rejected by the group, this will be far from therapeutic; being 'sent to Coventry' is a terrible experience, and such rejection usually makes the person leave the company. If a group member deviates from group norms he will be under group pressure to conform; this has the effect of increasing physiological indices of anxiety, until he gives way by conforming. Workers who are placed under pressure to work harder or in a different way feel more strain (Wolfe, cited by Zander and Quinn, 1962). If a group member fails to do as well as other members of the group he is likely to form a low opinion of his performance and of himself, especially if he has internalized the goals or levels of performance in question (Zander *et al.*, 1960). The importance of the working group probably varies according to the nature of the work. In groups exposed to stress, e.g. trawlermen, miners or steelworkers, the group is more important than it is in manufacturing industry. The group has a small effect on mental health in Detroit factories: for middle-aged men who did not like their fellow workers 47 per cent were in poor mental health, compared with 36 per cent for those who did like them (Kornhauser, op. cit.).

Supervision. We have seen that job satisfaction is greater when supervisors look after their men and allow participation in decisions. Supervisors can affect mental health by being too authoritarian, applying too much pressure for high standards of work, and can damage self-confidence by being unskilled in giving appraisal interviews. Again the effect of different kinds of supervision on mental health probably varies with the setting, and is rather small in mass production industry.

Role conflict. As we have seen, a person will be in a state of role conflict if two or more other people or groups in the organization, with whom he is linked in the system of roles, have differing expectations or demands about what he should do. Thus a supervisor may be exposed to different demands from managers and subordinates, or a salesman may be exposed to different demands from customers and suppliers. It has been found that industrial employees in role conflict had more tension stemming from their work, lower job satisfaction, and less confidence in the organization (Kahn *et al.*, 1964). Role ambiguity occurs where there is no clear definition of what a person's role is. Kahn and his colleagues found that this results in greater tension, reduced job satisfaction, feelings of futility and low self-confidence. Role conflict was much more disturbing for those who were generally neurotic, and for those who were concerned about status.

It has been suggested that status incongruence, e.g. where a person's income, education, or job status are out of line with each other, can lead to psychosomatic complaints. However, Kornhauser (op. cit.) found that high mental health went with higher job status, education, and income level in childhood, with no evidence of such effects of incongruence. Indeed some kinds of incongruence might be experienced as beneficial, such as getting a better job or being paid more than might have been expected.

CHAPTER 10

THE SOCIAL PSYCHOLOGY OF WORK AND THE FUTURE OF WORK

The social psychology of work – creating optimal working conditions – leisure and the future of work.

THE SOCIAL PSYCHOLOGY OF WORK

HUMAN nature shows a nice adaptation between the propensity to work and the need to maintain a complex material culture. In order to survive, man needs clothes, houses and cultivated food. To provide this there has to be persistent striving for the achievement of goals, and cooperation in groups. There is a long period of socialization in the family, so the acquired ways of doing things – the culture – can be learnt by children. In addition to the biological part of human nature there is the acquired part, learned from the culture. Cultural attitudes to work have varied greatly, depending on circumstances. When large numbers of slaves were available to do it, work was despised. When fortunes could be made from setting up the first factories, hard work became morally praiseworthy. It would no doubt be possible for us to make a further cultural adaptation to automation, to form a 'post-industrial society', whose values and social structure are based on leisure activities.

Work is the setting for several kinds of basic social behaviour – cooperation and helping in groups, supervisory relationships, negotiation and bargaining, assessment and appraisal. These kinds of behaviour each call for special social skills, which have to be learned. And these forms of social behaviour take place in a complex environmental setting, which contains technology, incentive schemes and social organization, where people are all placed in definite relationships to one another, each pursuing his career over many years.

In simpler societies work is done in a way that gives satisfaction to those who do it, and there is no clear division between work and leisure. Under the conditions of modern industry many do not enjoy their work. The conditions of work in Britain, Europe and the U.S.A. since 1800 have left a great deal to be desired, and caused many people to believe that work, particularly manual work, must be unpleasant. Yet many people enjoy their work, including many manual workers. While it was once believed that 'happy workers work harder', surveys have found very small, though positive, correlations between these variables (p. 238 f.). It is certainly possible to create conditions which maximize one at the expense of the other. Under a tyranny with total control over enslaved workers, there can certainly be high productivity – though such unwilling workers are uncooperative in many ways and their management is very difficult. One could also imagine a regime devoted solely to the contentment of workers, where no demands were made for them to do much work.

However, social factors may affect productivity in several ways. The alteration of the composition of working groups, styles of supervision, incentives and the nature of the work can produce increases in the rate of work, or the productivity of labour, of the order of 10–40 per cent, though such increases are less if work is machine-paced. The alteration of the composition of working groups, supervision, and participation in decisions has a considerable effect on absenteeism and labour turnover – which may be reduced to one quarter under more favourable conditions. The construction of work-teams, introducing democratic supervision, participation in management, and arousal of intrinsic motivation all increase cooperation and reduce conflict inside the organization.

CREATING OPTIMAL WORKING CONDITIONS

At the beginning of this book we discussed some of the main problems of work as it is arranged today – widespread dissatisfaction and alienation, lack of motivation and cooperation, and difficulties of communication. This is partly a heritage of the Industrial Revolution, with its creation of large numbers of meaningless, repetitive jobs, and an unfamiliar and uncongenial social structure. These effects have been partly alleviated by the automation revolution, which has abolished some of these jobs, and may ultimately abolish many more. Social science research has played a minor but helpful role, mainly in bringing about less punitive and authoritarian styles of leadership, via training courses for supervisors and managers. It is interesting to note that the Japanese industrial revolution went much more smoothly, by making use of traditional social structures, and stepping straight into the age of automation.

From the evidence reviewed in earlier chapters it is possible to list the optimal conditions for maximizing both productivity and job satisfaction. Although this research was mostly done in the U.S.A., Britain or western Europe, the findings appear to apply over a wide variety of cultural conditions.

Nature of the work. (*a*) *Varied and meaningful work.* There is no problem about professional, managerial, craftwork or other highly skilled work; the difficulty comes with unskilled, repetitive manual and clerical work. We have seen that these jobs can be modified by job enlargement, rotation or enrichment, and that this leads to increased productivity and satisfaction (p. 34). A minority of alienated workers prefer boring jobs (p. 230); this is perhaps just as well since not all jobs can be improved. Improved preparation for work during the educational period should result in most people preferring interesting work. Maslow (1954), and Herzberg and his colleagues (1959) have offered a revised view of human nature; they maintain that people have potentialities for growth, and want to develop their skills and personalities. These ideas should perhaps be regarded not as empirically testable hypotheses, but rather as ideals about what work should be like. This emphasis on growth and the development of skill and personality also appears in the writings of those who have seen craftsmanship as the ideal form of work (Mills, 1951).

(*b*) *Freedom to choose pace and working conditions.* This is one of the main differences between 'work' and 'leisure' (see below), and one of the main obstacles to industrialization in developing countries. Such freedom is least in assembly-line and other machine-paced work. It is greater in less technically sophisticated craftwork. It is also greater under more technically sophisticated automated systems. Fortunately the jobs most easy to automate are those which require men to behave like machines. Here the second industrial revolution is abolishing the unpleasant jobs created by the first.

(c) *Work appropriate to the worker's abilities and interests.* This is achieved by vocational guidance. What firms do is personnel selection – which differs from guidance in looking primarily at abilities rather than interests and needs. Personnel selection could be modified to take more account of these factors, which are important sources of job satisfaction.

Incentives and inspiration. (a) *Sufficient security, pay and status.* Security is one of the most important factors in job satisfaction. It is now being sought by the unions, though it is difficult to achieve in a rapidly changing industrial scene, in view of redundancies created by automation. It has been achieved in Japan, with no apparent loss in efficiency, simply by adopting a policy of planning the work to employ all the people on the payroll. Under some conditions such a policy would involve using human labour rather than automated equipment.

Wage incentives certainly make people work but cause a lot of friction and are widely being replaced by a guaranteed wage for an agreed rate of work. Relatively high pay is an important source of job satisfaction, but how can everyone have it? In the kibbutzim there is equality of wages, in Japanese factories the managers only get 50 per cent more than manual workers. On the other hand, wage differentials probably act as incentives, at any rate to those with careers in which they can be promoted. Perhaps the differentials might be reduced from those commonly found in the U.S.A. and Europe – 10:1 – to a lower figure.

Relatively high status is also sought by all, and can act as an incentive. Under the organizational changes recommended below – fewer ranks, and more democratic leadership – status differences would be greatly reduced.

(b) *Intrinsic motivation.* We have seen the desirability of making use of forms of intrinsic motivation, as well as or instead of purely economic motivation. This can be done by participating in decisions, by aligning workers' goals with those of the organization, or by the strength of their identification with the community, as in the kibbutz. It can also be done when the work itself requires the use of valued skills, or offers challenging goals which will arouse achievement motivation. Under present conditions it is only managers and professional staff who are motivated in these ways. It can be done, too, when the work fits the interests and personality of the worker.

Working groups. (a) The formation of small and cohesive groups. Workers at all levels of skill prefer to work in a small and cohesive group. Productivity is often higher too, though this varies with the task. People who are isolated are likely to leave, groups that are too large divide into sub-groups, groups that are too heterogenous are often discontented and uncooperative.

(b) *The use of functional groups.* We saw earlier (p. 120) that job satisfaction and productivity are both greater in working groups that are small, cohesive, cooperative, and have small status differences within them. These principles can be made use of by constructing 'functional work groups'; instead of putting people in a group because they do similar jobs (e.g. secretarial, electronics, sales), groups are formed from those people who need to cooperate because they are engaged in the same project. Such a group should be formed so that the following conditions hold: the members need to communicate frequently in order to cooperate effectively; they must have the necessary skills to carry out the job between them; they may have different skills, but status differences must be small; the working relationships between them must be helpful and rewarding.

One example of the formation of such groups is the regrouping of miners reported by Trist and his colleagues (p. 44f.). Another is the regrouping of Indian textile workers reported by Rice (p. 45f.), also of the Tavistock Institute. Similar principles have been applied in the design of American projects in advanced technology, such as nuclear and space research. A further development is the 'systems' approach in which the membership of a team changes continuously as it comes to different phases of its work (Bass, 1965).

Supervision and management. We saw earlier that certain styles of supervision produce much higher levels of job satisfaction, cut absenteeism and labour turnover to one quarter of that found under other supervision, and can increase output by 10–25 per cent. The optimum style of supervision is a combination of initiating structure, consideration and democratic-persuasive skills (p. 146f.). Field experiments have been carried out in which the style of supervision has been changed in these ways, and which have had very successful results.

Changes of supervisory style will change the organizational structure without changing the organization chart. They can be brought about by training supervisors accordingly, as in the Morse and Reimer study (p. 209), though this needs to be supported by appropriate changes in the behaviour of senior managers – since styles of leadership are imitated and flow downwards through an organization.

Organizational structure. (*a*) *Decentralization.* Many of the problems of organizations can be solved by making the organizational units smaller – communication is easier, people can participate more in decisions, and there are fewer levels in the hierarchy; satisfaction is greater, absenteeism and turnover lower (p. 198f.).

(*b*) *Reducing the number of levels in the hierarchy.* This follows from decentralization, but the number of levels can also be reduced by increasing the span of control. This has been found to be advantageous, especially in small organizations (p. 199f.). Some degree of hierarchical structure seems to be unavoidable, but the harmful consequences can be minimized by reducing the number of levels. It is also possible to reduce the social distance between levels by reducing differences of pay and status.

(c) *Participation in decision-taking.* There is extensive evidence from American field experiments, and from large-scale schemes like those in use in Germany and Yugoslavia, that worker participation by means of committees with elected representatives generates a more cooperative spirit, better teamwork, fewer strikes, etc. For such schemes to work successfully the committees must have real power, especially over wages, and all levels must be represented.

Preparation for work. (a) *Education.* Many young people do not know what work is for or why they should do it, after years of education. It would be useful for such facts of life to be spelt out more clearly. This book is indeed an attempt to do it. Schools do teach some of the skills needed at work; it would be very useful if they could also give some training in the social skills needed at work.

(b) *The transition to work,* from school, is often found difficult. It is very desirable for young people to try out one or two jobs in vacations so that they can be initiated gradually. Employers need to handle their young intake with particular care and understanding.

(c) *Vocational guidance.* Many young people have very little idea of what different jobs are like. It would be most useful if they could see or try out for themselves the main jobs open to them in their area. Selection procedures, as well as vocational guidance, should consider the individual's personality and interests, as well as his abilities.

LEISURE AND THE FUTURE OF WORK

One possible future of work is that most of it will disappear, as the result of indefinite extensions of automation. The question is, would people enjoy this state of affairs, and what would they do instead? We can get further insight into this problem by considering how people do spend their free time, and asking what exactly the differences are between work and leisure.

There are twenty-four hours a day, of which people spend about eight sleeping, and eight working – for five and a half days a week, apart from holidays, which leaves about eleven hours per day free on average. Some of this is spent dressing, eating, travelling, etc., but this leaves quite a lot of time in which people can do more or less what they like. What do they do with it?

Constructive leisure is perhaps the most interesting type of leisure activity for our purposes. This is directed towards the achievement of goals, and is often conducted in groups, i.e. is much the same as work. In fact very similar activities are carried out as work by other people (or even by the same people). Examples of these are gardening (horticulture, agriculture); arts and crafts (arts and crafts); home decoration (decoration); do-it-yourself (carpentry); repairing cars, motor cycles (garage work); voluntary work (social work); church work (work of the clergy); committee work (administrative work); and motoring (lorry driving).

It is interesting that a variety of forms of work, including manual work, are voluntarily chosen by some people as leisure activities. Constructive leisure is often sought by men after retirement.

Cultural pursuits include further education, serious reading, artistic creation, listening to and performing serious music, and so on. This is somewhat similar to the work of professional academics, musicians and artists.

Sport. Exercise is obtained, tensions may be relieved, and social activities are enjoyed, but this is different from work because nothing is produced – sport is an end in itself.

Family-centred leisure – looking after children and the home, going on outings, visiting relations, etc.; much of this is more like work, especially for mothers. Domestic activities take up much of the spare time of adults between 25 and 40, and they often have little time or energy for much else.

Social activity. Friendship is one of the main kinds of social relationship and part of leisure is taken up by talking, eating and drinking, or playing games with friends. The aim is to have enjoyable social interaction with them, and activities are chosen which will generate the desired kinds of interaction. This is one of the main forms of leisure activity among adolescents, and the chosen activities are listening to music, dancing and talking about personal problems. Among older people social life can be a highly organized affair, and becomes more like work, in that a lot of organized cooperative activity is entailed.

Relaxation. Quite a lot of leisure time is spent in low pressure activities like watching television, going to the cinema, reading magazines and novels, or just sitting in a stupor. This is partly to recover from the exertions of work, but partly also because there is nothing else to do, because people have not been prepared to deal with so much free time, and they have to resort to blotting-paper activities which simply absorb time (Riesman, 1958).

Unfortunately there have been no studies of leisure-satisfaction or leisure-productivity and it is not known quite how leisure differs from work. Firstly, of the six kinds of leisure activity the first four are similar to work in that they involve the expenditure of considerable effort and are directed towards specific goals; the fifth – social activity – sometimes has this quality. It would be useful for research to be carried out on the differences between the ways in which identical tasks are performed when they are done for work or leisure, e.g. gardening v. horticulture. Perhaps they differ in the following ways. Most leisure activities are performed when and how one chooses – apart from team games, amateur theatricals, committee work, and other organized activities. Most leisure pursuits are carried out unsupervised – again apart from organized pursuits. Leisure is entirely voluntary and intrinsically motivated; a leisure task is not done at all unless it carries its own reward. The product, if any, is one's own property.

Some leisure activities are carried out in the company of family or friends, but this is not true of all, and most work is carried out in the company of people who may become friends. Some leisure activities have an air of 'fun', 'excitement' or 'challenge', but this is true of some work as well. It may be suggested that social activity and relaxation do not provide the kinds of satisfaction that the more active kinds of leisure provide. It has often been observed that those who do not work, and have no organized leisure activities, become depressed, lose their sense of identity and purpose in life, and become mentally or physically ill. This has been found with the unemployed and among alienated youth. Retired men are most upset by loneliness, loss of their peer group, loss of status and identity, and idleness – the loss of constructive activities (Cumming and Henry, 1961). Work appears to have a psychologically stabilizing effect – as is shown by the extensive use of occupational therapy for mental patients. It looks as if leisure, to be satisfying in any important sense, must be a kind of 'moral equivalent for work', though it may also differ from work in certain ways.

It has been argued by some observers of the current industrial scene that work should be allowed to disappear or become a minor aspect of life, and workers should be encouraged to seek satisfaction in leisure. For this to be successful there would have to be considerable expansion of leisure facilities and training for leisure. Unfortunately those people best prepared for leisure tend to be those who are busiest working, and who will be the last to be dispensed with as automation proceeds. At present our social structure and social order consist of relationships largely based on work; they would have to be replaced by some different kind of social structure. At present our identities and sense of meaning and purpose in life are mainly based on work; these too would have to be replaced by identities and purposes based on leisure pursuits. There would, of course, be quite a lot of work still to be done, much of it boring, so that there would be the paradoxical combination of meaningless work and meaningful leisure. There are some people today who have boring jobs but interesting leisure – like assembly-line workers who keep pigeons. However, this is not the normal pattern, and most observers think that the quality of work affects the quality of leisure (Blauner, 1964).

A more constructive approach would be to modify the character of work so that it provided maximum satisfaction, and incorporated as many of the properties of leisure as possible. In primitive and medieval village communities there was little distinction between work and leisure; work was intermingled with social, religious and other activities and met a variety of needs. To some extent this has already happened. The work of academics, artists, writers and others is indistinguishable from their leisure. They have no set hours of work, their social activities are bound up with their work, and they often have no clear leisure activities apart from their work – it would be difficult to classify professional social occasions such as conferences as either work or leisure. Similar considerations apply to many managers, whose work life includes lunches and other agreeable social gatherings, and whose leisure includes entertaining colleagues and clients. Leisure values can be found in the working life of clerical and manual workers – in long coffee breaks, informal social groupings, and general fooling about (p. 112f.).

Could work be made even more like leisure? Consider the differences noted above. Leisure activities are carried out when and how one chooses. This approach has been used successfully with African workers: an informal group of workers are given a job to do in their own time and they are paid when they have done it. This kind of freedom is normal in research and similar work, but is difficult to allow for in regular industrial production. Automation is however freeing workers from the more strictly machine-paced work, and gives them some control over the pace at which they can work and over methods, though not over hours. Most leisure pursuits are carried out unsupervised. Job enrichment incorporates inspection and other aspects of supervision; the new style of supervision we have recommended creates a changed relationship with supervisors. Leisure is intrinsically motivated. We have recommended that work too should be intrinsically motivated, as far as is possible. The products of leisure, if any, are one's own property. Writers on craftsmanship have argued that 'if the producer does not legally own the product he must own it psychologically in the sense that he knows what goes into it by way of sweat, skill and material . . . and sees the place of his part in the whole' (Mills, 1951, p. 221). It should be possible to build up a feeling of pride and identification with the product. Examples of work which meets these criteria are craftwork and other highly skilled manual work, research and other academic work, work in hospitals and other highly dedicated organizations.

It appears that work should have many of the properties of leisure to be most satisfying, and that this is consistent at nearly every point with the pursuit of high productivity. It also appears that for leisure to be satisfying it must have some of the main properties of work. People will seek activities of a certain kind, whether they are called work or leisure, because these are the conditions for human satisfaction: completing interesting and meaningful tasks, which use basic skills and abilities, giving adequate recognition and social status, performed under considerate and democratic-persuasive supervision (or no supervision), in cohesive groups and in small organizations with full participation in their management (or no organization).

The abolition of work is going to be a very slow process, and will never be more than partial. It is important, therefore, that the conditions of work should be improved to make it more satisfying for everyone, both as an end in itself, and to increase cooperation and efficiency. Industry cannot hope to continue to make a profit if a large proportion of employees are basically discontented and uncooperative, with high rates of absenteeism, labour turnover and strikes. Yet Riesman (1958) reports he found it 'impossible to get either unions or management in the least interested in making work more humanly satisfying' (p. 372). It is curious that the unions are exclusively concerned with increasing the extrinsic rewards for work. From the evidence presented above it would be in the interests of both management and unions to reform the decision-taking structure of industry to introduce more industrial democracy; to reform the organizational structure, e.g. by changing pay differentials, improving promotion prospects, making the organization flatter and more decentralized; to control automation so that the maximum advantages for both company and employees are realized; to increase job satisfaction, by bringing in job enrichment, better supervision, and better arrangements of working groups; and to carry out surveys to locate the sources of low satisfaction in different sections.

During their increased leisure it seems likely that people will continue to turn to constructive activities like arts and crafts, gardening, decoration, do-it-yourself, and other hobbies which have the essential components of work. Perhaps education should prepare people more for such activities, and local authorities should provide better facilities for them. Alternatively, our methods of socialization could be changed, so that the Protestant ethic totally disappears, and future generations will be perfectly contented doing nothing. However, from our own cultural standpoint this is not an attractive prospect – because basically we regard work and its moral equivalents as the most worthwhile form of human activity.

REFERENCES

Abegglen, J. C. (1958), *The Japanese Factory*, Asia Publishing House, Bombay.

Acton Society Trust (1953), *Size and Morale*, Acton Society Trust, London.

Adams, J. S. (1965), 'Inequity in social exchange', *Advances in Experimental Social Psychology*, vol. 2, pp. 267–99.

Adams, J. S. and Rosenbaum, W. B. (1962), 'The relationship of worker productivity to cognitive dissonance about wage inequalities', *Journal of Applied Psychology*, Vol. 46, pp. 161–4.

Albrecht, P. A., Glaser, E. M. and Marks, J. (1964), 'Validation of a multiple-assessment procedure for managerial personnel', *Journal of Applied Psychology*, vol. 48, pp. 351–60.

Allen, G. C. (1965), *Japan's Economic Expansion*, Oxford University Press, London.

Allen, V. L. (1954), *Power in Trade Unions*, Longmans, London.

Argyle, M. (1953), 'The relay assembly test room in retrospect', *Occupational Psychology*, vol. 27, pp. 98–103.

— (1967, 1972, 1978), *The Psychology of Interpersonal Behaviour*, Penguin Books, Harmondsworth.

— (1969), *Social Interaction*, Methuen, London.

Argyle, M., Gardner, G. and Cioffi, F. (1958), 'Supervisory methods related to productivity, absenteeism and labour turnover', *Human Relations*, vol. 11, pp. 23–45.

Argyle, M., Smith, T. and Kirton, M. (1962), *Training Managers*, Acton Society Trust, London.

Argyle, M., Salter, V., Nicholson, H., Williams, M. and Burgess, P. (1970), 'The communication of inferior and superior attitudes by verbal and non-verbal signals', *British Journal of Social and Clinical Psychology*, vol. 9, pp. 222–31.

Argyle, M. and Williams, M. (1969), 'Observer or observed? A reversible perspective in person perception', *Sociometry*, vol. 32, pp. 396–412.

Argyle, M. and Little, B. (1972), 'Do personality traits apply to social behaviour?', *Journal for the Theory of Social Behaviour*, 2, 1–35.

REFERENCES

Argyris, C. (1964), *Integrating the Organization and the Individual*, Wiley, New York.

Atkinson, J. W. (ed.) (1958), *Motives in Fantasy, Action and Society*, Van Nostrand, Princeton, New Jersey.

Babchuk, N. and Goode, W. J. (1951), 'Work incentives in a self-determined group', *American Journal of Sociology*, vol. 16, pp. 679–87.

Bakke, E. W. (1940), *Citizens without Work*, Yale University Press, New Haven.

Bass, B. M. (1965), *Organizational Psychology*, Allyn & Bacon, Boston.

Beals, R. L. and Hoijer, A. (1965), *An Introduction to Anthropology*, Collier-Macmillan, London.

Behrend, H. (1951), *Absence under full employment*, University of Birmingham, Department of Commerce (roneoed).

Benedict, R. F. (1934), *Patterns of Culture*, Routledge, London.

Bendix, R. (1956), *Work and Authority in Industry*, Wiley, New York.

Bennett, E. B. (1955), 'Discussion, decisions, commitment and consensus in "group decision"', *Human Relations*, vol. 8, pp. 251–73.

Bennett, J. W. and Ishino, I. (1963), *Paternalism in the Japanese Economy*, University of Minnesota Press, Minneapolis.

Berlyne, D. E. (1960), *Conflict, Arousal and Curiosity*, McGraw-Hill, New York.

Bingham, W. V. (1932), 'Making work worth while', *Psychology Today*, pp. 262–4, University of Chicago Press.

Birney, R. C. (1968), 'Research on the achievement motive', in Borgatta, E. F. and Lambert, W. W. (eds.), *Handbook of Personality Theory and Research*, Rand McNally, Chicago.

Blake, R. R. and Mouton, J. S. (1961), 'Power, people and performance reviews', *Advanced Management*, vol. 26, pp. 13–27.

— (1964), *The Managerial Grid*, Gulf Publishing Company, Houston.

Blau, P. M. (1955), *The Dynamics of Bureaucracy*, University of Chicago Press.

Blau, P. M. and Scott, W. R. (1963), *Formal Organizations*, Routledge & Kegan Paul, London.

Blauner, R. (1960), 'Work satisfaction and industrial trends in modern society', in Galenson, W. and Lipset, S. M. (eds.), *Labor and Trade Unions*, Wiley, New York.

265

Blauner, R. (1964), *Alienation and Freedom*, University of Chicago Press.

Blood, M. R. and Hulin, C. L. (1967), 'Alienation, environmental characteristics, and worker responses', *Journal of Applied Psychology*, vol. 51, pp. 284–90.

Blumberg, P. (1968), *Industrial Democracy: the Sociology of Participation*, Constable, London.

Bolster, B. I. and Springbett, B. M. (1961), 'The reaction of interviewers to favourable and unfavourable information', *Journal of Applied Psychology*, vol. 45, pp. 97–103.

Borgatta, E. F. and Lambert, W. W. (eds.) (1968), *Handbook of Personality Theory and Research*, Rand McNally, Chicago.

Bradford, L. P., Gibb, J. R. and Benne, K. D. (1964), *T-Group Training and Laboratory Method*, Wiley, New York.

Brayfield, A. H. and Crockett, W. H. (1955), 'Employee attitudes and employee performance', *Psychological Bulletin*, vol. 52, pp. 396–424.

Bright, J. R. (1958), *Automation and Management*, Harvard Graduate School of Business Administration.

Brown, J. A. C. (1954), *The Social Psychology of Industry*, Penguin Books, Harmondsworth.

Brown, R. (1965), *Social Psychology*, Free Press, New York.

Brown, R. K. (1967), 'The Tavistock's industrial studies', *Sociology*, vol. 1, pp. 33–60.

Burns, T. (1966), 'On the plurality of social systems', Lawrence, J. R. (ed.), *Operational Research and the Social Sciences*, Tavistock, London.

Burns, T. and Stalker, G. M. (1961), *The Management of Innovation*, Tavistock, London.

Campbell, J. P. and Dunnette, M. D. (1968), 'Effectiveness of T-group experiences in management training', *Psychological Bulletin*, vol. 70, pp. 73–104.

Caplow, T. (1954), *The Sociology of Work*, University of Minnesota Press, Minneapolis.

Centers, R. and Bugenthal, D. (1966), 'Intrinsic and extrinsic job motivation among different segments of the working population', *Journal of Applied Psychology*, vol. 50, pp. 193–7.

Chapanis, A. R. E. (1965), *Man-Machine Engineering*, Tavistock, London.

Chapple, E. D. and Sayles, C. R. (1961), *The Measure of Management*, Macmillan, New York.

Chen, S. C. (1937), 'Social modification of the activity of ants in nest-building', *Physiological zoology*, vol. 10, pp. 420–36.

Clegg, H. (1960), *A New Approach to Industrial Democracy*, Blackwell, Oxford.

Coch, L. and French, J. R. P. (1948), 'Overcoming resistance to change', *Human Relations*, vol. 1, pp. 512–32.

Cofer, C. N. and Appley, M. H. (1964), *Motivation: Theory and Research*, Wiley, New York.

Cumming, E. and Henry, W. E. (1961), *Growing Old*, Basic Books, New York.

Cumming, L. L. and El Salmi, A. M. (1968), 'Empirical research on the bases and correlates of managerial motivation: a review of the literature', *Psychological Bulletin*, vol. 70, pp. 127–44.

Cyert, R. M. and MacCrimmon, K. R. (1968), 'Organizations', in Lindzey, G. and Aronson, E., *Handbook of Social Psychology*, vol. 1, Addison–Wesley, Reading, Massachusetts.

Dalton, M. (1948), 'The industrial rate-buster: a characterization', *Applied Anthropology*, vol. 7 (1), pp. 5–18.

— (1959), *Men Who Manage*, Wiley, New York.

Darlington, C. D. (1969), *The Evolution of Man and Society*, Allen & Unwin, London.

Davidson, M. A. and Hutt, C. (1964), 'A study of 500 Oxford student psychiatric patients', *British Journal of Social and Clinical Psychology*, vol. 3, pp. 175–85.

Davis, J. H. (1963), *Great Aspirations*, Vol. 1, Chicago National Opinion Research Center.

Davis, L. E. and Valfer, E. S. (1966), 'Studies in supervisory job design', *Human Relations*, vol. 19, pp. 339–52.

Davison, J. P. *et al.* (1958), *Productivity and Economic Incentives*, Allen & Unwin, London.

Diggory, J. C. (1966), *Self-Evaluation: Concepts and Studies*, Wiley, New York.

Doll, R. & Jones, F. A. (1951), *Occupational Factors in the Aetiology of Gastric Duodenal Ulcers*, His Majesty's Stationery Office, London.

Dubin, R. (1958), *The World of Work*, Prentice-Hall, Englewood Cliffs, New Jersey.

Dunnette, M. S. (1966), *Personnel Selection and Placement*, Tavistock, London.

Economist (1963), *Consider Japan*, Duckworth, London.

Edholm, O. G., (1967), *The Biology of Work*, Weidenfeld and Nicolson, London.

Elder, G. H. (1968), 'Adolescent socialization and development', in Borgatta, E. F. and Lambert, W. W. (eds.), *Handbook of Personality Theory and Research*, Rand McNally, Chicago.

Emery, F. E. and Thorsrud, E. (1969), *Form and Context in Industrial Democracy*, Tavistock, London.

Erikson, E. H. (1956), 'The problem of ego identity', *American Journal of Psychoanalysis*, vol. 4, pp. 56–121.

Etzioni, A. (1961), *A Comparative Analysis of Complex Organizations*, Free Press, New York.

Evans, C. E. and Laseau, La, V. N. (1950), *My Job Contest*, Personnel Psychology Inc., Washington.

Evans, M. G. (1970), 'The effects of supervisory behaviour on the path–goal relationship', *Organisational Behavior and Human Performance*, vol. 5, pp. 277–98.

Eysenck, H. J. (1967a), 'Personality patterns in various groups of businessmen', *Occupational Psychology*, vol. 41, pp. 249–50.

— (1967b), *The Biological Basis of Personality*, Thomas Springfield, Ohio.

Eysenck, H. J. and Eysenck, S. B. G. (1969), *Personality Structures and Measurement*, Routledge & Kegan Paul, London.

Faucheux, C. and Moscovici, S. (1960), 'Études sur la créativité des groupes: II Tache, structure des communications et réussite', *Bull. CERP*, vol. 9, pp. 11–22.

Faunce, W. A. (1958), 'Automation in the automobile industry: some consequences for in-plant social structure', *American Sociological Review*, vol. 23, pp. 410–17.

Feldman, H. (1937), *Problems in Labor Relations*, Macmillan, New York.

Fiedler, F. E. (1967), *A Theory of Leadership Effectiveness*, McGraw-Hill, New York.

— (1970), 'Leadership experience and leader performance – another hypothesis shot to hell', *Organisational Behavior and Human Performance*, vol. 5, pp. 1–14.

Fleishman, E. A. (1965), 'Attitude versus skill factors in work group productivity', *Personnel Psychology*, vol. 18, pp. 253–66.

Fleishman, E. A. (1965), 'The description and prediction of perceptual-motor skill learning', in Glaser, R. (ed.) *Training Research and Education*, Wiley, New York.

Fleishman, E. A. and Harris, E. F. (1962), 'Patterns of leadership behavior related to employee grievances and turnover', *Personnel Psychology*, vol. 15, pp. 43–56.

Fox, A. (1971), *The Sociology of Work*, Collier-Macmillan, London.

Frager, R. (1970), 'Conformity and anti-conformity in Japan', *Journal of Personality and Social Psychology*, vol. 15, pp. 203–10.

Fraser, R. (1947), *The Incidence of Neurosis among Factory Workers*, Medical Research Council, His Majesty's Stationery Office.

French, E. G. (1958), 'Effects of interaction of motivation and feedback on task performance', in Atkinson, J. W. (ed.), *Motives in Fantasy, Action and Society*, Van Nostrand, Princeton, New Jersey.

French, J. R. P. (1950), 'Field experiments: changing group productivity', in Miller, J. G. (ed.), *Experiments in Social Process*, McGraw-Hill, New York.

Friedmann, G. (1961), *The Anatomy of Work*, Heinemann, London.

— (1965), *The End of the Jewish People?*, Hutchinson, London.

Froomkin, J. N. (1968) 'Automation', *International Encyclopedia of the Social Sciences*, vol. 1, pp. 480–89.

Furneaux, W. D. (1962), 'The psychologist and the university', *Universities Quarterly*, vol. 17 (1), pp. 33–47.

Gage, N. L., Runkel, P. J. and Chatterjee, B. B. (1960), *Equilibrium Theory and Behavior Change: an experiment in feedback from pupils to teachers*, Bureau of Educational Research, Urbana.

Georgopoulos, B. S., Mahoney, G. M. and Jones, N. W. (1957), 'A path–goal approach to productivity', *Journal of Applied Psychology*, vol. 41, pp. 345–53.

Gilbreth, F. B. (1909), *Bricklaying System*, M. C. Clark, New York.

Ginsberg, E. *et al.* (1951), *Occupational Choice: an Approach to a General Theory*, Columbia University Press, New York.

Glanzer, M. and Glaser, R. (1961), 'Techniques for the study of group structure and behavior: II empirical studies of the effects of structure in small groups', *Psychological Bulletin*, vol. 58, pp. 1–27.

Goffman, E. (1961), *Asylums*, Anchor Books, New York.

Goldsen, R. K. *et al.* (1960), *What College Students Think*, Van Nostrand, Princeton, New Jersey.

Goldthorpe, J. *et al.* (1968), *The Affluent Worker*, Cambridge University Press.

Goodman, P. S. (1967), 'An empirical examination of Elliott Jaques's concept of time-span', *Human Relations*, vol. 20, pp. 155–70.

Grove, E. A. and Kerr, W. A. (1951), 'Specific evidence on origin of halo effect in measurement of employee morale', *Journal of Social Psychology*, vol. 34, pp. 165–70.

Gurin, G., Veroff, J. and Field, S. (1960), *Americans view their Mental Health*, Basic Books, New York.

Haberstroh, C. J. (1965), 'Organisation design and systems analysis', in March, J. G. (ed.) *Handbook of Organisations*, Rand McNally, Chicago.

Haines, D. B. and Eachus, H. T. (1965), 'A preliminary study of acquiring cross-cultural interaction skills through self-confrontation', Aerospace Medical Research Laboratories, Wright-Patterson Air Force Base, Ohio.

Haire, M. (1955), 'Role-perceptions in labor–management relations: an experimental approach', *Industrial Labour Relations Review*, vol. 8, pp. 204–16.

Hall, D. T. and Nougaim, K. E. (1968), 'An examination of Maslow's need hierarchy in an organizational setting', *Organisational Behaviour and Human Performance*, vol. 3, pp. 1–11.

Halpin, A. W. and Winer, B. J. (1952), *The Leadership Behavior of the Airplane Commander*, Ohio State University, Columbus.

Harbison, F. (1959), 'Management in Japan', in Harbison, F. and Myers, C. A. (eds.), *Management in the Industrial World*, McGraw-Hill, New York.

Heinecke, C. and Bales, R. F. (1953), 'Developmental trends in structure of small groups', *Sociometry*, vol. 16, pp. 7–38.

Hemphill, J. K. (1960), *Dimensions of Executive Positions*, Bureau of Business Research monograph 98, Ohio State University, Columbus.

Herzberg, F., Mausner, B., Peterson, R. O. and Capwell, D. F. (1957), *Job Attitudes: Review of Research and Opinion*, Psychological Service of Pittsburgh, Pittsburgh.

Herzberg, F., Mausner, B. and Snyderman, B. B. (1959), *The Motivation to Work*, Wiley, New York.

Hespe, G. W. A. and Little, A. J. (1971), 'Some aspects of employee participation', in Warr, P. B., *Psychology at Work*, Penguin Books, Harmondsworth.

Hewitt, D. and Parfit, J. (1953), 'A note on working morale, and size of group', *Occupational Psychology*, vol. 27, pp. 38-42.

Himmelweit, H. and Whitfield, J. (1944), 'Mean intelligence scores of a random sample of occupations', *British Journal of Industrial Medicine*, vol. 1, pp. 224-6.

Hobert, R. D. (1965), 'Moderating effects in the prediction of managerial success from psychological test scores and biographical factors', University of Minnesota Ph.D. thesis (cited by Dunnette, 1966).

Hobhouse, L. T., Wheeler, G. C. and Ginsberg, M. (1915), *The Material Culture and Social Institutions of the Simpler Peoples*, Routledge & Kegan Paul, London.

Hoffman, L. R. (1965), 'Group problem-solving', *Advances in Experimental Social Psychology*, vol. 2, pp. 99-132.

Hoppock, R. (1935), *Job Satisfaction*, Harper, New York.

Hudson, L. (1968), *Frames of Mind*, Methuen, London, and Penguin Books, Harmondsworth.

Hulin, C. L. and Blood, M. R. (1968), 'Job enlargement, individual differences, and worker responses', *Psychological Bulletin*, vol. 69, pp. 41-55.

Hulin, C. L. and Smith, P. (1967), 'An empirical investigation of two implications of the two-factor theory of job satisfaction', *Journal of Applied Psychology*, vol. 51, pp. 396-402.

Humble, J. W. (1968), *Improving Business Results*, McGraw-Hill, Maidenhead.

Hutchins, D. W. (1963), *Technology and the Sixth Form Boy*, Oxford University Department of Education.

Ingram, J. K. (1926), 'Slavery', in *Encyclopedia Britannica*, 13th edition, vol. 25, pp. 216-27.

Jacobsen, H. R. and Roucek, J. S. (eds.) (1959), *Automation and Society*, Philosophical Library, New York.

Jaques, E. (1951), *The Changing Culture of a Factory*, Tavistock, London.

— (1961), *Equitable Payment*, Heinemann, London.

Jurgensen, C. E. (1948), 'What job applicants look for in a company', *Personnel Psychology*, vol. 1, pp. 443-5.

Kahn, R. L. *et al.* (1964), *Organizational Stress: Studies in Role Conflict and Ambiguity*, Wiley, New York.

Kanter, R. M. (1968), 'Commitment and social organization: a study of commitment mechanisms in utopian communities', *American Sociological Review*, vol. 33 (2), pp. 499-517.

Kasl, S. V. and French, J. R. P. (1962), 'The effects of occupational status on physical and mental health', *Journal of Social Issues*, vol. 18 (3), pp. 67–89.

Katz, D. *et al.* (1951), *Productivity Supervision and Morale among Railroad Workers*, Institute for Social Research, Ann Arbor, Michigan.

Katz, D. and Kahn, R. L. (1966), *The Social Psychology of Organizations*, Wiley, New York.

— (1952), 'Some recent findings in human relations research', in Swanson, E., Newcomb, T. M. and Hartley, E. (eds.), *Readings in Social Psychology*, Holt, Rinehart & Winston, New York.

Katz, D., Maccoby, N., and Morse, N. (1950), *Productivity, Supervision and Morale in an Office Situation*, Institute for Social Research, Ann Arbor, Michigan.

Kay, E., Meyer, H. H. and French, J. R. P. (1965), 'Effects of threat in a performance appraisal interview', *Journal of Applied Psychology*, vol. 49, pp. 311–17.

Kelley, H. H. and Thibaut, J. W. (1969), 'Group problem solving', in Lindzey, G. and Aronson, E. (eds.), *Handbook of Social Psychology*, vol. 4, Addison-Wesley, Reading, Massachusetts.

King, N. (1970), 'Classification and evaluation of the two-factor theory of job satisfaction', *Psychological Bulletin*, vol. 74, pp. 18–31.

Kirchner, W. K. and Dunnette, M. D. (1957), 'Identifying the critical factors in successful salesmanship', *Personnel*, vol. 34, pp. 54–9.

Kluckhohn, C. (1954), 'Culture and behavior', in Lindzey, G. (ed.), *Handbook of Social Psychology*, Addison-Wesley, Cambridge, Massachusetts.

Kogan, N. and Wallach, M. A. (1967), 'Risk-taking as a function of the situation, the person and the group', in *New Directions in Psychology*, vol. 3, Holt, Rinehart & Winston, New York.

Kolaja, J. (1965), *Workers' Councils: the Yugoslav Experience*, Tavistock, London.

Kornhauser, A. (1965), *Mental Health of the Industrial Worker*, Wiley, New York.

Lahiri, D. K. and Srivasta, S. (1967), 'Determinants of satisfaction in middle-management personnel', *Journal of Applied Psychology*, vol. 51, pp. 254–65.

Landsberger, H. A. (1961–2), 'The horizontal dimension in bureaucracy', *Administrative Science Quarterly*, vol. 6, pp. 299–332.

REFERENCES

Lanzetta, J. T. and Roby, T. B. (1956), 'Effects of work-group structure and certain task variables on group performance', *Journal of Abnormal and Social Psychology*, vol. 53, pp. 307–14.

Lawler, E. E. (1968), 'Equity theory as a predictor of productivity and work quality', *Psychological Bulletin*, vol. 70, pp. 596–610.

Lawler, E. E. and Porter, L. W. (1963), 'Perceptions regarding management compensation', *Industrial Relations*, vol. 3, pp. 41–9.

Lesieur, F. S. (1958), *The Scanlon Plan*, Wiley, New York.

Levine, S. B. (1958), *Industrial Relations in Postwar Japan*, University of Illinois Press, Urbana.

Likert, R. (1961), *New Patterns of Management*, McGraw-Hill, New York.

Lippitt, R. (1940), 'An experimental study of the effects of democratic and autocratic atmospheres', *University of Iowa Studies in Child Welfare*, vol. 16, pp. 45–195.

Lott, A. J. and Lott, B. E. (1965), 'Group cohesiveness as interpersonal attraction: a review of relationships with antecedent and consequent variables', *Psychological Bulletin*, vol. 64, pp. 259–309.

Lowin, A. (1968), 'Participation in decision-making: a model, literature critique, and prescriptions for research', *Organizational Behavior and Human Performance*, vol. 3, pp. 68–106.

Lupton, T. (1968), 'Beyond payment by results?' in Pym D. (ed.), *Industrial Society*, Penguin Books, Harmondsworth.

Lynn, R. (1971), *Personality and National Character*, Pergamon Press, Oxford.

McClelland, D. C. *et al.* (1953), *The Achievement Motive*, Appleton-Century-Crofts, New York.

McClelland, D. C. (1961), *The Achieving Society*, Van Nostrand, New York.

— (1962), 'On the psychodynamics of creative physical scientists', in Gruber, H. E. *et al.* (eds.), *Contemporary Approaches to Creative Thinking*, Atherton Press, New York.

McClelland, D. C. and Winter, D. G. (1969), *Motivating Economic Achievement*, Free Press, New York.

McGregor, D. (1960), *The Human Side of Enterprise*, McGraw-Hill, New York.

McGuire, W. J. (1969), 'The nature of attitudes and attitude change', in Lindzey, G. and Aronson, E. (eds.), *Handbook of Social Psychology*, vol. 3, Addison-Wesley, Reading, Massachusetts.

Mace, C. A. (1935), *Incentives – some experimental studies*, Industrial Health Research Board, Report No. 72, His Majesty's Stationery Office, London.

Mahone, C. H. (1960), 'Fear of failure and unrealistic vocational aspiration', *Journal of Abnormal and Social Psychology*, vol. 60, pp. 253–61.

Maier, N. R. F. (1958), *The Appraisal Interview*, Wiley, New York.

Mann, F. C. (1957), 'Studying and creating change: a means to understanding social organization', *Research in Industrial Human Relations*, vol. 17, pp. 146–67.

Mann, F. C. and Baumgartel, H. J. (1953), *Absences and Employee Attitudes in an Electric Power Company*, Institute for Social Research, Ann Arbor, Michigan.

Mann, F. C. and Hoffman, L. R. (1960), *Automation and the Worker*, Holt, Rinehart & Winston, New York.

Mann, F. C. and Williams, L. K. (1962), 'Some effects of the changing work environment in the office', *Journal of Social Issues*, vol. 18 (3), pp. 90–101.

Mann, R. D., *et al.* (1967), *Interpersonal Styles and Group Development*, Wiley, New York.

Mannheim, H. and Wilkins, L. T. (1955), *Prediction Methods in Relation to Borstal Training*, Her Majesty's Stationery Office, London.

Marriott, R. (1968), *Incentive Payment Systems*, Staples, London.

Maslow, A. H. (1954), *Motivation and Personality*, Harper, New York.

Massie, J. L. (1965), 'Management theory', in March, J. G. (ed.), *Handbook of Organizations*, Rand McNally, Chicago.

Mayo, E. (1933), *The Human Problems of an Industrial Civilization*, Macmillan, New York.

— (1945), *The Social Problems of an Industrial Civilization*, Harvard University Graduate School of Business Administration, Boston.

Meehl, P. E. (1954), *Clinical versus Statistical Predictions*, University of Minnesota Press, Minneapolis.

Merton, R. K. (1957), *Social Theory and Social Structure*, Free Press, Glencoe, Illinois.

Merton, R. K. *et al.* (1957), *The Student-Physician*, Harvard University Press.

Metzner, H. and Mann, F. C. (1953), 'Employee attitudes and absence', *Personnel Psychology*, vol. 6, pp. 467–85.

Miller, D. C. and Form, W. H. (1962), *Industrial Sociology*, Harper & Row, New York.

Miller, E. J. and Rice, A. K. (1967), *Systems of Organization: the Control of Task and Sentient Boundaries*, Tavistock, London.

Mills, C. W. (1951), *White Collar*, Oxford University Press, New York.

Minsky, M. *et al.* (1968), 'Machines like men', *Science Journal*, vol. 4, no. 10.

Mischel, W. (1969), *Personality and Assessment*, Wiley, New York.

Misumi, J. (1959), 'Experimental studies on "group dynamics" in Japan', *Psychologia*, vol. 2, pp. 229–35.

Modern Industry (April 1946), 'Pay plans for higher production', p. 51 f. Cited by Viteles (1954).

Moon, G. G. and Hariton, T. (1958), 'Evaluating an appraisal and feedback training program', *Personnel*, vol. 35, pp. 34–41.

Moreno, J. L. (1953), *Who Shall Survive?* (2nd ed.), Beacon House, Beacon, New York.

Morrison, A. and McIntyre, D. (1971), *Schools and Socialization*, Penguin Books, Harmondsworth.

Morrison, R. F. *et al.* (1962), 'Factored life history antecedents of industrial research performance', *Journal of Applied Psychology*, vol. 46, pp. 281–4.

Morse, N. C. (1953), *Satisfaction in the White Collar Job*, Institute for Social Research, University of Michigan, Ann Arbor.

Morse, N. C. and Reimer, E. (1956), 'The experimental change of a major organizational variable', *Journal of Abnormal and Social Psychology*, vol. 52, pp. 120–29.

Morse, N. C. and Weiss, R. R. (1955), 'The function and meaning of work and the job', *American Sociology Review*, vol. 20, pp. 191–8.

Mosel, J. N. and Cozan, L. W. (1952), 'The accuracy of application blank work histories', *Journal of Applied Psychology*, vol. 36, pp. 365–9.

Mulder, M. (1960), 'Communication structure, decision structure and group performance', *Sociometry*, vol. 23, pp. 1–14.

Mulford, H. A. and Salisbury, W. W. (1964), 'Self-conceptions in a general population', *Sociological Quarterly*, vol. 5, pp. 35–46.

National Institute of Industrial Psychology (1952), *Joint Consultation in British Industry*, Staples, London.

Nealey, S. M. and Blood, M. R. (1968), 'Leadership performance of nursing supervisors at two organizational levels', *Journal of Applied Psychology*, vol. 52, pp. 414–22.

Nealey, S. M. and Fiedler, F. E. (1968), 'Leadership functions of middle managers', *Psychological Bulletin*, vol. 70, pp. 313–29.

Neff, W. S. (1968), *Work and Human Behavior*, Atherton Press, New York.

Odaka, K. (1963), 'Traditionalism and democracy in Japanese industry', *Industrial Relations*, vol. 3, pp. 95–103.

Opinion Research Corporation (1947), *Public Opinion Index for Industry*. Cited by Viteles (1954), p. 303f.

Parkinson, C. N. (1957), *Parkinson's Law*, Murray, London.

Paul, G. L. (1966), *Insight v. Desensitization in Psychotherapy*, Stanford University Press.

Pelz, D. C. (1952), 'Influence: a key to effective leadership in the first-line supervisor', *Personnel*, vol. 3, pp. 209–17.

— (1957), 'Motivation of the engineering and research specialist', *American Management Association General Management Series*, No. 186, pp. 25–46.

Peter, L. J. (1969), *The Peter Principle*, Samuel Press, London.

Pollard, S. (1965), *The Genesis of Modern Management*, Arnold, London.

Porter, L. W. and Lawler, E. E. (1965), 'Properties of organization structure in relation to job attitudes and job behavior', *Psychological Bulletin*, vol. 64, pp. 23–51.

— (1968), *Managerial Attitudes and Performance*, Homeword, Illinois.

Prawer, J. and Eisenstadt, S. N. (1968), 'Feudalism', *International Encyclopedia of the Social Sciences*, vol. 5, pp. 393–402.

Pugh, D. S. and Hickson, D. J. (1968), 'The comparative study of organizations', in Pym, D. (ed.), *Industrial Society*, Penguin Books, Harmondsworth.

Read, W. H. (1962), 'Upward communication in industrial hierarchies', *Human Relations*, vol. 15, pp. 3–16.

Rennie, T. A. C. and Srole, L. (1956), 'Social class prevalence and distribution of psychosomatic conditions in an urban population', *Psychosomatic Medicine*, vol. 18, pp. 449–56.

Remitz, U. (1960), *Professional Satisfaction among Swedish Bank Employees*, Munksgaard, Copenhagen.

REFERENCES

Revans, R. W. (1958), 'Human relations, management and size', in Hugh-Jones, E. M. (ed.), *Human Relations and Modern Management*, North Holland Publishing, Amsterdam.

Rice, A. K. (1958), *Productivity and Social Organization: The Ahmedabad Experiment*, Tavistock, London.

— (1963), *The System and its Environment*, Tavistock, London.

Riesman, D. (1958), 'Work and leisure in post-industrial society', in Larrabee, E. and Meyersohn, R. (eds.), *Mass Leisure*, Free Press of Glencoe, Illinois.

Roe, A. (1964), 'Personality structure and occupational behavior', in Borow, H. (ed.), *Man in a World of Work*, Houghton Mifflin, Boston.

Roethlisberger, F. J. and Dickson, W. J. (1939), *Management and the Worker*, Harvard University Press, Cambridge, Massachusetts.

Rosenberg, M. (1957), *Occupations and Values*, Free Press of Glencoe, Illinois.

Rosenberg, S. and Hall, R. L. (1958), 'The effects of different feedback conditions upon performance in dyadic teams', *Journal of Abnormal and Social Psychology*, vol. 57, pp. 271–7.

Roy, D. (1955), 'Efficiency and "the fix": informal intergroup relations in a piece-work machine shop', *American Journal of Sociology*, vol. 60, pp. 255–66.

Rushing, W. A. (1966), 'Organizational size, rules, and surveillance', *Journal of Experimental Social Psychology*, pp. 11–26.

Sayles, L. R. and Strauss, G. (1966), *Human Behavior in Organizations*, Prentice-Hall, Englewood Cliffs, New Jersey.

Scanlon, J. N. (1948), 'Profit-sharing under collective bargaining: three case studies', *Industrial and Labour Relations Review*, vol. 2, pp. 58–75.

Schuchman, A. (1957), *Codetermination: Labor's Middle Way in Germany*, Public Affairs Press, Washington.

Scott, W. D. *et al.* (1941), *Personal Management*, McGraw-Hill, New York.

Seashore, S. E. (1954), *Group Cohesiveness in the Industrial Work Group*, Institute for Social Research, University of Michigan, Ann Arbor.

Seeman, M. (1959), 'On the meaning of alienation', *American Sociological Review*, vol. 24, pp. 783–91.

Selvin, H. C. (1960), *The Effects of Leadership*, Free Press, New York.

Sewell, W. H. and Orenstein, A. M. (1965), 'Community of residence and occupational choice', *American Journal of Sociology*, vol. 70, pp. 551–63.

Sherif, M. *et al.* (1961), *Intergroup Conflict and Cooperation: the Robbers Cave Experiment*, University Book Exchange, Norman, Oklahoma.

Shimmin, S. (1968), postscript to revised edition of Marriott (1968).

Sidney, E. and Argyle, M. (1969), *Selection Interviewing*: films and training kit distributed by Mantra Ltd.

Sofer, C. (1970), *Men in Mid-Career*, Cambridge University Press.

Stagner, R. (1956), *Psychology of Industrial Conflict*, Wiley, New York.

Stewart, R. (1967), *Managers and their Jobs*, Macmillan, London.

Super, D. E. (1957), *The Psychology of Careers*, Harper, New York.

Super, D. E. and Overstreet, P. L. (1960), *The Vocational Maturity of Ninth-grade Boys*, Bureau of Publications, Teachers College, Columbia University, New York.

Tawney, R. H. (1926), *Religion and the Rise of Capitalism*, Penguin Books, Harmondsworth.

Taylor, D. W., Berry, P. C. and Block, C. H. (1958), 'Does group participation when using brainstorming facilitate or inhibit thinking?', *Administrative Science Quarterly*, vol. 3, pp. 23–47.

Taylor, F. W. (1947), *Scientific Management*, Harper, New York.

Thibaut, J. W. and Kelley, H. H. (1959), *The Social Psychology of Groups*, Wiley, New York.

Thomas, E. J. and Fink, C. F. (1963), 'Effects of group size', *Psychological Bulletin*, vol. 60, pp. 371–84.

Thomas, K. (1964), 'Work and leisure in pre-industrial society', *Past and Present*, no. 29, pp. 50–66.

Thorndike, R. L. and Hagen, E. (1959), *Ten Thousand Careers*, Wiley, New York.

Tiffin, J. and McCormick, E. J. (1966), *Industrial Psychology*, Allen & Unwin, London.

Tiger, L. (1969), *Men in Groups*, Nelson, London.

Tilgher, A. (1931), *Work*, Harrap, London.

Trist, E. L. *et al.* (1963), *Organizational Choice*, Tavistock, London.

Trower, P., Bryant, B. and Argyle, M. (1978), *Social Skills and Mental Health*, Methuen, London.

Tuckman, B. W. (1965), 'Developmental sequence in small groups', *Psychological Bulletin*, vol. 63, pp. 384–99.

Turner, A. N. and Lawrence, P. (1966), *Industrial Jobs and the Worker*, Harvard Graduate School of Business Administration, Cambridge, Massachusetts.

Tyler, L. E. (1964), 'Work and individual differences', Borow, H. (ed.), *Man in a World of Work*, Houghton Mifflin, Boston.

Udy (1959), *The Organization of Work*, Human Relations Area Files, New Haven.

Ulrich, L. and Trumbo, D. (1965), 'The selection interview since 1949', *Psychological Bulletin*, vol. 63, pp. 100–116.

Underwood, W. J. (1965), 'Evaluation of laboratory method training', *Training Directors Journal*, vol. 19 (1), pp. 34–40.

Van Zelst, R. H. (1951), 'Worker popularity and job satisfaction', *Personnel Psychology*, vol. 4, pp. 405–12.

Van Zelst, R. H. (1952), 'Validation of a sociometric regrouping procedure', *Journal of Abnormal and Social Psychology*, vol. 47, pp. 299–301.

Veness, T. (1962), *School Leavers*, Methuen, London.

Vernon, P. E. (1950), 'The validation of Civil Service Selection Board procedures', *Occupational Psychology*, vol. 24, pp. 75–95.

— (1964), *Personality Assessment*, Methuen, London.

Viteles, M. S. (1954), *Motivation and Morale in Industry*, Staples, London.

Vroom, V. H. (1960), *Some Personality Determinants of the Effects of Participation*, Prentice-Hall, Englewood Cliffs, New Jersey.

— (1962), 'Ego-involvement, job satisfaction, and job performance', *Personnel Psychology*, vol. 15, pp. 159–77.

— (1964), *Work and Motivation*, Wiley, New York.

Vroom, V. H., Grant, L. D. and Cotton, T. S. (1969), 'The consequences of social interaction in group problem-solving', *Organizational Behaviour and Human Performance*, vol. 4, pp. 77–95.

Walker, C. R. (1957), *Toward the Automatic Factory: A Case of Study of Men and Machines*, Yale University Press, New Haven, Connecticut.

Walker, C. R. and Guest, R. H. (1952), *The Man on the Assembly Line*, Harvard University Press, Cambridge, Massachusetts.

Walker, C.R. *et al.* (1956), *The Foreman on the Assembly Line*, Harvard University Press, Cambridge, Massachusetts.

Weber, M. (1904–5), *The Protestant Ethic and the Spirit of Capitalism*, Scribner, New York.

— (1923), *General Economic History*, Allen & Unwin, London.

Webster, E. C. (1964), *Decision-Making in the Employment Interview*, McGill University Industrial Relations Centre, Montreal.

Weingarten, M. (1962), *Life in a Kibbutz*, Jerusalem Post Press.

Weiss, E. C. (1957), 'Relation of personnel statistics to organization structure', *Personnel Psychology*, vol. 10, pp. 27–42.

Werts, C. E. (1968), 'Parental influence on career choice', *Journal of Counselling Psychology*, vol. 15, pp. 48–52.

Wherry, R. J. (1958), 'Factor analysis of morale data: reliability and validity', *Personnel Psychology*, vol. 11, pp. 78–89.

Whitehill, A. M. and Takezawa, S. (1961), *Cultural Values in Management–Worker Relations: Gimu in Transition*, University of North Carolina School of Business Administration.

Whittemore, I. C. (1924–5), 'Influence of competition on performance: an experimental study', *Journal of Abnormal and Social Psychology*, vol. 19, pp. 236–53, vol. 20, pp. 17–33.

Whyte, W. F. (1948), *Human Relations in the Restaurant Industry*, McGraw-Hill, New York.

— (1955), *Money and Motivation*, Harper, New York.

— (1957), *The Organization Man*, Simon & Schuster, New York; Penguin Books, Harmondsworth.

Wiener, N. (1961), *Cybernetics*, Massachusetts Institute of Technology Press, Cambridge, Massachusetts.

Wilkins, L. T. (1950–51), 'Incentives and the young male worker', *International Journal of Opinion and Attitude Research*, vol. 4, pp. 540–61.

Wolpe, J. (1958), *Psychotherapy by Reciprocal Inhibition*, Stanford University Press.

Woodward, J. (1960), *The Saleswoman*, Pitman, London.

— (1965), *Industrial Organization: Theory and Practice*, Oxford University Press, London.

Woodward, J. (1965), *Industrial Organization: Theory and Practice*, Oxford University Press, London.

Wyatt, S. (1934), *Incentives in Repetitive Work*, Industrial Health Research Board, Report No. 69, His Majesty's Stationery Office, London.

Zajonc, R. B. (1965), 'Social facilitation', *Science*, vol. 149, pp. 269–74.

REFERENCES

Zaleznik, A., Christenson, C. R., and Roethlisberger, F. J. (1958), *The Motivation, Productivity and Satisfaction of Workers: a Prediction Study*, Harvard Graduate School of Business Administration, Boston, Massachusetts.

Zander, A., Natsoulos, T., and Thomas, E. J. (1960), 'Personal goals and the group's goal for the member', *Human Relations*, vol. 13, pp. 333–44.

Zander, A. and Quinn, R. (1962), 'The social environment and mental health: a review of past research at the Institute for Social Research', *Journal of Social Issues*, vol. 18 (3), pp. 48–66.

Zweig, F. (1959), *The Israeli Worker*, Herzl & Sharon, New York.

NAME INDEX

SUBJECT INDEX

abilities, 55 f., 254
absenteeism, 120, 136, 240
achievement motivation, 18,
23 f., 68 f., 93 f.
activity, need for, 92 f.
adolescence, 63 f.
affiliative motivation, 101
Africa, 13, 62 f., 261
age, 61 f., 237
agriculture, 15 f., 25 f.
alienation, 1 f., 225 f.
ancient civilizations, 17 f.
animals, work in, 7 f., 107
ants, 8, 108
anxiety, 93
appraisal interview, 161 f.
assembly-lines, 34, 48
authoritarians, 175 f.
authority, attitudes to, 61, 180,
185 f.
automation, 49 f., 260 f.

biographical information, 77
biological needs, 8 f., 56 f.
brain, size of, 11
brain-storming, 131
bureaucracy, 188

capitalism, 22 f.
careers, 66
chairmanship, 133 f., 167 f.
classical organization theory, 28,
84 f., 185 f.
clinical selection method, 78 f.
codetermination, 206 f.
collective bargaining, 197
collective ownership, 100 f.
committees, 129 f.

in Israeli kibbutzim, 213 f.
in Yugoslavian factories, 216 f.
communication, difficulties of, 4 f.
downward, 194
in organizations, 192 f.
lateral, 193 f.
structures, 42 f., 181 f.
upward, 194 f.
company, and job satisfaction,
236
competition, 248
conflict between groups, 195 f.
consideration, 147 f.
cooperation, 36, 118 f.
co-partnership, 100
craft guilds, 22
craftsmen, 21 f., 67
craftwork, 35, 48, 262
creativity, 56
culture, 13 f.

decentralization, 199, 256
democratic-persuasive skills,
148 f.
dependency, need for, 102 f.
developing countries, 94 f.
division of labour, 14 f., 180
doctors, 65
domestic system, 21 f.
drop-outs, 64

economic
growth, 6, 23 f., 69, 93, 218
motivation, 84 f.
education for work, 257
encounter groups, 174
engineers, 70
entrepreneurs, 26, 66, 184

288